# A+

# in Cooking

Favorite recipes from former students and families
and collected by Cleone Colvin.

ISBN 0-9640246-0-8

Printed in the USA by

**WIMMER**

The Wimmer Companies, Inc.

Memphis

# INTRODUCTION

This book is a unique collection of recipes from families and pupils I've taught over the past 44 years. It is not a regional cookbook because the recipes come from many places. The search for former students was an adventure within itself. Students were found all the way from Hawaii to Germany, from California to Florida, from Michigan to Utah, from Arkansas to New Mexico, from Oklahoma to Louisiana, and many, many points in between. And then, there were the surprises right in my "backyard" — one found at a check out counter in the grocery store, another in a receiving line at a wedding. Then there was the isolated trip to the post office on Saturday morning (I never go to the post office on Saturday mornings!) when I was reacquainted with a student I had in 1955. Once I asked a former pupil if he knew the "whereabouts" of a certain girl. His reply, "Yes, I married her!" Because of so many changes, it was often difficult to place an adult figure with that child-like face you once knew. While on a visit to our local hospital, a nurse asked if I remembered she had been one of my students. She was another piece of the puzzle. A 1949 student from New Mexico so aptly phrased it, "Everyone has a story to tell."

The letters and phone calls were rewarding and heartwarming. I rejoiced at my students accomplishments and grieved over their losses and sorrows. In all, more than 70% of the former students were located. I am tremendously grateful for their encouragement and support during this project. The response was far beyond my wildest dreams. Because of their input, the following recipes represent what they grew up on and other new-found favorites.

This book is a tribute to each of you and to what you have meant to me during my life. May your life be filled with A+ IN LIVING!

The names of parents and students follow each recipe; the date represents the year the child enrolled in my room as a sixth grader ('49-'80) or fifth grader ('81-'87).

# ACKNOWLEDGEMENTS

To all who spent their time in any way toward the collection of the recipes in *A+ In Cooking*, I want to say a big thank you.

My sincere appreciation to all who submitted the hundreds of recipes to me. I regret I was unable to incorporate all of the recipes due to the numbers and the similarity and lack of space.

The illustrator of *A+ in Cooking*, Pamela Fisher, lives in Andrews with her husband and three children. She has taught elementary art in Midland, Texas and served as a teaching assistant in the art department of Texas Tech University from which she holds a master's degree. Currently, the artist is an elementary art teacher in Andrews.

My deepest gratitude goes to Pam (Piper) Fisher who worked so hard on the artwork for this book. She is not only a fine artist and teacher of art in the Andrews Independent Schools, she just happened to be one of my former pupils back in 1963.

# Table of Contents

## ANDREWS
## INDEPENDENT SCHOOL DISTRICT
DEVONIAN ELEMENTARY SCHOOL

## REPORT CARD

PUPIL ___Jane Dough___

SCHOOL YEAR ___1937 - 1987___

TEACHER ___Mrs. Colvin___

**EXPLANATION OF GRADES**
A+ Very Good

# Appetizers and Beverages

The Cracker-eating Contest 1923

# Cracker Eating Contest — 1923

The first recollection I have of school involves food.

A few weeks before school was out in the spring, 6-year-olds could start to school and go until school was out. This was to let the child experience school and to see how he or she liked it. (Don't you know the teachers loved it and US!)

One spring afternoon after I had started, the teacher had a Cracker-Eating Contest. The one who could eat 5 crackers and then whistle first was the winner. All of those that wanted to enter lined themselves up in front of the room and each was given his 5 crackers. I do not remember the others who entered the contest or who won. I do not even remember the "Whistle". That was not my concern or intent. My concern was an afternoon snack that consisted of at least 5 crackers — win or lose. Whistle or no whistle!

# ARTICHOKE DIP

1 (14-ounce) can artichoke hearts, drained and chopped
1 cup Parmesan cheese
1 cup mayonnaise
Garlic powder to taste

Mix all ingredients. Heat in 350 degree oven for 20 minutes. Spread on crackers or use as dip.

Mixture may be stored up to 12 hours in refrigerator before heating.

*Diana Henderson: Latisha Atwood '84*

# AVOCADO DIP

1 small onion
1/2 cup mayonnaise
1 (3-ounce) package cream cheese
2 real ripe avocados
Bit of Worchestershire sauce

Mix all ingredients in blender.

*Ray and Doris Flowe: Rita '68*

# BEAU MONDE DIP

1-1/3 cups mayonnaise (not salad dressing)
1-1/3 cups sour cream
1 tablespoon dill weed
2 tablespoons finely minced onion
2 teaspoons Spice Island Beau Monde seasoning

Combine mayonnaise and sour cream. Add remaining ingredients. Stir and mix well.

Note: This dip, which can be used on crackers or fresh vegetables, is best prepared 8 hours before use in order for the flavors to blend. It's pretty served in a hollowed-out round loaf of rye bread.

*Keith and Marcella Harding: Barbara '65*

# CHEESE DIP

1 pound hamburger meat
Morton Chili Blend
Garlic salt
1 (2-pound) box Velveeta cheese
1 can Rotel tomatoes, diced

Brown meat in iron skillet; season with chili blend and garlic salt (to taste). Cut cheese in small pieces and put in 2-1/2 to 3 quart pan with tomatoes. On low heat, stir until cheese melts. Add meat. (If you like your dip hot, add 2 or 3 jalapeno peppers.)

*Robert and Lana Moon: Greg '80*

# CHILI CON QUESO MEXICAN DIP

| | |
|---|---|
| 1 pound ground round | 1 can Rotel tomatoes |
| 1 small onion, chopped | 1 small can tomato sauce |
| 1 pound American cheese | 1 small can green chilies |

Brown meat and onion. Melt cheese. It is best to use a double boiler. Add all other ingredients. Mix well. Serve with tortilla chips while warm.

*Fred and Brenda Lindsey: Chris '80*

# NACHO CHEESE DIP

| | |
|---|---|
| 2 cans Cheddar Cheese soup | Small box Velveeta cheese |
| 1/2 can Picante Sauce | (1/2-pound box) |
| 1/2 cup milk | |

Place ingredients in double boiler. Stir while cheese melts. Great for nachos or as a dip. Also great on hamburgers.

*Paul and Ann Hodge: Paula '80; David '85*

# WELCH RAREBIT

| | |
|---|---|
| 1 tablespoon butter | 1/2 teaspoon mustard |
| 1/2 pound American cheese, | 1 cup milk |
|    grated | 1 egg, slightly beaten |
| Dash of salt, pepper and | |
|    Worchestershire sauce | |

Melt butter in top of double boiler. Add cheese, seasonings. When melted, add milk slowly, stirring constantly. When mixture is well blended, add a little mixture to the eggs. Gradually add egg to first mixture; blend well. Serve on hot, crisp toast.

*Granville and Mary Porter: Granville '58*

# OKLAHOMA DIP

| | |
|---|---|
| 1 pound hot sausage (mild is | 2 pounds Velveeta cheese |
|    good also) | 2 cans Rotel tomatoes, drained |
| 1-1/4 pounds hamburger meat |    and juice reserved |
| 1 medium onion | |

Combine sausage, hamburger and onion and cook; drain. In a crock pot melt Velveeta, Rotel tomatoes, and add other ingredients. Add juice as desired. Mix well and serve with chips.

*Linda Henderson Parmley: Lisa Parmley '74; Greg Parmley '75*

# DEMOSTHENES DIP

1 can tomato soup
1 small package lemon Jello
1 cup celery, chopped
1-1/2 cups bell pepper, chopped
1-1/2 cups green onion, chopped
1 (4-ounce) jar pimientos

1 (8-ounce) package soft cream
 cheese
1/2 cup salad dressing
1/2 teaspoon salt
1 teaspoon Accent
1/8 teaspoon pepper

Heat together tomato soup and jello, stirring until dissolved. While this cools, chop finely celery, bell pepper, green onions, and pimientos. Add cream cheese and salad dressing to soup with mixer. Add salt, Accent, and pepper. Add and fold in vegetables. Refrigerate overnight. It can also be frozen and used later. IT IS DELICIOUS SERVED WITH RAW VEGETABLES!

*Charles and Wanda Dye: William '80; Chad '83*

# MARSHMALLOW FRUIT DIP

1 (8-ounce) jar marshmallow
 cream
1 (8-ounce) package cream
 cheese, softened

2 to 3 tablespoon orange juice or
 enough to make desired
 consistency for dip

Soften cream cheese and add other ingredients; mix until smooth. Good with fresh fruit, melon balls, (party food).

*Teacher's Pet: Cleone Colvin*

# FRUIT DIP
## (Weight Watchers)

1/4 cup unflavored yogurt
1 teaspoon vanilla
1 package sweetener

2 teaspoons diet strawberry
 preserves
2 tablespoons Cool Whip (or
 LaCreme)

Mix.

*Teacher's Pet: Cleone Colvin*

# RELISH DIP

3 fresh tomatoes, chopped
1 bunch green onions, chopped
1 can tomatoes and green chilies
1 can Jalapeno relish

3 tablespoons oil
1 tablespoon vinegar
1 dash garlic powder
1 can pitted ripe olives, chopped

Mix and serve.

*Billy and Pat Morrison: Bill '77*

# TEX-MEX DIP

3 medium-sized ripe avocados
2 tablespoons lemon juice
1/2 teaspoon salt
1/4 teaspoon pepper
1 cup sour cream
1/2 cup mayonnaise or salad dressing
1 package (1-1/4 ounce) Taco Seasoning Mix
2 cans (10-1/2 ounce) plain or jalapeno-flavored bean dip

1 large bunch green onions, with tops, chopped (1 cup)
3 medium tomatoes, cored, halved, seeded, and coarsely chopped (2 cups)
2 cans (3-1/2 ounce) pitted ripe olives, drained, coarsely chopped
1 (8-ounce) package sharp cheddar cheese, shredded
Large round tortilla chips

Peel and mash avocados in a medium sized bowl with lemon juice, salt, and pepper.

Combine sour cream, mayonnaise, and Taco Seasoning; mix.

**To assemble:**

Spread bean dip in a large shallow serving platter; top with avocado mixture. Layer with sour cream/taco mixture. Sprinkle with chopped onions, tomatoes, and olives. Cover with shredded cheese. Serve chilled or at room temperature with tortilla chips.

*Melvin and Katie Spear: Brenda '52*

# SHRIMP DIP

1 package unflavored gelatin
1/4 cup warm water
3/4 cup chopped green onions
3/4 cup chopped celery

1 cup chopped shrimp
1 cup mayonnaise
1 can tomato soup (no water)
1 (8-ounce) package cream cheese

Mix gelatin and warm water; set aside. Mix onions, celery, shrimp, and mayonnaise. Mix together the tomato soup and cream cheese. Combine all of the above and chill.

*E. B. and Rose Forbess: Dale '85*

# SPINACH DIP

1 box frozen chopped spinach
2 cups mayonnaise
1/2 cup green onions, chopped

1/2 teaspoon salt
Juice of 1 lemon

One box of frozen spinach is equal to 1 cup of spinach. Thaw and drain spinach. Mix with other ingredients; mix well. Chill before serving.

*Frank and Carol Bice: Susan '80*

# VEGETABLE DIP

1 cup mayonnaise, (not
substitute)
4 teaspoons soy sauce
1 teaspoon ginger

2 teaspoons dehydrated minced
onion
1 teaspoon vinegar

Combine all ingredients and refrigerate 24 hours before serving. Wonderful with cauliflower, broccoli, mushrooms, bell peppers, carrots, etc. Makes 1 cup.

*J. Roy and Shirley McAdams: Shell '73*

# GAZPACHO DIP

3 tablespoons oil
1-1/2 tablespoons cider vinegar
1 teaspoon salt
1/2 teaspoon garlic powder
1/4 teaspoon pepper
1 (4-ounce) can chopped black
olives and liquid

1 (4-ounce) can chopped green
chilies and liquid
1 can chopped Rotel tomatoes
4 to 5 green onions, finely
chopped

Blend oil and vinegar. Add salt, garlic powder, and pepper. Stir. Mix with remaining ingredients and chill for several hours for flavors to mix. Serve cold with tortilla chips.

*Teacher's Pet: Lana Albers, daughter*

# CHEESE BALL

1 (8-ounce) package cheddar
cheese, grated
2 small packages cream cheese
Chopped onion, small amount
Chopped green pepper, small
amount
1 small jar pimientos, chopped

1 tablespoon lemon juice
1 to 2 tablespoons
Worchestershire sauce
Mayonnaise, to moisten
Dash of cayenne
Dash of salt
Pecan crumbs.

Mix all ingredients well; mold into ball and chill 1 hour or longer. Roll in pecan crumbs. Serve with crackers.

*Doc and Ramona Sharp: Nancy '71*

**God gives us the ingredients for our daily bread,
But he expects us to do the baking.**

# CHEESE BALL

2 (8-ounce) packages cream
  cheese
1 (8-ounce) can crushed
  pineapple, drained

1/2 cup bell pepper, finely
  chopped
1/2 cup onion, finely chopped
2 cups chopped pecans

Mix all ingredients; blend well. Shape into 2 balls. Roll in pecans that have been finely chopped.

*George F. and George Ann Baker: Steven '78*

# BAKED OLIVE CHEESE BALLS

2 cups grated cheddar cheese
1 stick oleo
1 cup flour

1 teaspoon salt
1 teaspoon paprika
1 jar small stuffed olives

Have cheese and oleo at room temperature. Cream together. Add the sifted dry ingredients and mix well. Drain and wipe olives dry. Roll cheese mixture around olives, making small balls. Place on cookie sheet and freeze. After frozen keep in a plastic bag until ready to use. Cook 15 minutes in 375 degree oven. (Party sandwiches and dainties.)

*Al and Maxine Hays: Steve '62*

# CHEESE LOG

1 pound Velveeta cheese
1 clove garlic
2 cups chopped pecans

1 (3-ounce) package cream cheese
1 tablespoon Worchestershire
  sauce

Grind Velveeta, garlic, and pecans. Add cream cheese and Worchestershire sauce. Shape in rolls and roll in chili powder (long rolls). Wrap in wax paper and freeze. Slice while frozen and serve on small crackers.

*Darrell and Charlotte Jackson: Valerie '66; Kevin '71*

**Manners are the happy way of doing things.**

## CREAM CHEESE ROLL

1 (8-ounce) package cream
   cheese, softened
1/2 cup small curd cottage cheese,
   drained

2 teaspoons Italian salad dressing
   mix (packaged)
1 (4-1/2 ounce) can deviled ham
1/2 cup snipped parsley (flakes)
1/2 cup chopped nuts

Blend cream cheese, cottage cheese, and salad dressing mix. Spread on foil-lined sheet 3/8" thick; chill overnight. Spread ham on top of mixture; combine parsley and nuts. Sprinkle 1/2 of mixture over ham. Roll jelly-like fashion with a narrow spatula. Roll outside of roll in remaining nuts and parsley. Cover and chill until ready to serve.

*Robert and Faye Boone: Steven '82*

## OLIVE CHEESE ROLL

2 packages cream cheese
1 small jar chopped green olives
   with pimientos
1 teaspoon dried onion bits
2 teaspoons Parmesan cheese

1 teaspoon white pepper
1 teaspoon horseradish
2 packages thinly sliced smoked
   ham

Combine first 6 ingredients with blender until creamy. Place in refrigerator for 1 hour. On Saran wrap, place ham slices end to end, overlapping. Spread cheese mixture onto ham in long slender roll 1" in diameter. Roll cheese mixture in ham to form long roll. Wrap in Saran Wrap and refrigerate 1 to 2 hours. Slice and place on cracker with fresh parsley.

*Dan and Tina Newbrough: Heather '84*

## CHILI CHEESE

(Becky's Canape)
1 pound regular cheddar cheese,
   grated
1 large onion, finely chopped

1 cup mayonnaise
1 teaspoon salt
1 teaspoon chili powder

Mix and refrigerate. Before using, remove from refrigerator and soften until spreadable. Spread on triskits. Put under broiler for just long enough to bubble a little. Serve immediately.

*Johnny and Edith Smith: Becky '53*

Add a teaspoon of Love to every recipe.

## CHEESE SPREAD

4 ounce shredded cheddar cheese
4 ounce shredded Mozzarella
cheese
4-1/2 ounce can chopped ripe
olives

1/2 to 3/4 cup margarine
6 chopped green onions
Ritz crackers

Mix all ingredients. Best if mixed ahead of time so onion flavor can blend.

(This has never failed to be a hit at any gathering. I've never had any "left over." By the way, it tastes great with any kind of crackers.)

*Paul and Ruth Newman: Paula '52 (submitted by Paula Newman Ogden)*

## HOT PECAN SPREAD

*(SUPER! and I mean SUPER!)*

3 (8-ounce) packages cream
cheese, softened
6 tablespoons milk
3 packages Leo's sliced beef, cut
into small pieces
3/4 cup finely chopped green
pepper

6 tablespoons dried minced onion
1-1/2 teaspoons garlic salt
3/4 teaspoon pepper
1-1/2 cups sour cream
1-1/2 cups chopped pecans
6 tablespoons oleo

Combine cream cheese and milk; mix well. Stir in beef, green pepper, onion, and seasonings. Blend well. Fold in sour cream and spoon into 9x13" pan. (Can do ahead). When ready to serve, bake at 350 degrees for 20 minutes. Top with chopped pecans that have been sauteed in 6 tablespoons oleo. Serve hot with Wheat Thins.

*Teacher's Pet: Lana Albers/Donna Lambert (daughters)*

## PIMIENTO SPREAD

1 package Kraft pimiento cheese
(or your choice)

1 can Pet milk
1 small jar pimientos, chopped

Combine milk and pimiento in saucepan or double boiler. On low heat, heat and add cheese (cut into strips). Continue to heat to melt cheese. Good as a dip or over crackers. Peppers can be added to make it "HOT".

*John and Marie Hays: Johnny '49*

**Anger is only one letter short of Danger!**

# HOT TOPPERS
*(Hor d'ouevres)*

| | |
|---|---|
| 2 pounds hot sausage | 1 pound Velveeta cheese |
| 1 large onion, diced | 1 loaf wheat bread (party slices) |

Brown sausage (crumbled); add onion. Cook until onion is tender. Add cheese. Mix. Spread mixture on slices of bread and bake at 350 degrees for 5 minutes.

This can be made ahead and frozen. If so, cook at 300 degrees for 7 to 10 minutes.

*Tommy and Wilma Williams: Sherry '75; Danny '77*

# PIMIENTO CHEESE SPREAD

| | |
|---|---|
| 1 pound cheese, grated | 1/2 cup chopped pecans |
| 1 small jar pimiento, mashed | Enough salad dressing to moisten |
| 3 hard-boiled eggs, mashed | |

Mix well and store in refrigerator in tight container.

*Dovie Pace: Martha '55*

# CHEESE DO-DADS

| | |
|---|---|
| 2 sticks oleo | 1/2 tablespoon paprika |
| 1/2 pound sharp cheese | 2 cups flour |
| Tabasco sauce to taste | 3 tablespoons cold water |
| 1 cup chopped nuts | |

Grate cheese. Mix all ingredients. Roll like refrigerator cookies and chill. Slice into cookie thickness and bake at 350 degrees for 10 to 12 minutes. DO NOT GREASE COOKIE SHEET.

*Arlan and Ima Kellum: Becky '61*

All people smile in the same language.

## HOT PEPPER CHEESE SNACKS

1/2 pound oleo or butter
1 teaspoon salt
1/2 pound sharp cheese
1 cup ground pecans

1 or 1-1/2 teaspoons cayenne
pepper (1-1/2 makes them
HOT!)
2-1/2 cups flour

Leave cheese at room temperature all day, then grate. Cream oleo and salt; add cheese and other ingredients. Make into several rolls; wrap in wax paper and chill. Slice thin and bake at 350 degrees for 10 minutes.

*James and Sue Ulmer: Lois '61*

## JALAPENO CHEESE SQUARES

1 pound Monterey cheese, grated
1 pound sharp cheese, grated
1/4 to 1/2 cup chopped jalapeno

1/2 cup flour
2 eggs, beaten
1 can evaporated milk

Mix cheeses and jalapeno; press in 9x13" pan. Mix flour, eggs, and milk; pour over cheese mixture and bake at 325 degrees for 30 to 40 minutes.

*Frances and Ilaverne Tubb: Lynn Adele '49*

## SAUSAGE CHEESE BALLS

1 pound sausage
2 cups cheddar cheese

1 package Mexican Cornbread
Mix OR 2 cups Bisquick
1 egg

Mix all ingredients together. Roll into walnut-size balls. Bake for about 25 minutes at 350 degrees. Makes 30 to 40 balls.

*Note:* Great for Christmas Party; office party. Can be kept warm on warming tray.

*B. B. and Brooksie Stephens: Beckie '76*

## SAUSAGE BALLS

1 (10 ounce) package cheddar
  cheese

1 pound hot bulk sausage
2-1/2 cups Bisquick

Cut cheese into cubes. Melt in double boiler or microwave. Mix sausage, Bisquick, and melted cheese. Make into balls. Bake 15 minutes at 400 degrees.

*Note:* May be frozen before baking. Place on cookie sheet and freeze until firm. Store in freezer.

*L. B. and Phanshon Hudgens: Gary '72*

**May you never have so much
That you are a slave to what you own.**

# TORTILLA ROLL-UPS

1 (8-ounce) package cream
    cheese, softened
8 ounce sour cream
1 small can chopped green chilies
1 small jar chopped pimientos,
    drained

1/2 to 1 cup chopped pecans
1 "finely" chopped green pepper,
    optional
1 package Jumbo flour tortillas

Mix all ingredients thoroughly; spread mixture on individual tortillas and roll tightly. Wrap in Saran Wrap; secure by laying open side **down**. Refrigerate overnight. Slice in 1/2" thickness. Good party food!

*Rodney and Jane Noble: Carmen '78*
*Yvonne Vickery: Dawn '85*

# MICROWAVE CARAMEL CORN

1 cup brown sugar
1 stick margarine
1/4 cup white Karo

1/2 teaspoon salt
1/2 teaspoon soda
3 to 4 quarts popped corn

Combine all ingredients except soda and popped corn. Put in 1-1/2 or 2 quart dish. Bring to boil in microwave, then cook on full power for 2 minutes. Remove from microwave and add soda. Put corn in brown bag and pour syrup over corn. Close and shake. Cook in bag on high for 1-1/2 minutes. Shake and cook another 1-1/2 minutes. Pour into pan and cool.

*Bob and Paula Hamilton: Scott '80; Jeff '81*

# NUTS AND BOLTS

1 (15-ounce) box Cheerios
1 (15-ounce) box Wheat Chex
1 (8-ounce) box Rice Chex
1 (10-ounce) box pretzels
3 cups mixed nuts
2 tablespoons chili powder

1 tablespoon garlic salt
1 tablespoon salt
1-3/4 teaspoons Tabasco sauce
1 tablespoon Worchestershire
    sauce
1 cup oil

In large baking dish mix cereals and nuts; shake mixed dry seasonings over mixture. Heat sauces and oil and pour over mixture. Bake at 250 degrees for 2 hours, stirring every 15 minutes.

*Alex and Linda Catoe: Cody '81*

**A happy greeting from a friend**
**Puts courage in the soul.**

# PARTY MIX
## (TRASH)

2 cans Planters peanuts
1 (10-ounce) package pecans
1 package slim pretzels
1 package Rice Chex
1 box Cheerios
1 package Fritos
Sauce:
1 stick oleo

1/2 cup bacon drippings
2 tablespoons Tabasco
1 tablespoon Worchestershire
 sauce
2 teaspoons salt; 2 teaspoons
 Savor salt
2 teaspoons celery salt

Mix sauce and pour over first mixture. Roast in 250 degree oven 1-1/2 hours covered; uncovered 1/2 to 1 additional hours. Stir every 15 minutes.

*Al and Maxine Hays: Steve '62*

# CANDIED PECANS

1-1/2 cups sugar
1/2 cup water
1 cup honey

1/4 teaspoon salt
1/2 teaspoon vanilla
3-1/2 to 4 cups pecan halves

Mix sugar, water, honey, and salt and boil to a soft stage. Add vanilla. Stir in pecan halves. Stir until creamy. Place on waxed paper and separate with a fork. When cool break apart and store in container.

*Carroll and Estelee Derington: Michell Grissom '84; Lisa Grissom '86*

# PECAN SNACKS

1 tablespoon corn oil
2 cups pecan halves

1/2 teaspoon onion powder
1/2 teaspoon garlic salt

Heat oil in a heavy skillet over moderate heat. Add pecans, onion powder, and garlic salt. Stir constantly 1 minute. Remove from heat; drain on paper towel.

*Ronny and Linda Rice: Johnna '85*

# OVEN TOASTED PECANS

1 quart pecans
4 tablespoons Worchestershire
 sauce

2 dashes Tabasco sauce
4 tablespoons butter
Salt to taste

Combine all ingredients except salt. Mix well. Bake at 250 degrees for 30 minutes, stirring frequently. Drain on paper towel. Salt to taste.

*Paul and Ruth Newman: Paula '52*

# TOASTED PECANS

1/2 cup melted butter                    Salt to taste
3 cups pecan halves

Pour melted butter over pecans; stir to coat well. Arrange in single layer on cookie sheet. Sprinkle with salt. Bake 1 hour at 275 degrees. Stir and add salt occasionally. Makes 3 cups.

*Charles and Ethel Pope: Sherri '82; Ginger '86*

# SWEET TRASH

1 pound almond bark                    2 cups small pretzels
2 cups Rick Krispies                    2 cups salted peanuts
2 cups Captain Crunch

Melt bark in double boiler. Pour over mixed ingredients. Mix. Spoon onto wax paper by teaspoon.

*Randy and Reba Stilwell: Shannon '81*

# MERINGUE NUTS

1 large egg white                    1/8 to 1/4 teaspoon salt
1/2 cup sugar                    2 cups whole nuts
1 teaspoon cinnamon

Beat egg whites and gradually add sugar, cinnamon, and salt. Stir in whole nuts. Drop on greased cookie sheet. Bake 35 to 40 minutes at 300 degrees. Cool on wire rack.

*Note:* While cooking, watch carefully. They will turn a golden brown; take out pretty fast.

*James E. and Sara Jordon: Helen Mary '72; Daniel '76*

It takes both rain and sunshine to make a rainbow.

# ALMOND TEA

2 tablespoons Instant tea
  (sweetened, but without
  lemon)
2 cups cold water
2 cups hot water

1-1/2 cups sugar
2 small cans frozen lemonade
3 teaspoons vanilla
3 teaspoons almond extract
2 quarts water

Dissolve tea in cold water. Boil 2 cups of water with sugar until dissolved (about 5 minutes). "Dump" rest of ingredients together. Makes 3 quarts. ENJOY!

*Arlan and Ima Kellum: Becky '61 (submitted by Becky Kellum Menti)*

# BANANA PUNCH

6 cups water
4 cups sugar
1 (46-ounce) can pineapple juice
2 (12-ounce) cans concentrated
  orange juice

1 (12-ounce) can concentrated
  lemon juice
6 bananas, well mashed
1 large size 7-Up or Ginger Ale

Boil water and sugar 3 minutes to dissolve. Cool. Combine fruit juices and bananas and mix well with sugar and water mixture. Adjust to taste. Freeze overnight in 4 (1 quart) containers. One or two hours before serving, take out of freezer. Right before serving, add 1 bottle of 7-Up or Ginger Ale to mixture. The mixture should be slushy.

*Herbert and Vera Barnes: Ronnie '62*

# ORANGE BLUSH

1 (6-ounce) can frozen orange
  juice, undiluted
1 quart cranberry juice cocktail

1/4 to 1/2 cup sugar
1 quart club soda

Combine first 3 ingredients and mix well. Just before serving, add club soda and serve over crushed ice.

*Joseph and Lynn Lynch: Nathan '86*

# ORANGE SLUSH DRINK

1 (12-ounce) can frozen orange
  juice
1 cup milk
1 cup water

1 teaspoon vanilla
1/2 cup sugar
Several ice cubes

Mix all ingredients. Add ice cubes and pour into blender. Blend until a thick slush. DELICIOUS!

*Eddie and Betty McNett: Becky '82*

**"They say" is often proved a great liar.**

# HOT CRANBERRY PUNCH

4 sticks cinnamon
1 cup brown sugar
4 teaspoons cloves (whole)
1/4 teaspoon salt
9 cups cranberry juice

9 cups pineapple juice
4-1/2 cups water
1 tablespoon red food coloring,
  optional

Pour cinnamon, sugar, cloves, and salt in top of coffee pot. Place liquids in bottom of coffee pot. Brew.

*Al and Maxine Hays: Steve '62*

# PINEAPPLE WASSAIL

4 cups unsweetened pineapple
  juice
1 (12-ounce) can apricot nectar
2 cups cider

1 cup orange juice
6 sticks cinnamon, broken
1 teaspoon whole cloves

Combine all ingredients; heat to boiling. Simmer 15 to 20 minutes. Serve hot.

*Note:* Can be made in 30 cup coffee maker.

*Joe and Carolyn Weatherby: Randy '70*

# SLUSH PUNCH
### (can be made any color)

3 cups sugar
3 cups water
2 small packages jello, choice of
  color
3/4 cup real lemon juice

2 cups pineapple juice
2 teaspoons almond flavoring
4 cups hot water
4 quarts cold water

Boil sugar and water; add jello, lemon juice, pineapple juice, and almond flavoring. Add hot water, then cold water. Freeze. Set out before time to serve in time to make slush.

*Ernie and Anetta Reusch: Roxa '76*

# DOUBLE STRAWBERRY DREAM

1 (10-ounce) package frozen
  sliced strawberries
1/2 pint strawberry ice cream

1 large banana, cut up
2 cups milk
1 teaspoon vanilla

Combine strawberries, ice cream, banana, 1 cup milk, and vanilla in electric blender. Cover and blend. Stir in remaining milk and blend. Pour into 6 tall glasses. Garnish with several fresh strawberries.

*Odis and Rose Schoolcraft: Linda '67*

# HOT CHOCOLATE MIX

1 ( 8-quart) box powdered milk     1 (1-pound) box powdered sugar
1 (2-pound) box Nestles Quick     1 (11-ounce) jar Coffee Mate

Stir real well, then sift. Store in tight container. Use 2 to 3 heaping teaspoons in cup; add hot water. Stir.

*Robert and Lynda Blubaugh: Corey '83*

# HOT SPICED DRINK

*(Excellent in winter, plus it makes the house smell good)*

1 tablespoon whole cloves     1/4 teaspoon salt, optional
1/2 tablespoon whole allspice     3 cups water
3 sticks cinnamon, broken     3 cups pineapple juice
1/2 cup brown sugar, lightly
    packed

Pour water and juice in bottom of an electric 8 to 10 cup percolator. Place rest of ingredients in top basket. Let percolate through cycle.

*D.K. and Dessie North: Sheree '72; Terry '78*

# HOT TEA PUNCH

3 family-size tea bags     2 sticks cinnamon
9 cups boiling water     1/2 cup honey
1 can (6-ounce) frozen lemonade     1/2 cup sugar
    concentrate

Pour boiling water over tea bags and steep for 5 minutes. Remove tea bags. Stir in remaining ingredients and simmer and steep for 10 minutes. Makes 12 servings.

This will store in refrigerator; reheat to serve.

*William (Bill) and Sammie Jo Manes: Glenna '60; Paula '64*

# INSTANT SPICED TEA

2 cups Tang     1 package Twist Lemonade Mix
2 cups sugar     (or other)
1/2 cup Instant tea     1-1/2 teaspoons cinnamon
    1-1/2 teaspoons cloves

Mix well (can use blender). Store in tight container. Use 2 heaping teaspoons of mix per cup of hot water (or desired amount).

*Dean and Alice Crawley: Kelly '71*

---

**If "Life" Hands you a lemon...**
**Make lemonade.**

# Soups and Stews

Lunch with Friends 1923

*Reflections...*

# Lunch with Friends — 1923

School was always so much fun! Every day was met with excitement, just waiting for something wonderful to happen.

Besides the important part of learning, even the walk to and from school meant you could talk and talk with your neighbor-friends. If the weather was bad, we were taken to school; otherwise, we walked the mile or so.

An added joy at school was lunchtime. Lunch was often brought to school in a special little lard bucket. At noontime, we would go outside and sit under a shade tree, visit, and leisurely eat the lunch our precious mothers had prepared for us. I can still smell lunchtime when I smell peanut butter and crackers! A very special treat my mother often sent was fried chocolate pies. They were made like any other fried pie — only the inside was a sweet mixture of chocolate, sugar, and a pat of butter. I have never tried that delicious treat since those days.

I think I shall go NOW and try it!

No, I am afraid! I am afraid it will not taste like I remember it. I want to save the memory!

DO YOU HAVE A MEMORY YOU WANT TO SAVE?

# BLACK BEAN SOUP

4 cups black beans
3 quarts water
2 cups diced ham (ham bone,
  optional)
2 onions, finely chopped
1 green pepper, finely chopped
1/4 to 1/2 cup butter
2 teaspoons salt
2 bay leaves

1/2 teaspoon thyme
1/4 teaspoon cayenne
1/2 teaspoon oregano
1/2 teaspoon curry powder
3 tablespoons vinegar
1 cup white wine, rum, or
  cooking sherry
2 cups light cream
Lime

Rinse beans; add water. In soup pot, saute ham, onions, and green pepper in butter. When onions are soft, add all spices. Add beans, the water, and vinegar. Add ham bone, if used. Bring to a slow boil; cook 1 hour. Lower heat to simmer and cook 5 hours. Remove ham bone and allow beans to cool slightly. Puree in blender in batches. Return to pot; add wine and cream; heat slowly. Garnish with lime.

*Steve and Kelly Smith: Scott '81*

# BLACK-EYED PEA SOUP

1 pound ground round
3 to 5 cups fresh cooked
  black-eyed peas

1 can Rotel tomatoes
1/2 cup chopped onions
Salt and pepper to taste

Brown meat. Use fresh cooked black-eyed peas or you can use canned ones. Combine all in a large pot and simmer. Add salt and pepper to taste. Add water to cover. Cook "down" to make thick juice.

*Note:* To make it a little different, fresh cut and chopped okra can be cooked with it.

*Coker and Jane Lassiter: Lea Ann '76*

# BROCCOLI AND CHEESE SOUP

1 chopped onion
2 tablespoons butter
2 tablespoons flour
Salt and pepper to taste
Nutmeg to taste

2 cans Campbell's double rich
  chicken broth
1 package frozen chopped
  broccoli (1 cup or to taste)
1 (8-ounce) Half and Half milk
1 (8-ounce) grated cheddar cheese

Saute onion in butter; add flour and seasonings. Add chicken broth and broccoli and cook for 30 minutes. Add Half and Half and cook 5 minutes longer. Add grated cheese and simmer until cheese melts. Serve with toasted English muffins. WONDERFUL!

*C.E. and Lois Short: Camille '79*

# CREAM OF BROCCOLI SOUP

| | |
|---|---|
| 1 quart chicken stock | 1/2 teaspoon white pepper |
| 1 cup dry white wine | 1 tablespoon Tabasco |
| 1 bunch fresh broccoli | 1 cup light cream |
| 1 tablespoon lemon juice | 1/2 stick butter |
| 1/2 teaspoon salt | |

Combine all ingredients except butter and cream in a soup pot. Bring to a boil then lower heat and simmer 1 hour. Let cool and puree in blender. When ready to serve, add cream and butter and heat — **just to boiling point,** or until butter is melted. Serve with a slice of toasted French bread.

*Johnny and Edith Smith: Becky '53*

# CANADIAN CHEESE SOUP

*Talk about good in the wintertime*
*with a pan of cornbread!*

| | |
|---|---|
| 1/4 cup oleo | 1 quart chicken stock |
| 1/2 cup diced onions | (4 cubes=1 quart) |
| 1/2 cup diced carrots | 1-1/2 teaspoons salt |
| 1/2 cup diced celery | 1/8 teaspoon pepper |
| 1/4 cup flour | 1/8 teaspoon soda |
| 1-1/2 tablespoons cornstarch | 1 cup cheddar cheese, grated |
| 1 quart milk | 2 tablespoons chopped parsley, optional |

Melt oleo in large saucepan, and saute diced vegetables until tender. Add flour and cornstarch; cook until bubbly. Add milk and chicken broth, plus seasonings. Cook until sauce is smooth. Mix baking soda with grated cheese and add to soup mixture, stirring until cheese is melted. Cover and simmer 15 minutes, stirring from bottom of pan occasionally. Just before serving, add parsley. Makes 2 quarts.

*Joe and Chan Longley: Chad '78*

The door to happiness opens outward.

# CHEESE SOUP

1-1/2 cups celery, chopped
1-1/2 cups onions, chopped
1-1/2 cups bell pepper, chopped
1-1/2 cups carrots, chopped
1/2 cup butter
1/3 cup flour
2 tablespoons cornstarch

2 cans chicken broth
1 quart milk
1 pound box Velveeta cheese
1 bag Green Giant
    Broccoli-Cauliflower-Carrots
1-1/2 cups cooked chicken,
    chopped (or canned chicken)

Saute vegetables in butter. Stir in flour and cornstarch and mix well. Add chicken broth, milk, cheese, bag of vegetables, and chopped chicken. Heat until well heated. Very versatile. Can use different vegetables; use fresh instead of frozen.

*J.D. and Cozette Sanders: Debbie Sanders Ryals: '60 (submitted by Debbie)*

# CHICKEN SOUP

1 package chicken breast (about
    4) boiled with skin
1 cup chopped onions
1 cup chopped celery
1 cup shredded carrots, optional

1/2 cup uncooked converted rice
1-1/2 cups potatoes, cubed
Salt and pepper to taste
1/2 pound (or less) Velveeta
    cheese

Debone chicken. Boil onions and celery in broth. Add chicken pieces back to broth. Add carrots, rice, and potatoes. Cook until vegetables are done. Salt and pepper to taste. When done, add cheese before serving and let melt.

*Note:* Can add 1 cup bouillon or water if liquid is needed.

*Gary and Sidney Gaston: Whitney '85*

# EASY CHEESEY CHICKEN SOUP

3 boneless, skinless chicken
    breasts
1/2 cup chopped celery
1/2 cup chopped onions
1 can Cream of Mushroom soup

1 can Cream of Chicken soup
1 small can condensed milk
1 cup grated cheese, (your choice)
1 teaspoon pepper
Salt to taste

Cook (boil) chicken breasts until done and reserve 1/2 of broth. Dice breasts and set aside. Saute celery and onions in small amount of oil. To broth add soups, milk, and cheese. With wire whisk, stir until mixture is smooth. Add diced breasts, salt, pepper, sauteed celery and onions. Heat until hot. Serves 6.

*Ronnie and Nancy Purtell: Wade '82*

# CLAM CHOWDER

3 (7-1/2 ounce) cans chopped
  clams
6 ounce salt pork, minced
4 cups diced potatoes
1-1/2 cups water
1/2 medium onion, chopped

2 cups milk
3 tablespoons flour
1 cup Half and Half
1-1/2 tablespoons salt
Pepper to taste

Strain liquid from clams, reserving 1/2 cup. In saucepan, fry salt pork until crisp; remove pork and set aside. Add reserved clam liquid, potatoes, water, and onion to drippings in pan. Bring to boil and simmer until potatoes are tender (15 to 20 minutes). Stir in clams. Blend 1/4 cup milk into flour, then blend into remaining milk. Stir into chowder with Half and Half and cook, stirring until boiling. Add salt and pepper and sprinkle reserved pork bits on top.

*James and Elewese Crain: James '54; Jan '56; Rhonda '59*

# CORN CHOWDER

*(This is one of my favorite recipes!)*

1 pound thin-sliced bacon,
  cooked crisp; mince
1/4 cup bacon drippings
1 onion, chopped
2 (17-ounce) cans Cream style
  corn
2 cups cubed cooked potatoes

2 cups potato water
1 can evaporated milk
1 teaspoon salt
1/4 teaspoon garlic salt
1 half moon cheddar cheese,
  cubed

Cook bacon until crisp; saute onion in bacon drippings. In large pan, combine all other ingredients, except cheese. Simmer until hot. Add cheese and cook until melted.

*Bob and Nancy Campbell: Tammy '80; Steve '82*

# SPEEDY-DO CHOWDER

3 tablespoons butter
1-1/2 cups sliced celery
1 cup chopped onions
2 tall cans evaporated milk
1 can condensed tomato soup or
  Cream of Mushroom soup

1 can cut green beans, drained
1 can whole kernel corn, drained
1 can corn beef hash
1/4 teaspoon thyme
4 drops hot pepper sauce

Melt butter in soup kettle; add celery and onions. Cook slowly until tender but not brown. Stir in milk, soup, and drained vegetables. Add remaining ingredients. Mix well and heat. Yields 10 cups; 6 servings.

*Buford and Jackie Andrews: Johnny '66*

# FRENCH ONION SOUP

5 medium onions
4 tablespoons butter
1 teaspoon sugar
2 (10-3/4 ounce) cans condensed
    beef consomme
1 cup water

1/2 cup Holland House Red
    Cooking Wine
Grated Swiss cheese
Paprika
Croutons

Cut onions in half from root to stem ends; then cut to one-half moon shape slices (about 1/8" thick). In a saucepan, melt butter over medium heat; add onion slices and sugar. Saute about 5 minutes or until tender and golden brown. Add consomme, water, and wine. Reduce to low heat. Cover and simmer 15 minutes, stirring occasionally. Pour soup into individual crocks. Top each with croutons. Cover with Swiss cheese; sprinkle with paprika.

*Joe and Sue Summers: Debbie '79 (submitted by Debbie)*

# POTATO-CHEESE SOUP

4 chicken breasts or 1 whole
    chicken
4 to 6 sliced carrots
1 small chopped onion
4 to 6 sliced celery, optional
4 to 6 diced small potatoes

1 Cream of Chicken soup
1 cup milk
4 to 6 slices of any type cheese or
    1/4 pound Velveeta cheese
Salt and pepper to taste

Boil chicken, carrots, onions, celery, and potatoes until done. Remove chicken and debone. Add soup concentrate, milk, and cheese. Return chicken to broth. Simmer until cheese melts. Serve hot.

*WARNING:* Will scorch easily.

*Stan and Janis Payne: Neil '82*

**A good name is better than riches.**

# MAMMA LILL'S
# SHRIMP GUMBO

| | |
|---|---|
| 1/2 cup oil | 2 cans crab, optional |
| 1-1/2 cups flour | 1 pound shrimp (uncooked) and |
| 1 gallon water or chicken broth | peeled |
| 6 stalks celery, chopped | 1 chicken, cooked and deboned |
| 1/2 cup onions, chopped, optional | 1 teaspoon lemon juice |
| 2 cans tomatoes | 4 tablespoons file' |
| 1 large package okra | Salt and pepper to taste |

Cook until **very dark** (almost burned) oil and flour, stirring all the time. When almost burned, add 1 gallon of water or chicken broth, stirring constantly. Add celery, onions, canned tomatoes, and okra. Simmer for about 2 hours, then add crab meat, shrimp, and chicken. Turn off heat on stove. Add lemon juice and file'. Let stand for a couple of hours or overnight. The longer it sits, the better it gets. Serve with rice.

*Note:* Some people may worry about the uncooked shrimp, but they cook in the hot broth. My grandmother that raised me gave me this recipe when Joe and I were first married. She was French and raised in Louisiana in Cajun country. There are several other things that could be added to make it hot — such as hot sauce, but we like it mild.

*Joe and Chan Longley: Chad '78*

# VICHYOISSE POTATOES
## (Soup)

| | |
|---|---|
| 1/4 cup butter | 1-1/2 teaspoons salt |
| 2 cups chopped onions | 1/8 teaspoon pepper |
| 1/4 cup scallions | 1 cup light cream |
| 4 medium potatoes | 1 tablespoon parsley |
| 4 cups chicken broth (2 cans) | 1 tablespoon scallion |

Melt butter in saucepan; add chopped onions and chopped scallions; cook until tender, but not brown. Add potatoes, thinly sliced, chicken broth, salt and pepper. Simmer until vegetables are tender (10 to 15 minutes). Pour into blender and mix. Add cream; reheat, stirring. Add parsley and scallions. 6 servings.

*Floyd and Pat Garrot: Mike '69*

Tearing someone down
never lowers him to your size.

# HEARTY BEEF STEW

| | |
|---|---|
| 2 pounds beef, cut to bite size | 1 bay leaf |
| 6 carrots, cut | 1/4 teaspoon cayenne |
| 1 onion, chopped | 6 medium potatoes, cut |
| Salt to taste | Tomatoes or tomato sauce |

Braise beef in a very hot pan with enough oil to prevent sticking. Cover with water and cook until meat is almost tender. Add carrots, onions, salt, bay leaf, cayenne, and enough water to cover. Continue to cook. Add potatoes when carrots are nearly done. When potatoes are done, add tomatoes or tomato sauce. Simmer for about 15 minutes. Serve with a skillet of cornbread.

*Kenneth and Frances King: Kenny '58; Kelly '61*

# POLISH STEW

| | |
|---|---|
| 1 pound stew meat | 1 medium onion, chopped |
| Flour | 1 package frozen peas and carrots |
| 3 tablespoons oil | 1/4 cup flour |
| 4 cups water | 1/2 cup water |

Dice stew into 1" cubes; roll in flour. Brown in saucepan on all sides in oil. Add water and simmer about 1 hour or longer. Add vegetables and simmer another hour. Thicken with flour and water mixture (mixed into thin paste). GOOD OVER MASHED POTATOES. Makes a meal in one.

*Tom and Pat Harsh: Robert Harsh '75; John Currie '76*

# TEXAS STEW

| | |
|---|---|
| 1 pound hamburger meat | 1 large can Ranch Style beans |
| 4 cans (large) chunky vegetable soup | |

Brown hamburger meat until brown and crumbly. Drain meat. Mix beans and soup. Combine with meat; heat until hot. Serve with crackers or cornbread.

*Stanley and Brenda Morris: Kim '80*

Today is the tomorrow you worried about yesterday.

# TACO SOUP

1-1/2 pounds hamburger meat, browned
3 cans stewed tomatoes (1 can Rotel)
1 can Ranch Style Beans
1 can Pinto or Kidney Beans
1 can corn (I leave this out)
1 small can green chilies, chopped
1 package Ranch Style Dressing
1 package Taco Seasoning

Brown hamburger meat; drain. Open cans; pour into big pot. Sprinkle in Ranch Style Dressing mix and Taco Seasoning. Add meat. Heat for 30 minutes.

Serve with chips or cornbread. YUM! YUM!

*Gerard and Lulabel VanDuist: Ryan '79*

# VEGETABLE SOUP

1 pound ground meat (do not brown separately)
1 can Ro-Tel tomatoes
1 can whole kernel corn
1 can Veg-All
1 medium chopped onion
2 medium potatoes, cut in chunks (or more)
Salt and pepper to taste

Put all ingredients in large pan, using liquid from all canned foods. Add several cans of water and cook for at least 1 hour. Add salt and pepper to taste. Delicious with hush puppies.

*James and Faye Bearden: Karen '66*

# 5-CAN SOUP

3 cans Campbell Minestrone Soup
1 can Ranch Style Beans
1 can Rotel tomatoes
1/2 pound hamburger meat, browned

Combine and simmer for 1 hour or cook in crock pot on low for 6 hours. (My favorite recipe.)

*Francis and Ilaverne Tubb: Lynn Adele '49*

Life is like an onion...
You peel off one layer at a time,
And sometimes you weep.

*Salads*

Pop Delivery Truck 1924

*Reflections...*

# The Soda Pop Man — 1924

What child does not enjoy the colors of the rainbow? Who does not love the colors of jello? Popsicles? And soda pop?

When I was a very small child, my father owned a service station "over by the highway". Our house sat about a mile away inside a pasture with a winding road that led to the service station on the highway and many days my sisters and I would walk to the highway to do two things: pick up the mail (which always included the Fort Worth Star Telegram) and to stop by the service station to see if we could manage to get a cold soda pop from the ice box.

It was such a fun time to be there when the Soda Pop Man pulled his truck into the driveway and began to unload the new cases of colorful soda pop. There were all colors: lime green for the lime; red for the strawberry; purple for the Delaware punch; orange for the orange; and yellow for the lemon. When I'd see all those pretty colors coming off the truck, I wanted one of each. It was so hard to make a choice! Those were days that lingered long after we moved from that place.

# APRICOT AND PINEAPPLE SALAD or DESSERT

1 (8-ounce) can crushed
  pineapple, undrained
1 (3-ounce) package Orange Jello
3/4 cup sugar
2 (4-3/4 ounce) jars strained
  apricot baby food

1 (8-ounce) package cream
  cheese, softened
1 (8-ounce) carton Cool Whip
1 cup Chopped pecans

Combine pineapple, jello, and sugar in small saucepan. Stir over low heat until jello is dissolved. Remove from heat and add cream cheese and apricot baby food. Mix well but do not beat. Chill until slightly thickened. Fold in Cool Whip and spoon into bowl, sprinkle with chopped pecans. 8 servings.

*H.S. and Alice Earle: Margaret Ann '49*

# CREAMY APRICOT JELLO SALAD

1 small package Apricot Jello
1 small can crushed pineapple
1/2 cup hot water
1 small package soft cream cheese

1 cup Cool Whip
1 cup chopped pecans
1 cup chopped celery

Mix jello, pineapple, and hot water; bring to a boil; boil 10 minutes. Add cream cheese. Stir until dissolved. Add Cool Whip, chopped pecans, and celery. Refrigerate.

*John and Judy Blair: Leslie '79*

# GRANDMA LO'S BLUEBERRY SALAD

1 large package Raspberry Jello
1 cup boiling water
1 can blueberries, in heavy syrup

1 small can crushed pineapple
1/2 pint whipping cream
1/2 cup chopped nuts

Mix boiling water with jello. Add blueberries and pineapple and allow to gel. Stir well and add whipped cream and nuts. Mix thoroughly. Chill.

*Wayne and Lo Parker: Yates '62; Stan '64*

Don't ever eat at the house
where the cook is skinny!

# BLUEBERRY SALAD

2 (3-ounce) packages Blackberry
  or Black Raspberry Jello
2 cups boiling water
1 (15-ounce) can blueberries
  (drain but save liquid)
1 (8-1/4 ounce) can crushed
  pineapple (drain but save
  liquid)

Topping:
1 (8-ounce) package cream
  cheese, room temperature
1 carton sour cream
1/2 cup sugar
1/2 teaspoon vanilla
1 cup chopped pecans

Pour boiling water over jello and stir until dissolved. Drain fruit and measure liquid. Add enough water to make 1 cup; add to jello mixture. Stir in fruit. Pour into a 2-quart flat pan. Cover and place in refrigerator until almost set. For topping blend the first 4 ingredients and stir well. Beat in mixer until fluffy. Spread over congealed salad and sprinkle with pecans. Chill.

*George and Beatrice Pendleton: Sammy '52*
*(submitted by Gloria Pendleton, daughter-in-law)*
*Melvin and Colleen Timmons: Larry '75*

# CHERRY SALAD

1 package Cherry Jello
1-1/2 cups boiling water
1 can Cherry Pie Filling Mix

1 (3-ounce) package cream cheese
1 cup nuts, chopped

Mix jello and hot water. Add Cherry Pie Filling and cream cheese. Stir. Add nuts. Chill.

*Note:* May use frozen strawberries and strawberry jello.

*William and Ruth Phillips: Billie Ruth '53*

# CHERRY COKE SALAD

1 box Black Cherry Jello
1/2 cup Black Cherry juice
1/2 cup pineapple juice
8 ounce Coca-Cola

1/2 cup cherries
1/2 cup crushed pineapple
1/2 cup chopped pecans

Mix the liquids and bring to a boil. Pour over jello. Add remaining ingredients and refrigerate to jell.

*Mrs. Clara Roach, aunt: Roger Glover '50*

---

**The argument you win with your wife —
Isn't over yet!**

# COCA COLA DELIGHT

2 (3-ounce) packages Black
  Raspberry Jello
2 cups hot water
1 can black sweet cherries,
  drained; save liquid

1 (10-ounce) package frozen
  strawberries, drained
1 (6-ounce) coke
1 cup chopped nuts
1 cup miniature marshmallows
Whipped cream

Dissolve jello in hot water. Measure juice from fruit, coke, and enough water for 2 cups cold liquid. Pour into jello and hot water mixture. Partially jell. Add remaining ingredients except whipped cream. Pour into mold; stir occasionally to keep fruit from setting. Chill. Top with whipped cream.

*Jack and Oleta Greaves: Linda '61; Donna '63; Randy '66*

# COMPANY SALAD
## *(Lemon)*

1 package lemon gelatin
2 cups hot water
1 cup heavy cream, whipped
1 cup grated cheese

1 cup chopped nuts
1 small can crushed pineapple,
  drained
1 small bottle stuffed olives

Dissolve gelatin in hot water. Let stand in refrigerator until almost set and then whip until creamy. Fold in whipped cream, cheese, nuts, pineapple, and olives. Pour in mold and chill.

*Ernie and Joyce Higdon: Kim '73*

# CRANBERRY SALAD

1 quart cranberries, ground
1 orange, seeded, quartered and
  ground (rind included)
1 cup chopped pecans

1 cup chopped celery
2 cups sugar
2 packages Cherry Jello
2 cups hot water

Mix ground and chopped ingredients. Mix jello and hot water; add sugar and mix. Cool. Add first ingredients; mold or put in pint or quart jars. Keeps well.

*O.B. and Wanda Raburn: Rocky '62; Chuck '67*

**Life is fragile
Handle with prayer.**

## CRANBERRY-APPLE SALAD

2 cups cranberries
1 cup sugar
1 cup boiling water
1 package Cranberry Jello
1 cup hot water

15 marshmallows
1 cup diced celery
1 cup diced apples
1 cup chopped pecans

Combine cranberries, sugar, and boiling water. Boil 10 minutes. Dissolve cranberry jello in hot water. Add marshmallows to jello and stir until melted. Cool until thick and syrupy. Add celery, apples, and nuts. Mix with cranberry mixture. Chill.

*Note:* Strawberry jello may be used.

*Glen and Cleta Wieser: Karol '68; Kerri '74*

## RAW CRANBERRY SALAD

1 package Raspberry Jello or
    Strawberry Jello
1 cup boiling water
1 pound cranberries
1 orange

Pinch of salt
2 cups sugar
2 tart apples, diced
1 cup chopped celery
1 cup chopped nuts

Dissolve jello in hot water. Let cool. Grind cranberries and orange. Combine with sugar, apples, celery, and nuts. Add jello mixture. Chill.

*C.M. "Dick" and Carmen Williams: Gail '55*

## LIME JELLO

1 large package Lime Jello
1 cup boiling water
12 large marshmallows, chopped
    up
1 can crushed pineapple, drained

12 teaspoons vinegar or lemon
    juice
2 large packages cream cheese
    (or 1 cottage cheese)
1/2 pint whipped cream
1 cup chopped pecans

Mix jello in boiling water; mix marshmallows and let dissolve in hot jello. Partially cool. Add remaining ingredients. Chill.

*John and LaVelle Carrigan: Chuck '55*

---

**The company of a friend
seasons the meal!**

# MANDARIN FLUFF

1 large package Orange Jello
2 cups boiling water
1 small can frozen orange juice

1 pint orange sherbet
1 small can mandarin oranges

Dissolve jello in boiling water. Add juice and sherbet while jello is hot. Stir until all ingredients are melted. Add oranges. Chill until it sets.

*Marvin and Kathy Friemel: Randy '78*

# ORANGE SALAD

1 package Orange Jello
1 cup hot water
3/4 cup cold water
1 small can coconut

1 can mandarin oranges, drained
1 small can crushed pineapple, drained
1 carton whipping cream

Mix jello with hot water; dissolve. Add cold water. Let almost set. Beat until foamy. Add next 3 ingredients; mix. Add whipped cream. Return to refrigerator to jell.

*Bob and Johnnie Shannon: Neva Jo '51*

# RASPBERRY JELLO SALAD
## (Favorite)

1 large package Raspberry Jello
1 cup hot water
2 packages frozen raspberries
1 tablespoon lemon juice
1 cup applesauce

1 flat can crushed pineapple
16 marshmallows or 1 jar marshmallow whip (I prefer marshmallow whip)
1 cup sour cream

Dissolve jello in hot water. Add frozen raspberries (add while frozen). Add lemon juice, applesauce, and pineapple. Mix until berries are separated. Pour into mold. Chill until set.

Dressing:

Mix marshmallows and sour cream. Set in refrigerator overnight. Beat and mix before serving or beat the sour cream and blend.

Note: If you are in a hurry, use marshmallow whip.

*Lloyd and Margaret Faye Morgan: Susan '63; Nancy '64; Marsha '66*

---

Blessed are those who can give without
remembering...
And take without forgetting.

## STRAWBERRY JELLO SALAD

1 large box Strawberry Jello
2 cups hot water
2 small packages frozen
   strawberries

1 large can crushed pineapples,
   drained
Pecans, chopped
2 bananas
1 (8-ounce) carton sour cream

Mix jello, using only 2 cups of water. Add thawed strawberries, drained pineapples, and pecans. Pour 1/2 mixture in oblong serving bowl and jell. After set, spread with sliced bananas and sour cream in that order. Cover with remaining mixture and jell.

*Truman and Nadine Kidd: Kenny '72*
*Bob and Johnnie Shannon: Neva Jo '51*

## APRICOT DELIGHT

1 (No. 2-1/2) can apricot, drain;
   reserve juice
1/4 cup sugar
1/4 cup lemon juice
1/2 cup apricot juice

1 egg, beaten
1 small package miniature
   marshmallows
1/2 cup chopped pecans
1 cup whipping cream

Combine sugar, lemon juice, apricot juice, and beaten egg. Cook until thick and cool. Combine apricots, marshmallows, and pecans with sauce. Let refrigerate overnight. Fold in whipped cream before serving.

*Doyle and Faye Kelcy: Gordon '66*

## CHRISTMAS SALAD

1 package cranberries, ground
2 cups sugar
1-1/2 cups dark grapes, halved
   and pitted

1 pint whipped cream
1 cup chopped nuts

Grind cranberries; add sugar; let stand 30 minutes. Add rest of ingredients. Chill.

*Mrs. Wiley Bownds (Helen): Cheryl '67*

**Plan ahead...**
**It wasn't raining when Noah built the ark.**

# 5-CUP SALAD

1 cup pineapple tidbits, drained
1 cup Mandarin oranges, drained
1 cup coconut

1 cup miniature marshmallows
1 cup sour cream

Combine drained fruit with other ingredients. Mix and refrigerate overnight.

*Johnny and Edith Smith: Becky '53*
*Kenneth and Nancy Helvey: Valerie '76*

# LARGE CREAMY FRUIT SALAD

1 quart buttermilk
2 large Instant Vanilla Pudding
Mix
2 large cans fruit cocktail, drained

2 cups chopped pecans
1 large carton Cool Whip
Marshmallows, bananas, cherries
(optional)

Mix buttermilk and pudding mix until smooth. Add fruit cocktail and pecans. Mix well. Add Cool Whip.

*Note:* Reduce to half for 8 to 10 servings.

*Bob, Sr. and Ann Zugg: Bobby '73*

# PEACHY FRUIT SALAD

2 cups fresh or frozen peach
slices, thawed
1/2 cup marshmallow creme

3 ounce package cream cheese,
softened
1/8 teaspoon nutmeg

In food processor or blender, combine all ingredients and blend at medium-low speed until smooth, about 2 minutes. Serve over fresh fruit: grapes, strawberries, apples, bananas, peaches, kiwi, cantaloupe, anything!

*Teacher's Pet: Donna Lambert, daughter*

# QUICK FRUIT SALAD

1 (No. 303) can fruit cocktail
1 large can pineapple chunks
3 bananas

1 small package Instant Lemon
Pudding

Combine fruit cocktail, pineapple chunks and bananas, including juices from fruit. Add Instant Lemon Pudding. Mix well and chill.

*Lloyd and Maxine Stoebner: David '70*

Take care of the minutes,
And the hours will take care of themselves.

# 24-HOUR SALAD

1 can Fruit Cocktail, drained
1 can crushed pineapple, drained
1 can pineapple tidbits, drained
1 small package miniature
 marshmallows

1/2 pint whipping cream
1 small carton Cool Whip or 1/2
 pint whipped cream
Sliced bananas
Chopped pecans

Mix fruits and marshmallows. Mix in 1/2 pint whipping cream and refrigerate overnight. The next day, add Cool Whip or 1/2 pint of whipped cream. When ready to serve, add bananas and nuts.

*Glenn and Lou Ann Rex: Glen (Rusty) '61; Jimmy '66*

# PHILLY-PINEAPPLE SALAD

1/2 pint whipping cream,
 whipped
1 (No. 2) can crushed pineapple
 (sweet)
1/2 cup mayonnaise
2 tablespoons powdered sugar

4 ounces maraschino cherries,
 drained and halved
1/2 package miniature
 marshmallows
1 cup chopped pecans

Whip cream and add other ingredients in order given. Freeze. Put on lettuce leaf few minutes before serving.

*Jimmy and Vera Jones: Jimmy '67*

# PINK SALAD

1 (10-ounce) carton Cool Whip
1 can Eagle Brand Milk
1 can crushed pineapple, drained
1 cup miniature marshmallows

1 cup coconut
1 cup nuts
1 large can Cherry Pie Filling

Combine Cool Whip and Eagle Brand; mix. Add other ingredients. Chill.

*Ken and Mary Lin Stewart: Barry '73; Stephen '77*

**He who is not ready,
Will be less so tomorrow!**

# PINK CLOUD SALAD

1 large container whipped
    topping
1 (16-ounce) carton cottage cheese

1 (18-ounce) can crushed
    pineapple, drained
1 small package wild strawberry
    gelatin

Combine whipped topping and cottage cheese; mix well. Stir in pineapple. Add dry gelatin and mix well. Chill overnight.

*Jerry and Frieda Duggan: Kenny '71 (submitted by Ken and Janna Duggan)*

# FROZEN FRUIT SALAD

1 (No. 2-1/2) can fruit cocktail,
    drained
1 teaspoon unflavored gelatin
2 tablespoons lemon juice
1 (3-ounce) package cream
    cheese, softened

1/4 cup mayonnaise
Dash of salt
2/3 cups whipping cream, chilled
1/2 cup sugar
1/2 cup chopped nuts

Drain fruit cocktail. Soften gelatin in lemon juice, then dissolve over hot water. Blend cream cheese with mayonnaise and salt. Stir in gelatin. Whip cream until stiff, adding sugar gradually during last stages of beating. Fold in cheese mixture, nuts, and fruit cocktail. Pour into refrigerator tray or similar pan that has been lined with waxed paper. Freeze. Turn out on platter, remove paper, and cut into thick slices. Garnish with watercress. 8 servings.

*Note:* Let salad stand at room temperature for a few minutes just before serving; flavor and texture are ever so much better.

*Billy and Earlene Payne: Stan '59*

# SUPER FROZEN SALAD

3 mashed bananas
1 can crushed pineapple, drained
    (medium size)

1 cup sugar
1 (12-ounce) Cool Whip
1 cup buttermilk

Mix bananas, pineapple, and sugar; set aside for 10 minutes. Mix Cool Whip and buttermilk with fruit and freeze.

*Wayne and Frances Caraway: Kenny '64*

---

**A day of worrying is more exhausting
than a week of work.**

## AUNT MARIE'S
## FROZEN CRANBERRY SALAD

1 can cranberry (whole) sauce
1 (12-ounce) can crushed
   pineapple, well drained
3 bananas, mashed

1 cup chopped pecans
1 cup miniature marshmallows
1 cup whipped cream with 3
   tablespoons sugar

Mix and freeze.

*Russell and Maurene Austin: Sherry Kay '61*

## HOT FRUIT

1 pound canned peaches
1 cup dried apricots
1 can chunk pineapple, drained
1/2 cup brown sugar
1/2 teaspoon lemon peel

2 tablespoons lemon juice
1/3 cup orange juice
1 teaspoon orange peel
1 can dark cherries, drained

Mix all except dark cherries and bake at 350 degrees until apricots are tender. Add dark cherries and heat 10 minutes longer. Good served with meats.

*Teacher's Pet: Lana Albers, daughter*

## 3-BEAN SALAD

1 can French style green beans
1 can wax beans
1 can Kidney beans
1/2 cup onions, finely chopped
1/2 cup green peppers, finely
   chopped

1/2 cup vinegar
1/2 cup sugar
1/4 cup Crisco oil
1 teaspoon salt
1 teaspoon pepper

Drain all canned vegetables. Mix all vegetables with onions and pepper. In a separate bowl, mix vinegar, sugar, oil, salt, and pepper. Pour over vegetables. Let marinate for several hours or overnight in refrigerator. Serve cold.

*R.J. and Erie Walker: Sue '54*

### Ye are the salt of the earth.

# CARROT SALAD

3 cups shredded carrots
1-1/3 cups raisins
1 cup chopped celery
1 cup sour cream

1 teaspoon salt
2 teaspoons sugar
2 teaspoons lemon juice
1/8 teaspoon ground cloves

Combine carrots, raisins, and celery. Mix sour cream with remaining ingredients and blend into salad. Chill. 8 to 10 servings.

*Paul and Janice Hathaway: Marilyn Coryea '57*

# PINEAPPLE-CARROT SALAD

1 (7-ounce) can crushed pineapple
1 large carrot, grated

1/2 cup coconut
1/2 cup miniature marshmallows

Combine ingredients and toss lightly.

*Maurice and Marie Simmons: Jill '65*

# CHINESE COLE SLAW

1 large head cabbage, shredded
1 bunch onions, sliced
1 package (2-ounce) sliced
  almonds
1/4 cup sesame seeds

Oleo
2 packages Ramen noodles
  (chicken flavored and
  crushed)

Combine cabbage and onions. Brown almonds and sesame seeds in oleo. Add noodles, almonds, and sesame seeds right before serving. Mix in the seasoning that comes in the noodle package. Add dressing just before serving.

Dressing:
3/4 cup oil
6 tablespoons rice vinegar (or mild
  vinegar)

4 tablespoons sugar
1 tablespoon Accent or 1 teaspoon
  salt and 1 teaspoon pepper

*Everett and Virginia Maxwell: Jane '53*

# CAULIFLOWER-BROCCOLI SALAD

1 large head cauliflower, broken
  up
1 bunch fresh broccoli, chopped
1 bunch green onions, chopped
Green olives, chopped
Fresh tomatoes or use cherry
  tomatoes

3/4 to 1 cup mayonnaise
1/2 (4-ounce) package buttermilk
  salad dressing mix
2 tablespoons sugar
2 tablespoons vinegar

Mix all ingredients thoroughly. Toss and chill.

*Sam and Jenny Gantt: Judy '61*

# 8-DAY SLAW

| | |
|---|---|
| 1 large head cabbage, chopped | 3/4 cup oil |
| 2 medium onions, chopped | 2 teaspoons mustard seeds |
| 2 bell peppers, chopped | 2 teaspoons celery seed |
| 1 cup vinegar | 1/4 teaspoon pepper |
| 1 cup sugar | 2 teaspoons salt |

Mix cabbage, onions, and pepper. Heat vinegar and sugar. Add oil. Mix seasonings with cabbage mixture; pour vinegar mixture over all ingredients. Chill for at least 4 hours.

*J.B. and Susie Smith: Shelton '62*

# HARVEST COLE SLAW

| | |
|---|---|
| 1 cup Miracle Whip Salad Dressing | 1 cup unpeeled tomatoes, chopped |
| 1/4 cup French Dressing | 1/4 cup chopped celery |
| 1 teaspoon salt | 1/4 cup chopped green onion |
| Dash of freshly ground pepper | 1/4 cup sliced radishes |
| 4 cups shredded cabbage | 1/4 pound cubed cheese |

Combine Miracle Whip, French Dressing, salt, and pepper. Mix until well blended. Add remaining ingredients; toss lightly. 6 to 8 servings.

*Forrest and Oleta Noble: Rodney '54*

# CORNBREAD SALAD

| | |
|---|---|
| 1 pan cornbread, cooked | 8 slices bacon, cooked crisp and crumbled |
| 1 large purple onion, chopped | Salt and pepper to taste |
| 1 green pepper, chopped | Miracle Whip, enough to moisten |
| 1 large tomato, chopped | |
| 1 stem celery, chopped | |

Cook cornbread until brown; cool, crumble. Mix onion, pepper, tomato, celery, and bacon. Salt and pepper. Mix well and add cornbread. Add enough Miracle Whip to moisten. Place in mayonnaise greased oblong pan and refrigerate overnight. Cut into squares. Will keep in refrigerator for at least a week.

*N.E. and Sue Sherrill: Bill '72*

## Everything thrives on love.

## SHOE PEG CORN SALAD

| | |
|---|---|
| 1 can shoe peg corn, drained | 1 cup sugar |
| 1 can Lesueur small peas, drained | 3/4 cup vinegar |
| 1 bunch green onions, chopped | 1/2 cup vegetable oil |
| 1 bell pepper, chopped | Salt and pepper to taste |
| 1 small jar pimientos, diced | |

Mix corn, peas, onions, bell pepper, and pimientos. Mix sugar, vinegar, oil, salt and black pepper. Heat to a boil. Pour over vegetables; let set overnight covered. Then drain off all liquid.

*Willard and Loudine Turner: Alan '72*

## SHOE PEG CORN SALAD

| | |
|---|---|
| 2 cans white shoe peg corn, drained | 2 to 3 stalks celery, chopped |
| 2 ounces chopped pimiento | 1/2 cup sugar |
| 1/2 cup chopped green pepper, very fine | 1/2 cup cider vinegar |
| | 1/2 cup Crisco oil |
| 1/2 cup chopped onion | 1 teaspoon salt |
| | 1/2 teaspoon pepper |

Combine all vegetables; mix thoroughly. Combine sugar, vinegar, oil, salt and pepper. Pour over vegetables and marinate 3 to 12 hours. Keeps and gets better!

*Michael and Margaret Slagle: Jordan '86*

## ITALIAN VEGETABLE TOSS

| | |
|---|---|
| 1-1/2 cups of cooked macaroni | 1 cup sliced ripe olives |
| 2 cups broccoli flowerets | 1/2 to 1 cup chopped green onions |
| 1 cup cauliflower flowerets | 2/3 cup Italian salad dressing |
| 1 cup sliced fresh mushrooms | 1 medium avocado, sliced |
| 1 (6-ounce) can artichoke hearts, drained and chopped | 2 medium tomatoes, chopped |

Cook macaroni according to directions; drain. Combine and add other ingredients, except avocado and tomatoes. Toss with salad dressing. Add avocado and tomatoes; mix. Cover and chill several hours. Serves 6 to 8.

*Dalton and Katie Criswell: Vickie '62*

**Three may keep a secret, if two of them are dead.**
**-Poor Richard's Almanac**

## LAYERED LETTUCE SALAD

1 head lettuce, torn
1 cup diced celery
4 hard cooked eggs, sliced
1 (10-ounce) package frozen
  green peas, thawed
1/2 cup diced green pepper
1 medium onion, diced

8 slices bacon, cooked and
  crumbled
1-1/2 teaspoons sugar
2 cups mayonnaise
4 ounces cheddar cheese,
  shredded (1 cup)

Layer first seven ingredients in order given in 9x12" glass dish. Combine sugar and mayonnaise. Spread over top, sealing edges. Sprinkle with cheese. Cover and refrigerate 8 to 12 hours or overnight.

*Carroll and Estelee Derington: Michelle Grissom '84; Lisa Grissom '86*

## 24-HOUR DELICIOUS SALAD

*(Layered Vegetable)*

1 head lettuce, broken up
1 package Lesueur frozen peas
  (boil water and separate peas,
  drain)
1 bunch chopped green onions

1 can sliced water chestnuts
1 cup mayonnaise
1/2 cup (or more) sour cream
1 cup grated cheese
1/2 cup bacon chips

Put in layers in 9x13" casserole dish with lettuce on bottom; progressing to bacon chips on top. Refrigerate 6 hours.

*Teacher's Pet: Donna Lambert, daughter*

## MARINATED SALAD

1 cup finely chopped celery
1/2 cup finely chopped onions
1 finely chopped bell pepper
1 (2-ounce) jar chopped pimiento
1 can French Style green beans,
  drained
1 can small English peas
  (Lesueur)

1 teaspoon salt
Dressing:
1 cup sugar
1/2 cup salad oil
3/4 cup vinegar
2 tablespoons water

Combine all salad ingredients and toss with dressing. Refrigerate overnight, covered. Drain well before serving.

*Jay and Johnna Waldrop: Janae '86*

# POTATO SALAD

1-1/2 teaspoons mustard seed
1 teaspoon celery seed
3 tablespoons vinegar
5 potatoes, cooked and diced
(about 5 cups)
1/2 cup finely chopped green
onions and tops

2 hard boiled eggs, chilled and
diced
3/4 cup mayonnaise
1-1/2 teaspoons salt
Chopped pickles, to taste

Soak mustard and celery in vinegar for 20 to 30 minutes. Combine remaining ingredients in large bowl and toss; add vinegar and seeds. Stir. Chill.

*Note:* The addition of the mustard and celery is the secret for a very tasty salad. Adjust all ingredients to taste.

*Teacher's Pet: Cleone Colvin*

# COTTAGE CHEESE POTATO SALAD

3 hard-boiled eggs (use 1 for
garnish)
4 cups cooked potatoes, boiled,
cooled, and sliced
1 cup diced celery
1 cup large-curd cream style
cottage cheese

3/4 cup mayonnaise
1/2 cup sliced radishes
1/2 cup diced green pepper
1/2 cup sliced green onions
2 teaspoons salt
1/4 teaspoon pepper
Ripe olives

Boil eggs; peel, and chop. Mix with remaining ingredients except olives. Chill. Garnish with egg slices and olives.

*Nile and Janice Cole: Janis Claire '56*

# HOT CHICKEN SALAD

1 cup chopped chicken, or more
1 cup chopped celery
1/2 cup mayonnaise, mixed with
1/4 cup chicken stock

1/2 cup sliced almonds or 1 can
water chestnuts, sliced
1 cup crushed barbecued potato
chips
Sharp cheese, grated

Mix chopped chicken, celery, mayonnaise, stock, and almonds. Alternate a layer of chicken mixture and potato chips. Top with grated cheese. Bake 30 minutes at 350 degrees. Serve hot.

*Milton and Mildred Oswalt: Johnny '52*
*Lawton and Tommie Brevard: Paul '65*
*Howard and Myrtebel McLaughlin: Carole '62*

# TOMATO-ARTICHOKE ASPIC

4 envelopes unflavored gelatin
3/4 cup cold water
5 cups vegetable juice cocktail
   (V8)
1 tablespoon lemon juice
1 teaspoon Worcestershire sauce
1/4 teaspoon hot sauce (if you use
   plain V8)
1/4 teaspoon white pepper

5 carrots, finely chopped
1 (14-ounce) can artichoke hearts,
   drained, coarsely chopped
3/4 cup parsley, minced
3/4 cup celery, finely chopped
1/2 cup green pepper, finely
   chopped (red for color)
Optional: lettuce, lemon, paprika

Sprinkle gelatin over cold water; let stand 5 minutes. Boil V8 and dissolve gelatin/water mixture in it. Add lemon, Worcestershire, hot sauce, and pepper. Fold in vegetables. Spoon into lightly oiled 9-cup mold. Cover and chill until firm. Unmold on a lettuce-lined plate (or with parsley around it); garnish with lemon; sprinkle with paprika.

*Note:* It is more festive, in the Christmas sense, with parsley and omit the lemon garnish. Also the paprika adds nothing. Avocados may be substituted for the artichokes, if they are soft enough to dice.

*Charles and Elizabeth Roberts: Diana '53*

# GUACAMOLE

2 large avocados
1/4 cup chopped onion
1/2 teaspoon garlic powder
1/2 teaspoon Worcestershire sauce
1 large tomato, chopped

1 tablespoon lemon juice
1/8 teaspoon pepper
1/8 teaspoon Tabasco
1/2 cup sour cream
1 tablespoon mayonnaise

Chop and partially mash avocados. Combine rest of ingredients. Chill before serving.

*Ron and Sande Stover: Jason Neinast '84; Brad Neinast '85*

# MACARONI AND SHRIMP SALAD

2 cups cooked elbow macaroni
2 (4-1/2 ounce) cans shrimp
1 avocado, diced
1/2 cup diced celery
2 hard-boiled eggs, diced

2 tablespoons lemon juice
3/4 cup salad dressing
Lettuce cup
Paprika

Toss together all ingredients; spoon into lettuce cups and sprinkle with paprika.

*Sheila Ross Nelson: David '78*

# PASTA SALAD WITH PESTO

12 ounces pasta (linguini)
1/2 recipe of Pesto
1 tablespoon butter
1 tablespoon finely chopped
  shallots

3/4 pound mushrooms, thinly
  sliced
1 (10-ounce) package frozen baby
  peas
1/2 cup sliced ripe olives

Cook pasta; drain; rinse with cool water. Add pesto. Mix well and set aside. Melt butter and saute shallots 1 minute. Add mushrooms; saute 5 minutes. Drain and set aside. Cook peas according to directions; drain, and cool. When ready to serve, mix all ingredients. Serve at room temperature.

Pesto Sauce:
1/2 cup butter, softened
1/2 cup Parmesan cheese
1 cup chopped parsley

2 cloves garlic, crushed
2 teaspoons basil leaves
1 teaspoon marjoram
1/2 cup olive oil

Mix all ingredients in food processor or blender. Leftover can be stored in refrigerator.

*Steve and Kelly Smith: Scott '81*

# SEAFOOD RICE SALAD

8 ounces frozen or fresh cooked
  shrimp
8 ounces tuna, chicken, or turkey,
  chopped
3 cups cooked rice
1/2 cup chopped onions
1/2 cup chopped sweet pickles

1-1/2 cups chopped or thinly
  sliced celery
1/4 cup diced pimiento
3 hard-cooked eggs, chopped
1 tablespoon lemon juice
1 cup mayonnaise
Garnish: Tomato wedges, olives
  or parsley

Combine all ingredients and toss lightly. Season to taste. Chill. Serve on salad greens and garnish with tomato wedges, olives, or parsley.

*Hollis "Buddy" and Carol Luck: Holly '80*

# TACO SALAD

1 pound ground meat, browned
Taco seasoning
2 heads lettuce, torn to bite size
  pieces
2 bunches green onions, chopped
2 large avocados, chopped

2 large tomatoes, chopped
1 pound cheddar cheese, grated
2 cans Kidney beans, drained and
  rinsed
1 large package Doritos,
  "crunched"

Brown meat; season with "Taco" seasoning. Cool. Add other ingredients except Doritos. Add Doritos just before serving. Serve immediately.

*Bill and Mickey Green: Cindy '67*

# MEXICAN SALAD

1 large head of lettuce
1 pound Wisconsin rat cheese,
   grated
1 (15-ounce) can Ranch Style
   Beans, chilled

2 tomatoes, diced
1/2 onion, chopped finely
3/4 bottle Kraft Catalina
   Dressing, chilled
1 package Fritos, crushed

Prepare lettuce as for any tossed salad. Drain and wash chilled beans and add these, the diced tomatoes, chopped onions, grated cheese, and dressing. Chill 30 minutes to an hour before serving. Crushed Fritos are added and mixed well immediately before serving. Serves 12.

(Grand Prize Winner of Fort Worth Star-Telegram Recipe Contest in 1968)
*Francis and Ilaverne Tubbs: Lynn Adele '49*

# RICE TACO SALAD

1 pound hamburger meat
Onion and garlic
2 cups cooked rice
2 chopped tomatoes
1 chopped avocado

Grated cheese
1 teaspoon cumin
Salt and pepper
Taco shells

Brown meat with onion and garlic. Combine with cooked rice, tomatoes, avocado, and grated cheese. Season with cumin, salt and pepper. Can be spooned into taco shells.

*Chuck and Vanita Swift: Terry '83*

# WALDORF SALAD DRESSING

1 egg, beaten
1/2 cup sugar
1/2 cup milk

2 tablespoons vinegar
1 teaspoon butter

Mix all ingredients; bring to a boil and boil 30 seconds to 1 minute. Start to cook; thickens at a good boil. Use over Waldorf Salad (chopped apples, celery, pecans, or walnuts).

*Teacher's Pet: Cleone Colvin*

**I learned a long time ago never to wrestle with a pig.
You get dirty and besides the pig likes it!**

# *Breads*

The Chicken Funeral 1924

# Chicken Funerals — 1924

The coming of spring also brought the coming of little chicks — either by mail order or by the big incubator my mother operated in the storm cellar. How our curiosity mounted when the chicks arrived by mail or they began to hatch as the circumstance might be. Those fluffy bits of round fuzz with all their peeping and chirping, and the hustling and bustling was a big family affair. How we waited as they feathered out and became little chickens. Often times, though, the peepings and chirpings were silenced by death. And the big question was, "How do you take care of that situation?"

In child-like play, the most logical and spiritual thing to do was to have a chicken funeral.

In the corner of our backyard amidst the pebbles, grass, or weeds, we fashioned a tiny graveyard to take care of all the little chicks that died. Many a little chick was given a loving funeral with song service, preaching, and burial in a match box. I was always the preacher! And to be a preacher you must be a MAN!! To correct that major problem all I had to do was to stuff my dress down inside my big bloomers. I was in business! That was all it took.

That scenario was repeated time after time during our spring play.

# ANGEL BISCUITS

| | |
|---|---|
| 1 package dry yeast | 3 teaspoons baking powder |
| 2 tablespoons warm water | 1 teaspoon salt |
| 2-1/2 cups buttermilk | 1 teaspoon soda |
| 1/2 cup oil | 1/4 cup sugar |
| 5 cups flour | |

Dissolve yeast in warm water; add milk. Add oil with sifted dry ingredients. Work and blend with hands. Let rise or cook immediately or place in refrigerator, ready to cook when you like. Bake in greased pan at 425 degrees for approximately 30 minutes.

*Note:* Biscuits do not need to rise before baking, but it is good to make them out a little ahead of time.

*Morris and Barbara Grimes: Susan '70*

# CONFETTI BUBBLE RING

| | |
|---|---|
| 1/2 pound bacon | 1/4 cup chopped green bell |
| 2 cans biscuits | pepper |
| 1/3 cup melted butter | 1/4 cup Parmesan cheese |

Fry bacon until crisp; drain and crumble. Cut biscuits into 1/4's. In mixing bowl, combine all ingredients, mixing lightly with a fork. Pour into greased ring. Bake 20 minutes at 400 degrees.

*Robert and Cheryl Roark: Rachel '83*

# DENVER BISCUITS

| | |
|---|---|
| 1 quart sweet milk | Flour |
| 1 cup sugar | 1 teaspoon salt |
| 1 cup shortening | 2 heaping teaspoons baking |
| 3 packages dry yeast | powder |

Warm milk to lukewarm; add sugar, shortening, yeast, and enough flour to make dough the consistency of cake batter. Let rise about 2 hours in warm place; covered. Work down; let it rise one more time. Add salt, baking powder, and more flour until it is the consistency of biscuit dough. Do not make too stiff, just stiff enough to handle. Roll out, cut, and put on lightly floured cookie sheets and freeze. Store in plastic bags. When ready to use, place in greased pan, set oven at 400 degrees, and put in biscuits immediately. Bake about 20 minutes. MY FAMILY REALLY LIKES THEM!

*Tommy and Wilma Williams: Sherry '75; Danny '77*

## SECRET RECIPE BISCUITS

3 cups Bisquick                    Club soda
1 carton sour cream

Mix Bisquick and sour cream. Add just enough club soda to moisten; roll out on floured surface. Cut with biscuit cutter. Bake in oiled pan at 425 degrees for 10 minutes or until lightly browned. THESE ARE WONDERFUL! This is one of my favorite recipes.

*Bob and Nancy Campbell: Tammy '80; Steve '82*

## SOUR DOUGH BISCUITS

1 package yeast                    5 to 6 cups flour
1 cup warm water                   4 teaspoons baking powder
2 cups buttermilk                  1 teaspoon salt
1/2 cup sugar                      1/4 teaspoon soda
1/2 cup cooking oil

Dissolve yeast in warm water. Add buttermilk, sugar, and oil. Mix dry ingredients and add gradually to first mixture. Put in large bowl and cover tightly; place in refrigerator for 12 hours. (Not necessary to put in refrigerator, but appears to be better). Dough may be fairly soft and need extra flour at this time. Take out what is needed to use at the time. Pinch off and let rise 30 minutes or so or use at once. Cook in greased pan at 450 degrees for 20 minutes. Dough will keep in refrigerator for approximately one week.

*Byford and Jo Ann Sealy: Gayle '67; Kerri '72; Neal '76*

## CORNBREAD

1 egg                              1 tablespoon sugar
1 teaspoon salt (scant)            1 cup meal
1-1/2 to 2 teaspoons baking        1 cup flour
   powder                          Sweet milk

Mix in order given. Add enough milk to give right consistency. Pour into hot greased pan that has had a little bit of meal sprinkled on the grease while it is heating. Bake at 450 degrees until done.

*George and Evelyn Scroggins: George '59*

**Beware of half truths.
You may get the wrong half!**

# BROCCOLI CORNBREAD

1-1/2 sticks oleo
2 boxes Jiffy Cornbread Muffin
   Mix
4 eggs

1 (10-ounce) package chopped
   broccoli
1 (10-ounce) carton cottage cheese
1 medium onion, chopped

Melt oleo in pan and leave enough in bottom so cornbread won't stick. Drain broccoli; and squeeze out all excess water. Pat between paper towel to remove all moisture. (Chop in small chunks.) Pour all mixed ingredients over cornbread mix. Mix well. Cook at 350 degrees for 45 minutes or until top browns. Will freeze or keep in refrigerator a week.

*Bill and Vida Pinkston: Janis '64; Billy '67*

# MEXICAN CORNBREAD

1 cup yellow cornmeal
1/2 teaspoon salt
1/2 teaspoon soda
2 eggs
1 small can cream style corn
1 grated onion

1/4 cup bacon drippings
3/4 cup milk
1 small can chopped green chilies
1/2 pound American cheese,
   grated

Grease and heat pan. Mix all ingredients except cheese and chilies. Spread 1/2 of batter in pan. Sprinkle with cheese and chilies. Cover with remaining batter. Bake 45 minutes at 350 degrees.

*Fred and Jerry Piper: Paula '62; Pam '63*

# SWEET CORNBREAD MUFFINS

2/3 cup meal
1/3 cup flour
1 tablespoon baking powder
1/2 teaspoon salt

1/4 cup sugar
1 egg, beaten
1/2 cup milk
1 teaspoon shortening

Sift meal, flour, baking powder, salt, and sugar into mixing bowl. Mix egg with milk; add shortening and combine with other ingredients. Grease muffin tins and heat. Fill hot muffin tins about 2/3 full. Bake in hot oven at 350 degrees or 375 degrees. Makes 8 large muffins.

*Charles and Billie Burkett: Buz '62*

**May you always have the wisdom
To leave well enough alone.**

# MEXICAN CORNBREAD

1 cup cornmeal
1 cup sweet milk
1 (No. 2) can cream style corn
1/2 cup bacon chips and
    drippings
1/2 teaspoon soda

1 teaspoon baking powder
3/4 teaspoon salt
2 pods garlic, chopped (or less)
3 to 5 jalapeno peppers
1-1/2 cups grated cheese

Mix all except peppers and cheese. Pour in greased (hot) skillet (1/3 of the mixture at a time and sprinkle pepper and cheese between layers. Add rest of cheese and pepper on top and bake until brown. 350 degree oven.

*Mr. and Mrs. Frank Elkins: Annette '56*

# ALABAMA HUSH PUPPIES

1-3/4 cups cornmeal
4 tablespoons flour
1 teaspoon baking powder
1 teaspoon salt

6 tablespoons chopped onions
1 egg, beaten
1 cup boiling water

Mix and sift all dry ingredients. Add onions and egg. Pour boiling water over mixture, stirring constantly until smooth. Drop by teaspoon in hot deep grease.

*Wayne and Frances Caraway: Kenny '64*

# HUSH PUPPIES

1-1/2 cups cornmeal
1/2 cup flour
1 teaspoon salt
1 tablespoon sugar

1 small onion, grated
3/4 cup milk
1 egg

Sift and mix dry ingredients well. Add onion, milk, and egg. Mix lightly to stiff consistency. Allow to set for awhile. (May need to add hot water to bring to right consistency). Drop by spoonfuls into very hot grease. Cook until golden brown.

*Erven and Sue Vanderslice: Carol '68*

Never let yesterday use up today.

# JALAPENO HUSHPUPPIES

2 cups cornmeal
1 cup flour
2 eggs, beaten
3 teaspoons baking powder
1-1/2 teaspoons salt
Pinch of soda

1 small can cream style corn
3 jalapeno peppers, chopped
1/4 bell pepper, chopped
1 small onion, chopped
Buttermilk

Mix all ingredients. Use enough buttermilk to make the consistency of cornbread batter. Fry spoonful portions in medium hot grease.

If heavy and does not rise enough, use more baking powder. If hushpuppies are greasy and break apart, add more flour.

*Danny and LaDonna Ragsdale: Lance '80*

# CORN FRITTERS

1-1/3 cups flour
1-1/2 teaspoons baking powder
1 teaspoon salt

1 (17-ounce) can cream style corn
1 egg, beaten

Sift flour, baking powder, and salt. Mix corn and egg; add to dry ingredients. Drop by spoonful into heated oil.

*Ronny and Linda Rice: Johnna '85*

# CRACKLING BREAD

1-1/2 cups white corn meal
3/4 cup flour, sifted
2 teaspoons baking powder
1/2 teaspoon soda

1/4 teaspoon salt
1 cup sour milk
1 cup cracklings, diced

Mix dry ingredients. Add milk and stir in cracklings. Form into 8 to 10 small oblong cakes. Cook at 400 degrees on greased pan for 30 minutes.

*Donald and Judy Parker: Kevin '78*

Praise is a child's best vitamin.

# APPLE CINNAMON MUFFINS

2-1/4 cups oat-bran cereal
1/4 cup brown sugar
1-1/4 teaspoons cinnamon
1 tablespoon baking powder
1/4 cup chopped walnuts
1/4 cup raisins
1/2 cup skim milk

3/4 cup frozen apple juice
  concentrate
2 egg whites
2 tablespoons vegetable oil
1 medium apple, cored and
  chopped

Mix dry ingredients in large bowl. Mix milk, apple juice, egg whites, and oil in bowl or blender. Add to dry ingredients and mix. Add the chopped apples. Line muffin pans with paper cups and fill with batter. Bake at 425 degrees for 17 minutes. Makes 12 muffins. After cooling, store in large plastic bag to retain moisture and softness. Serve with applesauce or spread with apple butter.

*Leroy and Anna Moss: Debbie '65 (submitted by Debbie Moss Bookout)*

# REFRIGERATOR MUFFINS

2 cups Old Fashioned Oats
2 cups All-Bran
2 cups Shredded Wheat, crushed
3 cups boiling water
4 eggs, slightly beaten
3 cups dark brown sugar, packed

1 teaspoon salt
1 cup Crisco
1 quart buttermilk
5 teaspoons soda
5 cups flour

Combine oats, bran, and shredded wheat; add boiling water; set aside to cool. Add remaining ingredients. Mix well and place in tightly covered container. Place in refrigerator 12 hours. Grease muffin tins or use paper liners. Bake at 400 degrees for 20 minutes. Mixture will keep for 2 weeks in refrigerator.

*Ernest and Ann Thornton: Lane '76*

# BRAN MUFFINS
## (RAISINS)

15 ounces Raisin Bran cereal
1 quart buttermilk
1 cup oil
4 eggs

3 cups sugar
5 cups flour
2 teaspoons salt
2 teaspoons soda

Mix all ingredients. Will keep 6 weeks in tightly covered bowl in refrigerator. Spray or grease muffin tins; bake at 350 degrees for 20 minutes.

*Bill and Betty Luck: Terri '63*

## REFRIGERATOR BRAN MUFFINS

| | |
|---|---|
| 1 cup boiling water | 2-1/2 cups flour |
| 3 cups All-Bran cereal, divided | 2-1/2 teaspoons soda |
| 1 cup sugar | 1/2 teaspoon salt |
| 1/2 cup shortening | 2 cups buttermilk |
| 2 eggs | 3/4 cup raisins |

Pour boiling water over 1 cup cereal; stir to moisten cereal, and set aside to cool. Cream sugar and shortening until light and fluffy; add eggs, one at a time beating well. Combine flour, soda, and salt; add to creamed mixture alternately with buttermilk; stir lightly. Blend in cereal and water mixture, remaining 2 cups cereal, and raisins. Cover and store in refrigerator until ready to use, up to 5 or 6 weeks. When ready to bake, spoon batter into greased muffin tins, and bake at 400 degrees for 20 minutes. Makes 2 dozen.

(The secret to good muffins is to stir only long enough to moisten dry ingredients.)

*Gordon and Sharon O'Dell: Debbie '68; Kim '70*
*L.C. and Govie Maberry: Ronald '52*

## GOLD RUSH MUFFINS

| | |
|---|---|
| 1 cup flour | 1/2 cup finely chopped dried |
| 1/3 cup sugar | apricots |
| 1 tablespoon baking powder | 3 tablespoons vegetable oil |
| 1/2 teaspoon salt | 1 egg, beaten |
| 1 cup uncooked oats, Quick or | 1 cup milk |
| Old Fashioned | |

Sift dry ingredients; stir in oats and apricots. Add oil, beaten egg, and milk. Stir **ONLY** until dry ingredients are moistened. Fill greased muffin tins 2/3 full. Bake at 425 degrees 18 to 20 minutes. Frost with thin orange-water-powdered sugar mixture, if desired.

*Milburn and Marie Nichols: Keith '65*

## PUMPKIN RAISIN MUFFINS

| | |
|---|---|
| 1/4 cup butter or margarine | 1 teaspoon baking powder |
| 1/2 cup sugar | 1/2 teaspoon salt |
| 1 egg | 1/2 teaspoon cinnamon |
| 1/2 cup milk | 1/2 teaspoon nutmeg |
| 3/4 cup canned pumpkin | 1/2 cup raisins |
| 1-1/4 cups unsifted flour | |

Soften butter. Blend in sugar and beaten egg. Stir in remaining ingredients. Blend. Bake at 400 degrees for 20 minutes in lightly greased muffin pans.

*William and Neva Lee: Sheila '69*

## BOHEMIAN COFFEE CAKE

| | |
|---|---|
| 1 cup butter | 1 teaspoon soda |
| 1 cup white sugar | 1 cup buttermilk |
| 1 cup brown sugar | 1/4 teaspoon salt |
| 3 cups flour | 1 cup chopped dates |
| 2 eggs | 1 teaspoon vanilla |

Mix butter, sugars, and flour like pie crust and save out 1 cup for sprinkling on top. Add the rest to the eggs, buttermilk, and remaining ingredients. Pour into greased and floured oblong pan and sprinkle with topping. Bake at 375 degrees for 25 minutes or until done. Better to set overnight.

*Herman and Glenda Lawson: Vana '59*

## COWBOY COFFEE CAKE

| | |
|---|---|
| 2 cans refrigerator biscuits | 1/3 cup chopped pecans |
| 1/3 cup melted oleo | 1 teaspoon cinnamon |
| 1/3 cup brown sugar | |

Cut biscuits into quarters. Press into 9" round greased pan. Mix all other ingredients in another pan and cook over low heat for about 5 minutes. Pour over biscuits and spread to edges. Top should be covered. Bake at 350 degrees for 20 to 25 minutes.

*Raymond and Kathee Johnston: Dee Dee '86*

## EASY BUBBLE BREAD

| | |
|---|---|
| 1 cup brown sugar | 1 teaspoon cinnamon |
| 1/4 cup white sugar | 24 frozen rolls (Rhodes) |
| 1 package Butterscotch Pudding | 1 stick oleo |

Mix sugar, pudding mix, and cinnamon. Place frozen rolls in Bundt pan. Pour mix over rolls. Melt oleo and pour over rolls. Let stand overnight. Bake at 350 degrees for 30 minutes in greased pan.

*Jack and Gaynell Gregg: Joey '68*

A hug a day keeps the blues away.

# BUBBLE LOAF

1 cup scalded milk
1/2 cup cooking oil
1/2 cup sugar
1 teaspoon salt

2 yeast cakes or packages
2 beaten eggs
4-1/2 cups flour

Mix scalded milk, shortening, sugar, and salt. Cool to lukewarm. Crumble yeast into mixture. Add eggs and work in flour. Mix to soft dough; then turn out onto floured board and knead until smooth and elastic, but not sticky. Place in greased bowl and cover with damp cloth. Let rise until double in bulk. Punch down and let set for about 10 minutes. Make into small balls. Roll in sugar mixture. Place in greased Angel Food cake pan in staggered rows and layers. Let rise and then bake in 350 degree oven for 45 minutes. Be sure to use one-piece tube pan. Crunchy on the outside, moist inside.

Sugar Mixture:
1-3/4 cups sugar
2 sticks oleo

4 teaspoons cinnamon
1 cup chopped pecans
1/2 cup raisins, optional

Turn out on plate.

*Jack and Jo Gerald: Ann '66*

# EASY COFFEE CAKE
## *(Very Good!)*

Pecans, chopped
1 package frozen Parker House
    rolls
1 small box Jello Vanilla Pudding
    Mix (dry; not Instant)

Cinnamon, to taste
1 cup brown sugar, packed
1 stick oleo, cut up

Grease bundt pan with oleo. Sprinkle bottom and sides of pan with pecans. Add Parker House rolls on top of pecans. (Some will be up the side of the pan.) Sprinkle box of Jello Pudding Mix over rolls. Add cinnamon to taste. Next, crumble brown sugar over rolls. Add oleo, (cut up) over top. Cover with towel and let stand overnight to rise. (If weather is hot, make very late at night as it could rise over pan.) Bake at 350 degrees for 30 minutes. Turn out of pan onto plate immediately.

*Cecil and Marie Moore: Linda '53*

The smallest deed is better
than the grandest intention.

# APPLE BREAD

| | |
|---|---|
| 1 cup sugar | 1 teaspoon soda |
| 1/2 cup shortening | 1/2 teaspoon salt |
| 2 eggs | 2 cups chopped pared apples |
| 1 teaspoon vanilla | 1/2 cup chopped nuts |
| 2 cups flour | 1 tablespoon sugar |
| 1 teaspoon baking powder | 1/4 teaspoon cinnamon |

Heat oven to 350 degrees. Grease and flour 9x5x3" loaf pan. Mix sugar, shortening, eggs, and vanilla. Stir in flour, baking powder, soda, and salt until smooth. Stir in apples and nuts. Spread in pan. Mix sugar and cinnamon and sprinkle over batter. Bake 50 to 60 minutes. Immediately remove from pan. Cool completely. Store tightly covered. Makes 1 loaf.

*S.P. and Bernice Echols: Delilah '51*

# DOUBLE APRICOT BREAD

| | |
|---|---|
| 3 cups flour | 1 cup apricot preserves |
| 1 teaspoon cinnamon | 1 teaspoon soda |
| 1/2 teaspoon salt | 1 cup buttermilk |
| 1 cup oleo | 1 package dried apricot, chopped |
| 2 cups sugar | fine |
| 4 eggs | 1 cup chopped pecans |

Sift flour, cinnamon, and salt and set aside. Cream oleo and sugar. Add eggs one at a time. Stir in preserves. Dissolve soda in buttermilk. Add alternately with dry ingredients. Mix dried apricot and chopped pecans. Add and mix. Bake in 2 greased and floured loaf pans 1 to 1-1/4 hours at 325 degrees.

*Fred and Frankie Pack: Hazel (submitted by Hazel Pack Wood)*
*Oak Dale School '39*

# APPLE NUT BREAD

| | |
|---|---|
| 1-1/2 cups sifted flour | 1 cup chopped nuts |
| 2 teaspoons baking powder | 3/4 cups chopped apples |
| 1/2 teaspoon soda | 1 egg, slightly beaten |
| 1 teaspoon salt | 3/4 cup brown sugar, packed |
| 1/8 teaspoon allspice | 1-1/2 cups buttermilk |
| 1/4 teaspoon nutmeg | 2 tablespoons shortening |
| 1-1/2 cups crushed (ready-<br>    to-serve wheat cereal flakes) | |

Sift flour, baking powder, soda, salt, and spices. Add cereal, nuts, and apples. Combine egg, brown sugar, buttermilk and shortening. Add and mix just enough to moisten the dry ingredients. DO NOT BEAT. Turn into well-greased loaf pan (9x5x3"). Bake at 350 degrees for 1 hour.

*Louie and Betty Madison: Mike '59; Linda '61; Dona '65*

# BANANA BREAD

| | |
|---|---|
| 1/2 cup shortening | 2 cups flour |
| 1 cup sugar | 1 teaspoon soda |
| 2 eggs | 1/2 teaspoon salt |
| 1 cup ripe bananas, mashed | 1/2 cup chopped nuts |
| (about 3 good-sized ones) | |

Cream shortening and sugar. Blend in beaten eggs and bananas. Stir in mixed dry ingredients. Add nuts. Pour batter into (8x4") greased and floured loaf pans. Bake 1 hour at 350 degrees.

*Note:* You can bake them in muffin tins for 25 minutes.

*Jack and Alawayne Keen: Mary Beth '57; Jack '58*
*R.C. and Anita Yancy: Kim '67*

# BANANA BREAD WITH COCONUT

| | |
|---|---|
| 1-1/2 cups sugar | 2 cups flour |
| 1/4 cup oleo | 1 teaspoon baking powder |
| 2 eggs | 1 teaspoon salt |
| 2 mashed bananas | 1 teaspoon vanilla |
| 1/2 cup buttermilk | 1/2 cup chopped pecans |
| 1 teaspoon soda | 1/2 cup coconut |

Cream sugar, oleo, and eggs: add mashed bananas. Mix buttermilk and soda. Mix dry ingredients and add to creamed mixture, alternately with buttermilk. Add vanilla, pecans, and coconut.

Bake at 375 degrees for 45 to 50 minutes in greased and floured loaf pan.

*Bin and Pat Goolsby: Douglas '66*

# CARROT BREAD

| | |
|---|---|
| 2 cups sugar | 1/2 teaspoon salt |
| 1 cup Wesson oil | 1-1/2 teaspoons vanilla |
| 3 eggs, slightly beaten | 2 cups grated carrots |
| 2-1/2 cups flour | 1 small can crushed pineapple |
| 1 teaspoon soda | 1 cup chopped pecans |

Cream sugar and Wesson oil. Add slightly beaten eggs. Fold in the mixture of flour, soda, and salt. Fold in carrots, pineapple, and pecans. Bake in greased and floured loaf pans at 275 to 300 degrees for 2 hours. Makes 2 loaves. Slice when cool. WONDERFUL!

*Virgil and Bert Coffee: Larry '58*

# HO-BO BREAD

2 cups raisins
4 teaspoons soda
2-1/2 cups boiling water
Mix and let stand overnight.
1 cup brown sugar

1 cup white sugar
4 tablespoons salad oil
1-1/4 teaspoons salt
4 cups flour
1 cup chopped pecans, if desired

Mix above ingredients and combine with raisin and water. Pour into 3 greased and floured (1-pound) coffee cans. Bake at 350 degrees for 1 hour or until done. Let stand 15 minutes before removing from cans.

*James and Marie Mash: Jimmy '53*

# LEMON CREAM BREAD

2-1/2 cups flour
1 tablespoon baking powder
1 teaspoon salt
1-2/3 cups sugar
1/2 cup shortening
2 eggs

1 (8-ounce) cream cheese, cut into
    1/4" cubes
1 cup milk
1/2 cup chopped nuts
2 tablespoons lemon peel, grated
1/4 cup lemon juice

Sift flour with baking powder and salt. Add 1-1/2 cups (of the sugar) to shortening. Cream at high speed. Blend in eggs. Add dry ingredients. Fold in cream cheese, milk, nuts, and lemon peel. Bake in greased and floured loaf pans at 375 degrees for 50 minutes. Combine remaining sugar and 1/4 cup lemon juice. Brush over hot loaves. Cool 30 minutes.

*Danny and Ima Gene Thomas: Tammy '74*

# MANDEL BROT
## *(Bread)*

1 cup sugar
3/4 cup oil
3 eggs
3 cups flour

1/4 teaspoon salt
1/2 teaspoon anise
1 cup chopped walnuts

Mix and beat sugar, oil, and eggs. Add flour, salt, and anise. Mix well. Divide dough in half on a cookie sheet. With floured hands work into loaf shapes. Bake at 350 degrees 20 to 25 minutes. Remove from oven, slice, and return to oven and bake 15 to 20 minutes longer.

*John and Judy Blair: Leslie '79*

# MEXICAN APPLE

2 cups sugar
2 eggs
1-1/2 cups Wesson oil
3 cups peeled and chopped apples
3 cups sifted flour

1 teaspoon soda
1 teaspoon salt
2 teaspoons vanilla
1 cup pecans

Blend sugar, eggs, oil, and chopped apples. Sift dry ingredients and add. Add vanilla and pecans. Batter will be stiff. Spread in large ungreased sheet cake pan. Bake at 350 degrees for 1 hour and 15 minutes.

*Milton and Ann Brumley: Doug '73*

# MEXICAN SPOON BREAD

1 (1-pound) can cream corn
3/4 cup milk
1/3 cup melted butter
2 beaten eggs
1 cup cornmeal

1/2 teaspoon soda
1 teaspoon salt
1-1/2 cups grated cheese, divided
    equally
1 (4-ounce) can diced green chilies

In bowl mix corn, milk, butter, and eggs. Mix corn meal, soda, and salt, and add to first mixture. Pour half of the batter into a greased 9x9" pan or baking dish. Sprinkle with 3/4 cup of the grated cheese and the diced green chilies. Cover with remaining batter and 3/4 cup grated cheese. Bake at 400 degrees for about 45 minutes or until brown.

*Jess and Halya Barrera: Martha '79*

# ORANGE LOAF BREAD

1 cup oleo
2 cups sugar
4 whole eggs
1 tablespoon orange rind
3-1/2 cups flour
1 teaspoon soda
1 cup buttermilk

1/2 teaspoon salt
1 teaspoon vanilla
3 cups chopped pecans
1 cup coconut
1-1/2 small package orange slices,
    chopped

Mix all together. Bake 45 to 60 minutes in greased loaf pans at 350 degrees. Glaze.

Glaze:
1 cup orange juice

2 cups powdered sugar
Mix and pour over bread.

*Note:* You may want to warm glaze before spreading on loaves.

*Randy and Reba Stilwell: Shannon '81*

# POPPY SEED BREAD
## *(DELICIOUS!)*

2-1/4 cups sugar
1-1/8 cups Crisco oil
3 cups flour
1-1/2 teaspoons baking powder
1-1/2 teaspoons salt

1-1/2 cups milk
1 teaspoon butter flavoring
1-1/2 teaspoons almond flavoring
1-1/2 teaspoons poppy seeds

Cream sugar and oil. Sift and add dry ingredients alternately with milk to creamed mixture. Add remaining ingredients. Pour into 3 greased and floured loaf pans and bake at 350 degrees for 1 hour.

Glaze (optional):
1/2 cup sugar
1/2 teaspoon almond flavoring

1/2 teaspoon butter
1 teaspoon vanilla
1/4 cup orange juice

Mix well and pour over warm loaves. Freezes well.

*Leland and Mona Hamilton: Angela '63; Julie '77*

# POPPY SEED CAKE
## *(DELICIOUS!)*

1 box Duncan Hines Yellow
    Butter Cake Mix
1/2 cup sugar
3/4 cup Wesson oil

1/4 cup poppy seed
1 cup sour cream
4 eggs

Mix well and add four eggs one at a time. Bake in lightly greased and sugared Bundt pan for 1 hour at 350 degrees. (May also bake in 2 small Bundt pans; will cook in about 30 minutes. Eat one; give one.

*Teacher's Pet: Donna Lambert, daughter*

# PUMPKIN BREAD

1 cup corn oil
3 cups sugar
4 eggs
2 cups pumpkins
2/3 cup water
3-1/2 cups flour

1 teaspoon cinnamon
1/2 teaspoon nutmeg
1/2 teaspoon cloves
1-1/2 teaspoons salt
1-1/2 to 2 teaspoons soda
1 cup chopped pecans

Cream oleo, sugar, and eggs. Add pumpkins and water. Continue to beat. Mix dry ingredients and add. Fold in nuts (dredged in flour). Bake in 3 (1-pound) coffee cans at 350 degrees for 1-1/2 hours.

(These can be baked in greased and floured 9x5" loaf pans at 350 degrees for 1 hour.)

*Mike and Lavern Fetner: Gina '80*
*Miles and Lorena Luttrall: Melva '57*
*T.E. and Novaline Owens: Theresa '61; Tim '71*

# STRAWBERRY BREAD

3 cups flour
1 teaspoon soda
1 teaspoon salt
1 tablespoon cinnamon
2 cups sugar

4 eggs, beaten
1-1/4 cups cooking oil
2 (10-ounce) packages frozen
strawberries, thawed
1-1/4 cups chopped pecans

Mix and sift dry ingredients into large bowl. Mix and add remaining ingredients and pour into 2 large or 3 small, greased and floured loaf pans. Bake at 350 degrees for 55 to 60 minutes. (May save 1/2 cup strawberries and mix with 1 (8-ounce) package cream cheese. Mix and spread over bread.)

*Paul and Katherine Leffingwell: Brent '82*
*Jack and Carol Carlson: Rebecca '79*
*Morris and Pat Pope: Byron '79; Gwen '83*

# ZUCCHINI BREAD

2 medium zucchini
3 eggs
2 cups brown sugar
1 cup cooking oil
2 tablespoons orange juice

3 cups unsifted flour
1 teaspoon baking powder
1 teaspoon soda
1 teaspoon cinnamon
1 cup chopped nuts

Peel and cut zucchini into chunks. Whip eggs in blender and add zucchini a little at a time and blend. Pour into mixing bowl. Beat in brown sugar, oil, and orange juice. Mix dry ingredients and add slowly to batter. Beat well. Add nuts. Bake in 2 greased and floured 9x5x3" loaf pans for 1 hour at 325 degrees.

*Variation:* 2 cups white sugar may be substituted for the brown sugar, or use 1 cup brown and 1 cup white sugar.

*Nora Dalton: Don '55*

# APRICOT BREAD

1 cup dried apricots
1 cup sugar
1/2 cup brown sugar
2 tablespoons butter
1 egg
1/4 cup water

1/2 cup orange juice
2 cups flour
2 teaspoons baking powder
1/2 teaspoon soda
3/4 teaspoon salt
1/2 cup chopped nuts

Soak apricots 30 minutes; drain, then cut up. Mix sugars, butter, egg, water, and juice. Sift dry ingredients and blend into creamed mixture. Stir in chopped nuts and apricots. Let stand 20 minutes. Bake 60 minutes at 350 degrees.

*James and Lois Ketcham: Kristin '85*

# APPLE PANCAKES

| | |
|---|---|
| 3 apples, | 2 tablespoons sugar |
| Butter | 1 teaspoon baking powder |
| Sugar | 2 eggs, beaten |
| Pancakes: | 2/3 cup milk |
| 3/4 cup flour | 1/3 cup water |
| 1/2 teaspoon salt | 1/2 teaspoon lemon rind |

Peel, core, and chop fine 3 apples; fry in butter and a little sugar. Make pancake, putting some of the apple on top of batter as you cook each one, then add another layer of batter. Cook, flip over and cook as usual. Serve with powdered sugar sprinkled on top.

*G.L. and Carol DuBose: Amy '80; Jason '83*

# GERMAN APPLE PANCAKES

| | |
|---|---|
| 1/2 cup butter | 1/2 cup flour |
| Fresh sliced apples | 1/2 cup milk |
| 3 eggs | Powdered sugar |
| 1/2 teaspoon salt | |

Preheat oven to 450 degrees and melt butter in 10" pan. Line pan with fresh sliced apples. Mix remaining ingredients, making a batter. Pour batter over apples and butter. Reduce heat to 350 degrees and bake until crisp and brown (approximately 30 to 40 minutes). Cut in wedges and sprinkle with powdered sugar. Serve with sausage. Approximately 4 servings.

*Ed and Mickie Snook: Leland '74*

# COTTAGE CHEESE PANCAKES

| | |
|---|---|
| 1 cup cottage cheese | 1 tablespoon sugar |
| 1 cup sour cream | 1/2 teaspoon salt |
| 4 eggs | Butter |
| 3/4 cup flour | |

Combine cheese and sour cream; add eggs. Mix flour, sugar, and salt. Add to cheese mixture. Fry in butter. Serve with warm MAPLE SYRUP.

| | |
|---|---|
| Maple Syrup: | 1/2 cup brown sugar |
| 1 cup white corn syrup | Few drops maple flavoring |
| 1/2 cup water | Butter |

Combine corn syrup, water, and sugar. Heat to boiling point; remove from heat and add flavoring. Add as much butter as desired.

*Noble and Evelyn Lytle: Kay '53 (submitted by Kay Lytle Schneider)*

# TED'S MOST FAVORITE PANCAKES

| | |
|---|---|
| 2 cups flour | 3 tablespoons sugar |
| 2 teaspoons soda | 3 tablespoons oleo |
| 1/2 teaspoon salt | 2 eggs |
| 2 teaspoons baking powder | Milk |

Mix all above; add milk for batter consistency. Cook on hot griddle.

*Victor and Joyce Willman: Ted '81*

# BASIC BATTER FOR CREPES

*Note:* Make batter in blender 24 hours before use (store in refrigerator).

| | |
|---|---|
| 2 fresh eggs | 1 tablespoon soft (whipped) |
| 1 cup whole milk | butter or margarine, melted |
| 1 cup sifted flour | Pinch of salt |

In blender beat eggs and add milk at low speed.

Add flour gradually and blend constantly on even speed until batter is smooth. Add melted butter and salt and blend until smooth as cream. Makes 16 to 18 (7" crepes).

This is a recipe I picked up somewhere over the years and is the best all around crepe batter I have ever tried.

*Othel and Flora Mae Ogden: Walker '52*

# MORNING CALL STYLE DOUGHNUTS

| | |
|---|---|
| 1 loaf frozen bread dough | Vegetable oil to deep fry |
| 1 cake dome (preferably glass) | Powdered sugar |

Just before going to bed (10:00-11:00 P.M.), take frozen bread from freezer and place under domed cover. Next morning the loaf will be enormous. Roll it out on floured surface until very thin. Cut in 1-1/2x2-1/2" pieces. Cover with damp cloth and let set 30 minutes. Heat oil to 375 degrees; drop doughnuts 3 at a time into hot oil. Fry until golden. Roll in powdered sugar. Serves 6 to 8.

*Noble and Evelyn Lytle: Kay '53 (submitted by Kay Lytle Schneider)*

# BANANA FRITTERS

1 cup sifted flour
1 teaspoon baking powder
1 teaspoon salt
2 eggs

1/2 cup evaporated milk
1 teaspoon vegetable oil
2 to 3 mashed bananas

Mix and sift dry ingredients; set aside. Mix eggs, milk, and oil; beat well. Add to dry ingredients. Blend in mashed bananas. Deep fry by using one tablespoon of mixture until golden brown. Drain on paper towel. Roll in powdered sugar.

*Variation:* Yams may be used instead of bananas.

*Dr. Armand and Dr. Lellani Wiltz: Marie '85*

# ORANGE FRENCH TOAST

## *Wonderful!*

3 eggs
1/2 cup milk
1/2 cup orange juice
2 tablespoons sugar
1 teaspoon orange peel, grated

1/4 teaspoon cinnamon
1/8 teaspoon allspice
Dash salt
8 slices, thick whole wheat bread
Melted butter or oleo

Grease cookie sheet. In medium bowl, beat eggs slightly. Add milk, juice, sugar, peel, and spices. Beat well. Dip each slice of bread in mixture and place on cookie sheet. Cover lightly with foil; freeze 1 to 2 hours until completely frozen. To store, place waxed paper between slices. Stack, wrap in foil, and return to freezer.

To serve, heat oven to 425 degrees. Remove desired amount from freezer; brush with melted butter. Place buttered side down on ungreased cookie sheet; bake 10 minutes. Brush top with butter; turn over. Continue to bake 5 to 10 minutes or until golden brown. Serve with powdered sugar and syrup. Calories: 190 per slice, 11 grams fat.

*Bill and Ruth Wyche: Nancy '58*

# BUTTERMILK WAFFLES

2 cups flour
3 teaspoons baking powder
1 teaspoon soda
1 teaspoon salt

4 beaten eggs
2 cups buttermilk
1 cup cooled melted butter or oleo

Mix dry ingredients. Beat eggs until foamy; add buttermilk. Combine the 2 mixtures, then add melted oleo. Mix well; pour batter onto hot griddle.

This makes 8 waffles.

*Victor and Joyce Willman: Ted '81*

# BREAKFAST PITA POCKETS

6 slices cooked bacon, crumbled
4 medium potatoes, peeled,
  diced, and fried
1-1/2 cups grated cheddar cheese

4 to 6 scrambled eggs
1 package Pita bread
Picante sauce

Combine the first 4 ingredients in a large bowl. Slice Pita bread in half; fill halves with mixture. Top with Picante sauce as desired.

*Don and Gail Leatherwood: Mike '83*

# EGG AND SAUSAGE CASSEROLE

6 to 8 slices bread, cubed
1 pound sausage, hot or mild
1 (8-ounce) package cheddar
  cheese, grated
6 eggs, beaten

1 teaspoon dry mustard
2 cups milk
1 teaspoon salt
Pepper to taste

Grease oblong casserole dish; Spread bread (remove edges) into dish. Cook sausage and crumble over bread. Sprinkle cheese over sausage. Beat eggs, mustard, milk, salt, and pepper and pour over other. Set in refrigerator overnight. Cook at 350 degrees for 30 minutes or until brown.

*T.W. and Dorothy Hendrick: Mr. Hendrick, principal*
*Cindy Arnold, School Secretary*

# FLUFFY CHEESE AND EGGS

4 eggs
1/4 cup milk
1/4 teaspoon salt

1/4 teaspoon pepper
1/2 cup American cheese, cut into
  little pieces

Break eggs into a bowl; add milk, salt, and pepper. Beat well. Add cheese. Pour mixture into a 1-quart greased baking dish. Bake at 350 degrees for 30 minutes. Eat right away before it falls. Makes 4 servings.

*Charles and Linda Latch: Larry '72*

Kissin' don't last forever; cooks do.

# BISCUIT AND SAUSAGE ROLLS

1 (10-ounce) can refrigerated
   biscuits
1/2 pound pork sausage
1 tablespoon chopped onion

1/4 cup apple, chopped fine
1/2 tablespoon brown sugar
1/4 teaspoon cinnamon
1 cup cheddar cheese, grated

Place biscuits on a floured surface in 3 rows of 3 each. Use extra biscuit to fill in spaces between biscuits as you pat and roll until seams are joined to make a square of pastry. Crumble sausage in a medium skillet; add onion and cook until sausage is no longer pink. Drain and spread evenly over biscuit dough. Mix apple, brown sugar, and cinnamon and sprinkle over sausage. Top with cheese. Carefully roll up dough and filling and cut into 8 slices. Place slices flat in sections of muffin tins. Bake at 400 degrees for 12 to 15 minutes or until cheese is bubbly and biscuits are lightly browned.

*John and Katherine Kniffen: Kelly Kniffen Johnson '75 (submitted by Kelly)*

# EASY DRESSING

1-1/2 cups flour
4 teaspoons baking powder
2 tablespoons sugar
2 teaspoons salt
1/2 teaspoon sage
1 teaspoon thyme
1-1/2 cups cornmeal
1-1/2 cups chopped onions

1-1/2 cups chopped celery
3 eggs, beaten
1 small jar pimiento, optional
Black pepper to taste
1-1/2 cups milk
1/2 cup Wesson oil
3 or 4 cans chicken broth

Mix all ingredients and bake in greased 9x13" pan at 350 degrees. This may be frozen and used at a later time. When ready to use, crumble and mix with 3 or 4 cans of chicken broth. Bake 35 to 40 minutes at 400 degrees.

*Jack and Oleta Greaves: Linda '61; Donna '63; Randy '66*

# TURKEY DRESSING

Mix in large roasting pan:
2/3 biscuits, crumbled
1/3 cornbread, crumbled
3 raw eggs
2 medium onions, chopped and
   sauteed

2 stems celery, chopped and
   sauteed
1 tablespoon poultry seasoning
Black pepper and salt to taste
Broth

Mix biscuit and cornbread in pan. Add beaten eggs. Add sauteed onions and celery. Mix in seasonings. Add plenty of broth to make dressing mixture very moist. (You may want to add some canned chicken broth, if needed. Also, sage may be added to taste — add about a teaspoon at a time.) Bake about 45 minutes to 1 hour.

*Teacher's Pet: My Mother, Mama Jenny*

# CRESCENT TIDBITS

| | |
|---|---|
| 1 stick oleo | Garlic powder, optional |
| Parsley flakes | 2 cans crescent rolls |
| Sesame seeds | Parmesan cheese |

Melt oleo in bottom of large jelly roll pan (or one similar). Sprinkle oleo freely with parsley flakes and sesame seeds. (Add garlic powder if you like.)

Slice each can of rolls into 8 slices; then cut each slice into fourths. Roll each fourth in bowl of Parmesan cheese. Place on buttered pan and bake at 375 degrees for 11 to 13 minutes.

*Teacher's Pet: Lana Albers, daughter*

# SOPAPILLAS

| | |
|---|---|
| 2 cups sifted flour | 1-1/2 tablespoons shortening |
| 2 teaspoons baking powder | 2 eggs |
| 1 teaspoon salt | Water, to make medium dough |
| 2 tablespoons sugar | |

Sift dry ingredients together. Cut in the shortening; add beaten eggs. Mix. Add water and make into dough. Let set 15 minutes. Roll out 1/8 to 1/4" thickness on lightly floured board. Cut into trapezoid shape. Fry in grease until golden brown, then turn them over. They puff up quite a bit. Serve with honey.

*Sergio and Frances Marquez: Ernie '77*

# BRENNAN'S GARLIC BREAD

| | |
|---|---|
| 1 loaf French bread | 1/4 cup grated Parmesan cheese |
| 4 cloves garlic | 1 tablespoon minced parsley |
| 1/2 cup melted butter | 1/2 teaspoon paprika |

Thoroughly rub outside crust of bread with 2 slightly crushed cloves of garlic. Split loaf in half lengthwise and place each half, crust down, on cookie sheet. Put remaining 2 cloves of garlic through garlic press and combine with melted butter; brush over cut surfaces. Mix remaining ingredients; sprinkle over buttered surface. Cut in 2" bias slices. Heat on baking sheet at 350 degrees 12 to 15 minutes, or until very hot.

*Mrs. Floyd and Pat Garrot: Mike '69*

---

Lord, make my words tender today
'cause tomorrow I may have to eat them.

# FLUFFY ROLLS

| | |
|---|---|
| 1 package yeast | 1/2 cup oil |
| 1/4 cup water | 2 eggs, well beaten |
| 1 cup milk, scalded | 4 cups flour |
| 1/2 cup sugar | 1/2 teaspoon soda |
| 1 teaspoon salt | |

Dissolve yeast in 1/4 cup lukewarm water. Add milk, sugar, salt, oil, and egg. Whip well. Add flour and soda; let stand overnight. LEAVE OUT! DON'T REFRIGERATE!

Next morning, dump on lightly floured board; divide dough in half. Roll out about size of pie — 1/2" thick. Cut in 12 wedges. Roll each wedge up — wide end first. Place in well greased sheet 1" apart. Let rise several hours or all day. Bake 12 to 15 minutes at 350 degrees.

*Danny and Ima Gene Thomas: Tammy '74*

# HAWAIIAN BREAD
## *SUPER!*

| | |
|---|---|
| 1 package yellow cake mix | 2-1/2 cups warm water |
| 2 packages yeast | 5 cups flour |
| 1/2 teaspoon salt | 4 tablespoons melted butter |

Combine cake mix and yeast. Next combine salt and water. Add cake mixture to water and salt mixture. Add flour; mix well, and knead lightly. Let rise 1 hour. Knead lightly again, pat out, and cut for rolls. Let rise until double. Bake at 375 degrees. When brown, brush with melted butter and bake a little longer. Makes 24.

*Teacher's Pet: Donna Lambert, daughter*

# QUICK BUTTERMILK ROLLS

(Total time: 1 hour)

| | |
|---|---|
| 1-1/2 cups buttermilk, scalded | 1/2 cup shortening |
| 2 yeast cakes | 1 teaspoon salt |
| 1/4 cup warm water | 1/2 teaspoon soda |
| 1/4 cup sugar | 4-1/2 cups flour |

Scald milk in double boiler; dissolve yeast in warm water and add to cooled (lukewarm) milk. Add sugar, shortening, and salt, then add sifted flour and soda mixture. Mix well. Let stand 10 minutes. Roll out and cut or shape as desired. Allow to rise until double in bulk (about 30 minutes). Bake at 425 degrees for 10 to 12 minutes. Makes 24 rolls.

*Don and Peggy Doyle: James '77*

# QUICK ROLLS

1/2 cup mashed potatoes
1/2 cup shortening
1/4 cup sugar
Salt
1 package yeast

1/2 cup warm water
3 to 4 cups flour
1 cup water
1 egg, beaten

Mix potatoes, shortening, sugar, and salt. Add yeast dissolved in warm water. Add flour, water, and egg. Add enough flour to make dough stiff. Let dough rise 2 hours. Knead dough down. Make into rolls; let rise 2 hours. Bake at 450 degrees for 25 minutes.

*Laymon and Dail Baker: Sheila '78*

# RED APPLE INN ROLLS

1 cup boiling water
1 cup butter
2/3 cup sugar
1 tablespoon salt

2-1/2 packages yeast
2 eggs
6-1/3 cups flour

Pour hot water over butter, sugar, and salt; cool. Dissolve yeast in warm water. Add beaten eggs to yeast mixture. Add approximately 6-1/3 cups flour and blend well. Set in refrigerator overnight. Take out 2 hours before baking. Melt butter and dip in rolls as you place in pan. Sprinkle with sesame or poppy seeds if desired. Let set out with towel on top. Bake at 425 degrees for 12 minutes.

*Wayne and Dodie McAdoo: Tonya '83*

# SOUR DOUGH ROLLS

2 cups buttermilk, lukewarm
1-1/2 packages dry yeast,
    dissolved in milk
1/4 cup sugar

5 teaspoons baking powder
1/2 teaspoon salt
6 cups all-purpose flour
1/2 cup corn oil

Place milk and yeast in large bowl. Add sugar, baking powder, and salt. Mix well with mixer. Add flour to make batter, then add corn oil and flour to make soft dough (use flour as needed). Place dough in bowl with tight lid in refrigerator. No need to let rise before baking. Use as needed. Make into rolls. Bake at approximately 400 degrees until done.

*A.L. and Lola Rhodes: Sue '49*

Character is what you are
when no one is looking.

# HOT WHEAT ROLLS

1. Small bowl:                    1/2 teaspoon salt
1 package yeast                   1/3 cup sugar
1/2 cup warm water

In small bowl mix and stir; let yeast activate 12 minutes.

2. Large bowl:                    Almost 1/3 cup Crisco oil
1 cup hot water                   1 cup whole wheat flour
1 teaspoon salt                   3-1/2 cups white flour
1/2 cup sugar

In large bowl mix water, salt, sugar, and oil. Mix contents of small bowl into large bowl; add 1 cup whole wheat flour and 3-1/2 cups white flour. Cover and let rise in a warm place about 2 hours. Spray pan(s) with Pam or grease. Pinch out rolls and place in pan. (This makes about 4 mini loaves.) Let rise for 2 hours and bake at 425 degrees for 12 minutes or until golden brown. Rub top with soft butter. Cover and serve.

*Donald and Dee Cox: Cary '85*

# WHOLE WHEAT BREAD
## *SO GOOD!*

1 envelope dry yeast              1-1/2 tablespoons each of
3/4 cup warm water, very warm         caraway, sesame seeds, and
1/2 teaspoon sugar                    cornmeal
1-1/2 cups warm water             1 egg, beaten
3 tablespoons butter or oleo      1-1/2 cups whole wheat flour
2-1/2 tablespoons brown sugar     3-1/2 to 4 cups white flour
2 tablespoons molasses            1/2 tablespoon salt

Combine dry yeast in very warm water and sugar. Let set until yeast foams or bubbles. Mix 1-1/2 cups warm water, oleo, brown sugar, molasses, caraway, sesame seeds, and cornmeal. Stir until butter melts. Add yeast mixture, egg, and whole wheat flour. Stir until smooth. Let rest in a warm place for 25 minutes. Add 3-1/2 to 4 cups white flour and salt. Knead until smooth. Place in greased bowl and let rise until double in bulk. Divide into 2 loaves, kneading each again. Place in greased 9x5" loaf pan. Let rise until double in bulk. Bake at 350 degrees for 35 to 45 minutes.

*Leo and Esther Osterout: Susan '65*

The smile is the most powerful instrument
that mankind has ever invented.

# YEAST BREAD

2 cups lukewarm water
1/2 cup sugar
1-1/2 teaspoons salt
2 packages dry yeast

1 egg
1/4 cup soft shortening
6-1/2 to 7 cups sifted flour

Mix lukewarm water, sugar, and salt. Add yeast. Stir in beaten egg and shortening. Mix in sifted flour. Let dough rise after making into 24 rolls or 2 loaves. Bake at 425 degrees in greased pans until brown.

*Note:* It only needs to rise the one time.

*Robert and Mary Lou Montgomery: Bobby '71*

# LEFSE

6 cups mashed potatoes
2 tablespoons sugar
2 tablespoons salt

3/4 cup cream
3 cups flour

Mix in order given. Chill at least 2 hours. Roll out thin on floured surface. Fry on lefse grill at 500 degrees until light brown.

*Looney and Mary Walls: Jill '54*

# CINNAMON ROLLS
### *(Enough for a hungry family)*

2 packages yeast
2 tablespoons sugar
1/2 cup warm water
1 cup scalded milk
1 stick oleo
1 teaspoon salt

1/2 cup sugar
2 beaten eggs
Flour
Softened butter
Cinnamon
Sugar

Dissolve yeast and sugar in warm water. Set aside. Scald milk; add oleo, salt, and 1/2 cup sugar. Cool until comfortable to touch. Place yeast mixture, milk mixture, and eggs in large mixing bowl. Add enough flour to make a soft dough. Cover and let rise. In evening, roll out dough on floured board. Spread with softened oleo, cinnamon, and sugar. Roll; then cut in 1" thickness. Place cut-side down in greased baking dish. Allow to rise in cool place overnight. Bake at 400 degrees until lightly browned. Drizzle with Butter Icing and serve hot.

**Butter Icing:**
2 to 3 tablespoons butter

3 tablespoons sugar
1/4 teaspoon cinnamon

Mix icing ingredients and brush top of hot cinnamon rolls.

*Jack and Helen Clements: Jon '70*

# FLOUR TORTILLAS

4 cups flour
4 tablespoons shortening
2 teaspoons baking powder

2 teaspoons salt
1-1/2 cups warm water

Combine all ingredients, add water a little at a time. Knead dough until it no longer sticks to your hands. Roll into 12 to 15 tortillas. Cook on griddle until brown on both sides.

*Fred and Ora Herrera: Freddie '78*

# MONKEY BREAD

2 cups warm water
2 packages dry yeast, dissolved
    in a little water
1/2 cup sugar

1/4 cup cooking oil
1 teaspoon salt
6 cups flour, approximately
1-1/2 sticks melted butter

Dissolve yeast in warm water. Add remaining ingredients except melted butter. Knead in enough flour to make a fairly stiff dough. Let rise. Roll out dough about 1/2" thick like dumplings. Cut in small strips or 2" or 3" triangles. Dip each piece in melted butter and layer in bundt pan, overlapping the pieces. Fill pan about 1/2 full. Let rise again (about 1-1/2 hours). Bake in 350 degree oven for 40 to 45 minutes. To serve, turn pan upside down on plate. It will come out like a cake. Just pull apart.

*Rex and Diana Hale: Rob '76*

# OATMEAL BREAD

1 yeast cake or 1 package dry
    yeast
1/4 cup warm water
1/4 cup sugar
1 cup milk

2 eggs
3-1/2 cups sifted flour
1 teaspoon salt
2 cups oatmeal
Raisins may be added

Mix yeast in warm water. Mix remaining ingredients. Let it rise like white bread. Makes 2 or 4 little loaves. Bake at 375 degrees for 40 minutes.

*G.L. and Carol Du Bose: Amy '80; Jason '83*

**Happiness is contagious —
be a carrier.**

# Main Dishes

Baptism in the Horse Tank, 1925

# Spiritual Gathering at the Stock Tank — 1925

First, let me say that in all my life, I have moved very few times. Living in the country meant you worked and played (in that order). There were four girls in our family, and as you might surmise, we became the boys in the field.

Even though we worked, there were many little things that brought memorable pleasures. Lightning bugs were chased and caught when night came. Playhouses with many rooms were built under (what we thought) huge trees. Then there were the paper dolls we carefully cut from the catalogue. The mere cutting was pleasure within itself. Whole families would be assembled in shoe boxes, and your playmate would assemble her family, also. For hours upon hours all kinds of play could take place using the entire families you had made.

Inside play often turned to outside play, especially when the cousins came. Just as we preached and buried the chickens, we likewise made sure we took care of the "spiritual" needs of each other.

I do not know why we spent so much of our time playing church; perhaps it was such an integral part of our life. We would have our singing, preaching, and "joinings"! Then we would move out to the watering tank. There in proper fashion, I would again attire myself befitting a preacher. I would tuck my dress inside my flowing bloomers and begin to baptize those who came for baptism! They were completely immersed in the Horse Tank! One could be baptized over and over to his heart's delight without ever having any side effects!!!

# BARBECUED BEEF ON BUNS

4 to 5 cups cooked roast beef
1-1/2 cups chopped onions
3 tablespoons shortening
1 cup water
1 beef bouillon cube
1 cup catsup

2 tablespoons vinegar
2 tablespoons brown sugar
1 tablespoon Worcestershire
  sauce
1-1/2 teaspoons salt
1 tablespoon mustard

Chip roast beef into small pieces. Lightly brown onions in shortening. Combine remaining ingredients; heat to boiling and simmer 5 minutes. Add meat and onions. Simmer 30 minutes or longer. Serve on buns.

*Ray and Doris Flowe: Rita '68*

# BAR-B-CUPS

1 pound ground beef
1 small onion, chopped
Salt and pepper to taste
2 or 3 tablespoons barbecue sauce

2 teaspoons brown sugar
1 large can Hungry Jack biscuits
  (10)
3/4 cups grated Longhorn cheese

Heat oven according to directions on biscuit can. Brown meat and onion. Salt and pepper to taste. Drain thoroughly. Add barbecue sauce and brown sugar. Simmer. Spray muffin tins lightly with Pam. Flatten biscuits between fingers until large enough to make a cup in the muffin tin. Stuff with meat and top with cheese. Bake at 400 degrees until edges of biscuits are lightly browned. Remove immediately.

*W. H. and Ruth Neal: Billy '60*

# BARBECUE ROAST

3 pound roast
Salt
Sauce:
1 cup catsup
3 heaping teaspoons chili powder
5 tablespoons vinegar

3 tablespoons Worcestershire
  sauce
1 teaspoon pepper
Pod of garlic or garlic salt, if
  desired
About 3 pints of water (or less)

Salt and roll roast in flour; brown. Make sauce and pour over roast. Add water. Cook as any other roast.

*A.E. and Evelyn McCarver: Jerry '54*

Catch the bear before you sell his skin.

# BARBEQUE ROAST

1 chuck roast
1 tablespoon vinegar
2 tablespoons chili powder
1-1/2 cups ketchup

1 tablespoon Worcestershire
    sauce
1 medium can tomatoes
1 bay leaf
1 medium onion, chopped

Brown roast. Combine other ingredients; pour over roast. Cook in 300 degree oven 2-1/2 hours or until meat falls apart.

*George and Winnie Satterwhite: Polly Satterwhite (Collins)* '52*

# BEEF STROGANOFF
## *(Delicious)*

4 pounds round steak, sliced 1/2"
    thick
2 cups sliced onions
1/2 cup oleo
1 pound mushrooms, sliced

1 cup bouillon (may be half
    white wine)
3 cups sour cream
Salt, pepper, mustard to taste

Pound steak until very thin, then cut in pieces about 3" long and 1/2" wide. Cut the onion slices in half and cook them in butter until wilted. Add mushrooms and beef and cook for 5 minutes. Pour in the bouillon and cover. Simmer about 45 minutes or until the meat is tender and the liquid is almost evaporated. Stir in the sour cream, season to taste; heat gently; do not boil.

*Joe and Cordie Dillard: Joe '66*

# BEEF STROGANOFF

1-1/2 pounds round steak
1 teaspoon salt
1/2 teaspoon pepper
1/2 teaspoon garlic powder
Flour
3 tablespoons shortening

1/4 cup onions, chopped
1 (2-ounce) can mushrooms
1 can Beef bouillon soup plus 2/3
    cup water
1 cup sour cream
Egg noodles, cooked

Cut beef into thin strips. Season with salt, pepper, and garlic powder. Sprinkle with flour. Heat shortening in pan and brown meat on all sides; brown onions slightly. Pour off excess grease; add mushrooms, beef soup, and water. Cover and simmer until meat is tender (about 1 hour). Stir in sour cream gradually and cook over low heat 5 minutes. Serve over cooked egg noodles.

*Carey and Carolyn Cook: Cheryl '71*

# BEEF STROGANOFF

1-1/4 pounds beef tenderloin, cut into thin strips
2 tablespoons butter
2 teaspoons paprika
Salt and pepper, to taste
6 tablespoons sweet butter
4 heaped teaspoons onions, finely chopped
1/2 teaspoon garlic, finely minced
1 teaspoon shallots, finely chopped
3/4 cup Marsala wine
1 package Brown Beef Gravy Mix
1-1/2 cups water
Noodles, cooked

Saute meat in butter. When nearly done, add paprika, salt, pepper, sweet butter, onions, garlic, and shallots. Cook until onions are golden and meat is cooked. Add Marsala wine and 1 cup water; simmer until meat is tender (about 30 minutes) Mix gravy mix with 1/2 cup water and add to meat, stirring constantly. Heat thoroughly and serve with noodles.

I adapted this recipe from a recipe from Red Lion Restaurant here in Vail, Colorado.

*Bob and Linda Isbell: Chris '86*

# BEEF STUFFING FOR CABBAGE LEAVES

1 large head green cabbage
1-1/2 tablespoons butter
1-1/2 tablespoons olive oil
1/2 cup chopped onions
1 clove garlic, finely minced
1 pound ground chuck
2 cups cooked rice
3 tablespoons finely minced parsley
1/2 teaspoon thyme
1 teaspoon salt
1/4 teaspoon black pepper
1 cup bouillon (I use powdered beef stock with 1 cup hot water)
1 can tomato sauce
1 bay leaf, optional (I use 1/2 leaf)
Lemon slices

Take cabbage head; core. Place in boiling water to cover. Boil 5 minutes. Take out and drain. Wilted.

In a skillet heat butter and oil; add onions and garlic. Cook until transparent. Remove to platter. Add meat to skillet and cook until lightly brown. Return onions and garlic to skillet. Add cooked rice, parsley, thyme, salt, and pepper. Mix well and fill cabbage leaves with mixture. (First use small leaf, then wrap larger leaf around the first.) Arrange in casserole and add combined bouillon and tomato sauce, and if desired, the bay leaf. Cover and bake 1 hour; adding more liquid if necessary. Transfer the cabbage to a warm serving platter; garnish each serving with a lemon slice and sprinkle with additional parsley. Surround with the sauce remaining in the casserole; discard bay leaf.

*Allan and Rena Faulk: Randy '69.*

# BRISKET

| | |
|---|---|
| 1 (5 to 6-pound) brisket, trimmed | Garlic salt |
| Meat tenderizer, optional | 1/2 small bottle Liquid Smoke |
| Celery salt | 1/2 to 1 small bottle |
| Onion salt | Worcestershire Sauce |

Rub brisket thoroughly with seasonings. Place brisket in foil lined cooking pan. Pour liquids over brisket; wrap tightly and marinate overnight. Baste several times. Bake at 250 degrees for 6 to 8 hours.

*Note:* A small brisket can be cooked in a crock pot in the same way.

*Louie and Betty Madison: Mike '59; Linda '61; Dona '65*
*Erven and Sue Vanderslice: Carol '68*

# CHICKEN-FRIED STEAK FINGERS

| | |
|---|---|
| 1 package cube steaks | 1 cup milk |
| Salt and pepper | 1 cup buttermilk |
| Crisco | 1-1/2 cups flour |

Cut steaks into steak finger strips. Salt and pepper. Mix milk and buttermilk. Dip steak fingers into flour, dip into milk, then into flour again. Cook in Crisco until done. (For a different flavor, substitute Lawry's Seasoned Salt for regular table salt. Serve with cream gravy, potatoes, and salad. ENJOY!

*B.B and Brooksie Stephens: Beckie '76*

# CHINESE HASH

| | |
|---|---|
| 1 small onion, chopped | 1 can Cream of Mushroom soup |
| 5 sticks celery, sliced | 1 can Cream of Chicken soup |
| 2 tablespoons butter | 1 cup rice, cooked |
| 1 pound ground beef, browned | 1 can Chow Mein Noodles, small |
| and drained | |

Saute onion and celery in butter until tender. Brown meat. Combine all ingredients in casserole dish, except Chow Mein Noodles. Bake at 350 degrees for 1 hour. Sprinkle top of casserole with noodles. 4 servings.

*Doris Tillis '63*

Lord, grant me patience
To endure my blessings.

# CHINESE PEPPER STEAK

| | |
|---|---|
| 1 pound beef tip round steak | 3 medium green peppers |
| 1 tablespoon cornstarch | 2 medium-small tomatoes |
| 1/2 teaspoon sugar | 2 tablespoons cooking oil |
| 1/4 teaspoon ginger | 1 clove garlic, minced |
| 1/4 cup light soy sauce | 1/4 cup water |

Partially freeze steak to firm and slice diagonally across the grain into very thin strips. Combine cornstarch, sugar, ginger, and stir in soy sauce. Set aside. Cut green peppers into 1" squares and cut tomatoes into wedges. Quickly brown beef strips (1/3 at a time) in hot oil and remove from pan. Reduce heat; add green peppers, garlic, and water to pan and cook until peppers are tender-crisp, (about 5 to 6 minutes). Stir in meat and tomatoes and heat through.

*Gibbs and Alma Benham: Billy '61 (submitted by Billy and Linda Benham)*

# SHEEP SHEARERS FAJITAS

| | |
|---|---|
| 2 beef skirts | MORTON Natures Seasoning |
| 3 limes | Salt |

Trim beef skirts and marinate with the lime juice and seasoning. Best if marinated overnight. Cook on grill. Slice very thin cross-grain and serve with all the trimmings. (The secret to good tasting fajitas is cooking on mesquite wood.)

| | |
|---|---|
| Trimmings: | Shredded lettuce |
| 8 flour tortillas | Grated cheese |
| Picante Sauce | Sour cream |

Steam tortillas until soft in steamer. Place steak slices on each tortilla. Top with trimmings; roll and eat.

*John and Jean Gilliam: Eric '79*

# GOULASH

| | |
|---|---|
| 1 pound ground beef | 1 can stewed tomatoes |
| Salt and pepper to taste | 1 can Ranch Style beans |
| 1 small chopped onion | |

Brown beef; salt and pepper. Add onion and saute. Add stewed tomatoes and beans. Simmer for about 10 minutes. 6 to 8 servings.

*Note:* You can add 1 can of whole kernel corn, if you wish.

*Howard and Mary Allen: Narva '73*

## HAMBURGER-BROCCOLI CASSEROLE

1-1/2 to 2 pounds ground beef
1/2 chopped onion
1/4 teaspoon garlic powder
1/4 teaspoon pepper
2 packages frozen chopped
    broccoli

1 can mushroom soup
1/2 soup can evaporated milk
1 cup grated American cheese or
    rind

Brown beef and chopped onion. Drain liquid and add garlic powder and pepper. Thaw broccoli. Make a sauce with mushroom soup and milk. Put broccoli in bottom of 9x13" pan. Then layer ground beef and onion, then 1 cup cheese. Top with sauce. Bake 40 minutes at 350 degrees.

*Len and Lynne Wilson: Mark '75; Kirk '78*

## HO-BO STEW

*(A good dish when everyone has to come in and
eat at a different time. Can be kept in oven.)*

Ground meat
Salt and pepper
Carrots, sliced long-ways

Potatoes, sliced in thin slices
Butter

Make patties in medium thickness; salt and pepper. Place sliced carrots on top. Place sliced potatoes on top of carrots. Salt and pepper and dot with butter. Wrap each patty and vegetable stack individually with foil. Seal. Set temperature according to what time you want to eat. . . 300 degrees for 1 hour is average. (Less temperature and longer, if you want to eat later.)

*Howell and Mary Furry: Mike '63*

## HOT PEPPER STEAK

1 flank or round steak, cut in 1/2"
    strips
2 tablespoons shortening
1 tablespoon flour
1/2 cup catsup
1/2 cup water

3 tablespoons soy sauce
1 beef bouillon
1/8 teaspoon pepper
1 large onion, sliced
1 can chopped mushrooms
2 green peppers, cut into rings

Brown meat in shortening; remove meat, pour off fat. Stir in flour, catsup, water, soy sauce, bouillon, and pepper. Heat to boiling and add meat and onions. Cover and simmer 30 minutes. Add mushrooms and pepper rings. Simmer an additional 10 to 15 minutes. Peppers should be crispy tender.

*Teacher's Pet: Cleone Colvin*

# LASAGNA

1/2 pound ground beef
1 cup chopped onion
2 large clove garlic, minced
2 teaspoons oregano, crushed
2 cans (10-3/4 ounce each) tomato
   soup
1/2 cup water
2 teaspoons vinegar

9 lasagna noodles (about 1/2
   pound) cooked and drained
1 pint cream style cheese (cottage
   cheese) or Ricotta cheese
5 slices (1/2-pound) Mozzarella
   cheese
Grated Parmesan cheese

In saucepan, brown beef and cook onions, garlic, and oregano until onion is tender. Add soup, water, and vinegar. Cook over low heat 30 minutes; stir occasionally. In shallow baking dish (12x8x2"), arrange 3 alternate layers of noodles, cottage cheese, meat sauce, and Mozzarella cheese. Sprinkle with Parmesan cheese. Bake at 350 degrees for 30 minutes. Let stand 15 minutes before serving. Makes 6 servings.

*Byford and Jo Ann Sealy: Gayle '67; Kerri '72; Neal '76*

# LASAGNA OLÉ

1 onion, chopped
2 pounds ground meat
1 package Taco Seasoning
1 (10-ounce) can tomatoes
1 (10-ounce) can Rotel tomatoes

1 (8-ounce) can tomato sauce
1 package flour tortillas
2 cups sour cream
3/4 cups cheese, grated
1-2/3 cups Parmesan cheese

Saute onion and meat; drain. Add Taco Seasoning, tomatoes, and tomato sauce. Mix. Layer tortillas, meat, sour cream, and cheeses twice in 9x13" pan. Cook at 325 degrees for 45 minutes. 9 to 10 servings.

*Johnie and Bobbie Griffin: Greg '73*

# MEAT LOAF

2 pounds lean ground meat
2 eggs
1 small onion, chopped
1 green pepper, chopped
   (optional)
1 (No. 2) can peeled tomatoes
   with juice

1 cup cracker crumbs
4 slices bread (more if mixture
   seems too juicy)
Catsup
Bacon slices

Mix all ingredients in large bowl (except catsup and bacon). Make into two loaves in large baking dish. Spread catsup on top of each loaf. Add a slice of bacon on top, if desired. Bake at 325 degrees for about 1 hour. Eat one and freeze one for a later time.

*Cecil and Marie Moore: Linda '53*

# MEAT LOAF

2 pounds extra lean ground chuck
1 medium onion, chopped
1 medium green pepper, chopped
Dash of garlic salt
2 teaspoons salt
1 teaspoon pepper
2 eggs, beaten
1 can tomato soup, undiluted
2 cups crushed crackers

Mix well and form into two loaves. Baste now and throughout cooking with following sauce. Bake at 350 degrees for about 1 hour.

Sauce:
2 cans tomato soup, undiluted
2 tablespoons brown sugar
2 tablespoons vinegar
2 tablespoons prepared mustard

Mix well and heat. Baste loaves.

*Teacher's Pet: Edna Jones, sister*

# MEAT AND RICE STUFF

1-1/2 pounds round steak, cut
   into thin strips
1/4 cup oil
1 large bell pepper, cut into thin
   strips
1 large white onion, sliced into
   thin rings
1 large can whole peeled tomatoes
1/2 teaspoon crushed red pepper
   (or to taste)
1 teaspoon salt
1/4 teaspoon pepper
1/2 teaspoon parsley
1/2 teaspoon lemon pepper
1/2 teaspoon seasoned pepper
1 tablespoon Worcestershire
   sauce
Rice

In large skillet brown strips of meat in oil. Add pepper and onions. When onion begins to change texture, add tomatoes. Add remaining seasonings and simmer for 45 minutes with a lid on the skillet. Stir frequently. Cook rice according to directions; serve with mixture on top of rice.

*Ronald and Mary Mullen: Cassie '81*

# PANCHO PIE

1 green pepper, chopped
3 cloves garlic
2 tablespoons shortening
1 pound ground beef
1 teaspoon chili powder
2 teaspoons salt
1/2 cup cornmeal
1 cup milk
1 cup mushrooms
Grated cheese, optional

Combine chopped pepper, garlic, and shortening in frying pan. Add beef, chili powder, and salt. Boil briskly, then stir in cornmeal, milk, and mushrooms. Pour into casserole and bake at 325 degrees about 1 hour until set. Top with grated cheese before baking if desired.

*Doyle and Faye Kelcy: Gordon '66*

# PLENTY FOR 20

3 pounds hamburger
2 or 3 medium onions, chopped
1 or 2 green peppers, chopped
1 can tomatoes
1 can Rotel tomatoes

1 can mild enchilada sauce
1 can corn
2 cans chopped ripe olives
1 package wide noodles, cooked
2 pounds Velveeta cheese

Brown hamburger, onions, and green peppers. Add tomatoes, Rotel tomatoes; simmer 30 minutes. Add enchilada sauce, corn, olives, noodles, and Velveeta cheese. Heat until cheese melts. Let stand 24 hours (you don't have to let it stand, but it's always better the second day.) Freezes well.

*Jerry and Kay McWilliams: Chris '77*

# PORCUPINE MEAT BALLS STUFFED IN PEPPERS

4 to 6 green bell peppers
1 pound ground meat
1 cup cooked rice

1/2 medium chopped onion
1 small can tomato sauce
Salt and pepper

Take green peppers; cut off tops and remove insides. Boil in water until tender; but not too long (slightly boil). While these are boiling, prepare stuffed pepper mixture. Mix ground meat with rice and onion. Add tomato sauce, salt, and pepper. Stuff peppers. Place peppers in a shallow pan with a little water in pan. Bake 45 minutes at 350 degrees.

*George and Evelyn Scroggins: George '59*

# FORGOTTEN ROAST

1 roast, your choice
Carrots, sliced
Onions, sliced
1 package dry Onion Soup Mix

1 can mushroom soup
1/2 can water
Salt and pepper

Combine roast, carrots and onion in foil lined pan. Sprinkle onion soup mix over top. Mix mushroom soup with 1/2 can water; pour over roast. Salt and pepper. Wrap foil tightly to seal. Cook about 6 hours at 250 degrees (depending on size of roast).

*May Slack (Merritt): Jeanna Slack '70; Brian Slack '73*

Don't resent growing old...
It is a privilege denied to many.

## ROAST BEEF TURNOVERS

2 loaves frozen bread dough,
    thawed
1 pound cooked roast beef,
    shredded in butter
2 cups fresh mushrooms, sliced
1 bunch green onions, chopped
Basil to taste
Oregano to taste
1 egg
2 tablespoons water

Thaw frozen bread dough. Shred cooked roast in butter. Slice mushrooms and mix with chopped onions in large skillet. Simmer mushrooms, onions, basil and oregano in butter until tender. Gradually add roast beef. Pinch each loaf into 3 pieces. Flatten out into circle. Add beef mixture; fold over, pinching ends to seal. Last top with beaten egg and water and make slits in top. Bake 30 minutes or until brown.

*Von R. and Wanda Brinkley: Rebecca '77 (submitted by Rebecca)*

## ROAST AND COLA

3 to 4 pound roast
2 to 4 tablespoons flour
Salt and pepper to taste
4 tablespoons shortening
1 bottle Coke

Dredge roast in flour; salt and pepper. Brown in shortening. Pour coke over roast and place over low heat. Cover and cook until tender. May be cooked inside oven at about 300 degrees.

*Buford and Jackie Andrews: Johnny '66*

## ROAST COOKED IN FOIL

3 to 4 pounds chuck roast, arm
    roast, or Pikes Peak
1 can Cream of Mushroom soup,
    undiluted
1 tablespoon Steak A-1 sauce
Salt and pepper to taste

Place roast in foil in pan. Cover roast with soup and seasonings. Close foil completely. Cook 3 hours at 325 degrees.

*Note:* Variations: 1 can tomato soup and 1 package onion soup. When using these, do not salt and pepper, if so, very lightly.

*Julius and Herta Fuhrmann: (grandparents) David '68*

---

**Friendship doubles your joys
and cuts your grief in half.**

# STEAK 'N TATERS

| | |
|---|---|
| 2 pounds round steak | 5 peeled potatoes, cut in halves |
| 1 teaspoon salt | 1/4 cup chopped onions |
| 1/4 teaspoon pepper | Dash of paprika |
| 1/3 cup flour | 1 can cream of mushroom soup |
| 1/3 cup oil | 1/2 can water |

Cut steak into serving pieces. Salt and pepper. Coat in flour; brown in oil in heavy skillet. Lay steak, potatoes, and onions in bottom of 9" casserole dish. Salt and pepper potatoes; then add a dash of paprika on top. Cover with mushroom soup diluted with 1/2 can of water. Bake at 350 degrees until potatoes are done, about 1-1/2 hours. Serves 5 to 6.

*Joe and Faye Dutton: Diane '75*

# STUFF

| | |
|---|---|
| 1 pound hamburger meat, browned and drained | Crushed corn chips |
| | Grated cheese or chili carne |
| 1 can Ranch Style beans | Lettuce, finely chopped |
| 1 can Spanish rice | Tomatoes, diced |
| 1 can diced Rotel tomatoes | |

Brown meat; add beans, rice, and Rotel tomatoes. Heat and serve over crushed corn chips. Top with grated cheese or chili carne, finely chopped lettuce, and tomatoes.

*Leland and Mona Hamilton: Angela '63; Julie '77*

# SWISS STEAK

| | |
|---|---|
| 2 pounds top round steak (1" thick) | 1/2 cup water |
| | 1 cup mushroom soup |
| 1 cup flour | 1 (8-ounce) carton sour cream |
| 2 teaspoons salt | 1 large sliced onion |
| Pepper to taste | 1 small can mushrooms, drained |
| 2 tablespoons shortening | |

Cut meat into serving pieces and dredge in seasoned flour. Melt shortening and brown meat on both sides. Add water, mushrooms, soup, and sour cream. Cover and bake at 350 degrees for 1 hour. Add sliced onions generously, then bake for another hour and 15 minutes or until meat is done. Add mushrooms. (Use mushroom liquid in place of 1/2 cup water.)

*Tom and Frances Fee: Carol '63*

## SWISS STEAK JARDINIERE

3-1/2 pounds round steak
1/2 cup flour
2 teaspoons salt
1/4 teaspoon pepper
1/3 cup shortening
4 sliced medium onions

2 cups grapefruit juice
2 tablespoons brown sugar
2 cups frozen vegetables
Noodles
Poppy seeds

Combine flour, salt, and pepper. Sprinkle on steak. Pound in; cut into 1" cubes. Reserve remainder of flour. In hot fat, brown steak, then remove. Brown onions lightly. Make paste with remainder of flour mixture, brown sugar, other salt, and some grapefruit juice. Add onion and fat. Makes a thickening. Gradually stir in remainder of grapefruit juice. Return steak to mixture (gravy). Cover and cook 1-1/2 hours at 350 degrees. (Can be frozen at this point. Add frozen vegetables; serve with noodles, sprinkled with poppy seeds.

*Eugene and Mary Demmler: Ricky '63*

## TALAGARENA

*(Good for a covered-dish dinner; freeze and heat up)*

1 large package noodles, boiled
2 medium chopped onions
3 minced garlic buttons
1 chopped bell pepper
2 pounds ground meat
2 tablespoons chili powder

1 can corn
2 small cans tomato sauce
18 ripe pitted olives
1 pound cubed American cheese
    (about 1/4" in size)
Salt and pepper to taste

Boil noodles in salt water until tender. Saute onions, garlic, and pepper in butter. Add meat and brown. Mix remainder of ingredients. Stir in noodles. Bake 30 minutes in moderate oven.

(Good to cook in skillet or good to put in casserole. Thaw and heat. Good dish to cook after school and have for supper.)

*Al and Maxine Hays: Steve '62*

## WESTERN SPAGHETTI

1-1/2 to 2 pounds round steak,
    cubed
5 cups tomato juice
2 cups water
1 cup chopped onion

1 package spaghetti, uncooked
1 cup green olives, chopped
1 cup ripe olives
Salt and pepper to taste
Grated cheese

Brown steak in a little oil, then put in large pan. Add tomato juice, water, and onion. Simmer until meat is tender. Add spaghetti and olives. When spaghetti is done, add cheese and mix until cheese is melted and well mixed.

*Lewis, Jr. and Louise Young: Paul '69*

# TASTY TURNOVERS

Make your favorite yeast roll recipe. Let rise to recipe directions. While bread is rising:

1-1/2 pounds ground beef
1/2 cup chopped onions
Salt and pepper

1-1/2 cups cheddar cheese
1/2 cup salad dressing

Scramble ground beef with onions. Drain fat from meat; sprinkle with salt and pepper. Grate approximately 1-1/2 cups cheddar cheese.

When dough is ready to be shaped, pinch off a small ball size piece. Roll into an oval on floured board. Place 2 spoonfuls of cooked beef on half of dough. Add some grated cheese; place 1 tablespoon dressing on cheese. Fold other half of dough over all ingredients and seal edges together. Place on greased cookie sheet. Allow to rise 30 to 35 minutes; then bake at 350 degrees until golden brown. Makes approximately 12 to 14 turnovers.

*Ben and Erma Hudman: Bennie '56*

# GRINGO BURRITOS

1 pound ground beef
1 onion, chopped
1/2 cup picante sauce
2 cans cream of chicken soup

1/2 can water
1 dozen flour tortillas
1/2 pound shredded Monterey
Jack cheese

Preheat oven to 350 degrees. Brown meat and onion. Add picante sauce, soup, and water. Mix thoroughly. Spread thin layer of mixture in bottom of 11x14" pan. Heat tortillas slightly. Roll some of the meat mixture in each tortilla. Arrange in pan. Cover with any remaining sauce and shredded cheese. Bake uncovered at 350 degrees for 15 minutes. Serves 6.

*Note:* Meat mixture can be prepared in microwave on high power. Rotate every 5 minutes.

*Tome and Jerry Rehders: Denesa '70; Dee Aun 63*

# DORITO CASSEROLE

*(Marvin's favorite)*

1 pound ground beef
1 small onion, chopped
1 teaspoon salt
1 can Cream of Mushroom soup

1 soup can milk
1 (4-ounce) can mild chilies
1 (5-1/2 ounce) package Doritos
8 slices American cheese

Brown meat and onion until tender; add salt, soup, milk, and chilies. Mix well. Put layer of Doritos in casserole dish. Add 1/2 of meat mixture and top with 4 slices of cheese. Repeat with another layer of meat mixture. Top with cheese and with few crushed Doritos. Bake 30 minutes at 350 degrees. Serves 5.

*Roy and Ola Stilwell: Marvin '55*
*Carl and Thelma Dunaway: Jimmy '59; Patsy '60*

# CHILI

2 pounds hamburger, browned
1 onion, chopped and fried with
    meat
2 tablespoons flour
2 teaspoons garlic salt

2 teaspoons cumin
5 tablespoons chili powder
1/2 teaspoon red pepper, optional
3-1/2 cups water

Brown meat and onions; drain and add remaining ingredients. Mix well. Simmer 1-1/2 hours.

*Calvin and Zella Wither: Linda '55*

# EARL ROBERTS CHILI

6 pound beef, cut into 1" squares
2 pound pork
2 teaspoons onion salt
2 teaspoons garlic salt
4 teaspoons salt
3 teaspoons pepper
1 teaspoon oregano

8 cups hot water, as needed
6 tablespoons white vinegar
10 tablespoons chili powder
8 cubes beef bouillon
1 teaspoon cumino
2 tablespoons paprika
4 tablespoons masa harina

Brown beef and pork. Put in pot with all other ingredients except masa harina. Cook until beef falls apart. Mix masa harina with 2 cups hot water. Stir into chili. Add beans if desired. Skim off grease if necessary.

*George and Susan Pearl Roberts: Earl Roberts '49; Joe '51*

# ELK OR DEER CHILI

4 pounds ground elk meat
1 pound hamburger
6 cloves garlic, diced
2 small onions
2 cans tomato sauce
1 can tomatoes

3 tablespoons cumino, ground
1/2 teaspoon hot chili (or more)
6 tablespoons chili powder
1 cup water (to start with)
1 teaspoon salt
1/2 teaspoon black pepper

In a very large pan combine all of the above ingredients. (I cook at a bubbly boil until it is nearly dry. Turn down fire. Add another cup of water and simmer 1 hour.) Add water, if needed.

*T.D. and Iva Richardson: Mike '72*

**Patience is the companion of wisdom.**

# CHILIES RELLENOS

Several green chilies                    2 tablespoons flour
2 eggs, separated                        Slices of cheese

Remove seeds and ribs from peppers by slicing down one side. Boil 10 to 15 minutes; drain. Beat 2 eggs, separately; whites to soft peak; yolks slightly. Add flour; fold in the beaten eggs. Place a slice of cheese inside each pepper (a meat mixture may also be placed inside pepper — ground meat, chicken, etc.)

Roll each pepper in egg batter; then flour if desired. Fry in pre-heated oil (400 degrees) until golden brown on each side.

*Jim and Terry Adams: Leslie '71*

# CHILIES RELLENOS
## (CASSEROLE)

2 cans green chilies, diced              1 can evaporated milk
1 to 1-1/2 pounds ground meat            1 tablespoon flour
Salt and pepper to taste                 1/2 teaspoon garlic salt
1 pound cheddar cheese                   1 small can tomato sauce with
1/2 pound Monterey jack cheese               tabasco sprinkled in
4 to 6 eggs

Preheat oven to 350 degrees. Drain chilies and spread in a 9x13" baking dish. Brown meat, salt and pepper to taste. Drain meat and spread over chilies. Grate cheeses and mix together; spread over meat. In mixing bowl, beat eggs slightly; add milk, flour and garlic salt. Mix well. Pour evenly over ingredients in dish.

Bake for 30 minutes at 350 degrees. Remove from oven and pour tomato sauce and tabasco mixture over casserole. Bake 5 additional minutes. Cut into squares. Serves about 10. GOOD!

*Bill and Marilyn Wheeler: Bryan '68*

# GREEN CHILI CASSEROLE

1-1/2 pounds ground beef,                1 (4-ounce) can green chili
    browned                                  enchilada sauce
1/2 cup chopped onions                   1 (12-ounce) can evaporated milk
1 can cream of mushroom soup             1 large package Doritos
1 can cream of chicken soup              1 pound grated cheese

Brown meat with onion. Add soups, green chilies, enchilada sauce, and milk. Mix well. Pour mixture over Doritos that have been emptied into a 9x12" pan. Cover with grated cheese. Bake in 350 degree oven for 30 minutes.

*Note:* Add no salt. Can divide and make 2 casseroles and freeze one. THIS IS EASY!

*Doc and Ramona Sharp: Nancy '71*
*Marie Hinds: Jack '74*

# GREEN CHILIE PATTIES

2 eggs, beaten lightly
1 cup flour
1 teaspoon salt

3/4 pound grated cheese
1 can chopped green chilies or
   fresh chilies

Beat eggs; add flour, salt, cheese, and chilies. Mix well. Drop by spoonfuls in greased pan and fry until golden brown.

*David and Sharon Walker: Kay Lynn '76*

# CREAMED ENCHILADAS

1 pound ground meat
1 large onion, chopped
1/4 stick oleo
2 cans Cream of Chicken Soup
1 canned milk

1 can chili
1 can tomatoes, chopped
2 dozen tortillas
1 (10-ounce) package grated
   cheese

Brown meat and onion in oleo; cook until tender. Add soup, milk, chili, and tomatoes. In a 9x13" pan, make a layer of tortillas, sauce, and grated cheese. Alternate until all is used. End with cheese. Bake at 350 degrees until done, about 30 minutes.

*Otis and Edith Carruth: Joveta '50*

# GREEN ENCHILADAS

1 pound lean ground beef
1 teaspoon salt
1/4 teaspoon minced garlic
1 can Cream of Chicken soup
3/4 cup evaporated milk
1/2 pound Velveeta cheese, grated
1 package Green Onion Dip Mix
   or Borden's French Onion
   Dip

1 small can chopped green chilies
1 small jar pimientos
1/2 pound Longhorn cheese,
   grated
1 cup chopped onions
1 dozen tortillas
1/2 cup corn oil

Season beef with salt and garlic. Brown. Set aside. To make cheese sauce, heat soup, milk, and grated Velveeta until cheese melts. Add onion dip, green chilies, and chopped pimientos. To browned meat, add grated Longhorn cheese and chopped onions. Mix well. Soften tortillas in hot oil and drain thoroughly on both sides. Fill each tortilla with some meat mixture, roll lightly. Place in shallow (8x10") baking dish. Pour cheese sauce over tortillas. Cover with foil. Bake at 350 degrees for 30 minutes. Serves 8.

*Darrell and Charlotte Jackson: Valerie '66; Kevin '71*

# HOT GREEN ENCHILADAS

3 medium green jalapenos, seeds
removed
Light gravy made with oil, flour,
and water
1 cup canned tomatoes

Dash of salt
1 medium chopped onion
1 pound grated Longhorn cheese
1 dozen corn tortillas

Remove seeds from jalapenos and boil 10 minutes. (For milder enchiladas, use mild long peppers). Grind jalapenos or blend in blender. Mix jalapenos with gravy (made with flour, oil, and water). Add the tomatoes and salt. Chop the onion; grate the cheese. Fry the tortillas (not crispy). Spread the tortillas. Add a small amount of both cheese and onion. Roll the tortillas. Place in a medium pan; spread the sauce and sprinkle some cheese and onion on top. Place in 200 degree oven 5 minutes; ready to serve.

*Sergio and Frances Marquez: Ernie '77*

# "SOUTH OF THE BORDER ENCHILADA DISH"

1 pound ground meat
1/2 teaspoon salt
1 (10-ounce) can (mild) enchilada
sauce
1/2 cup water

1 small chopped onion
1/2 pound mild cheese, grated
coarsely
6 to 8 tortillas

Place meat and salt in skillet to cook over low heat stirring until meat is crumbled well and cooked to medium done. Drain. Pour enchilada sauce and 1/2 cup water in larger skillet, letting come to boil while meat cooks. Place tortillas in hot sauce to soften (singly) and line baking dish with layer of tortillas, meat, onion, and cheese, ending with layer of meat, onion, and cheese. Pour remaining sauce over top. Bake at 350 degrees until heated through and cheese is melted.

*Ollie and Betty Schrank: Mark '66*

# HAMBURGER CHILIES

1 pound ground beef
1 chopped onion
2 (7-ounce) cans diced chilies (or
less)
1 pound Monterey Jack or
cheddar cheese, grated

1/2 cup flour
2 cups milk
2 beaten eggs
Salt to taste

Brown meat with onions; drain. Mix meat, onions, and chilies in greased baking dish. Mix grated cheese with flour; add milk, eggs, and salt. Mix well. Pour over meat mixture and bake at 350 degrees for 1 hour, uncovered.

*Herbert and Vera Barnes: Ronnie '62*

# MEXICAN CASSEROLE

2 pounds ground meat
1 large onion, chopped
1 garlic bud, chopped
2 cans cream of mushroom soup
2 cans Ranch Style beans

2 cans Ro-Tel tomatoes
1 pound Velveeta cheese,
  chopped
1 package flour tortillas

Brown meat, onions, and garlic in skillet. Drain off grease. Add all other ingredients and mix well. Pour into large casserole and bake at 400 degrees for 30 minutes.

*James and Betty Dillard: Johnny Chapman '70*

# MEXICAN HEAVENLY HASH

2 pounds ground meat
Salt, pepper, and garlic, to taste
1 large onion, chopped
1 can chopped green chilies
1 can tomatoes and green chilies
1 can enchilada sauce (hot or
  mild)

1 can cream of mushroom soup
1 can cream of chicken soup
1 can cheddar cheese soup
1 pound Longhorn cheese, grated
1 (11-ounce) package toasted corn
  Doritos, (tortilla chips)

Brown meat and onions with salt, pepper, and garlic. Add green chilies, and tomatoes and green chilies. Simmer 15 minutes. In separate pan, mix enchilada sauce and soups. Heat and stir to mix well. Place in casserole as follows: Doritos, meat, soup, and cheese. Sprinkle cheese on top. Cover with foil.

Bake at 350 degrees for 1 hour. Last 15 minutes remove foil.

Excellent for freezing. Thaw 1 hour before baking.

*Clarence and Shirley Parker: Marty '72*

# MEXICAN MACARONI

1 small package macaroni,
  cooked and drained
1 pound ground beef
1 tablespoon chili powder
1-1/2 cups chopped celery

2 medium onions, chopped
1 large sweet pepper, chopped
2 cans tomato sauce
Salt and pepper to taste
Grated cheese

Brown beef; add chili powder. Saute celery, onions, and pepper. Add cooked and drained macaroni and tomato sauce. Salt and pepper. Pour mixture into a pan or dish and top with grated cheese. Simmer until heated through and bubbly.

*William and Troy Lou Munn: Mary '55*

# STACK 'EM ON A PLATE
## (Mexican Dish)

Layer: Fritos (small size)
Layer: Chili, canned or made
Layer: Cooked rice
Layer: Chopped onions
Layer: Shredded lettuce
Layer: Chopped tomatoes

Cheese Sauce:
2 tablespoons butter
1 tablespoon flour
1" slice Velveeta
1 cup milk

Mix all ingredients; heat until desired consistency (thin gravy consistency). (Or use Cream of Cheese Soup.)

*Note:* Good for a party where everyone stacks and fixes his own Mexican dish.

*Kenneth and Mary Sacke: Schaun '66; Corbi '70*

# SPANISH RICE

1 pound ground round
1 cup Ranch Style beans
1 cup Rotel tomatoes with diced
    green chilies

1 package Taco Mix
1-1/2 cups water
1-1/2 cups Instant rice

Brown meat; drain. Transfer meat to 2 or 3 quart pot with tight fitting lid. Add all except rice. Mix well. Bring to a full boil and add rice; cover and let set 10 minutes.

*James and Vera Ulan: Michael '59; Debbie '60 (submitted by Debbie)*

# TACO PIZZA PIE

1 can pizza dough (in dairy case)
1 pound ground beef
1/2 medium onion, diced
1 small can taco sauce, hot or mild
1 small can enchilada sauce, hot
    or mild

1 (15-ounce) can refried beans,
    warmed
Cheddar cheese, shredded
Mozzarella cheese, shredded
Lettuce
Tomatoes
Onions

Prepare pizza dough (bakes well in 9x13" oblong pan). Brown ground meat with 1/2 onion; drain well. Add taco sauce mix. Pour most or all of enchilada sauce evenly over dough. Warm beans (they spread easier); spread evenly over sauce. Pour meat mixture over beans. Next top with both cheese (amount you like). Bake at 400 degrees until cheeses melt and dough is golden brown. Top with chopped lettuce, tomatoes, and onions.

*Walter and Rosa Renner: Nelva (Collins) '68 (submitted by Nelva)*

# CORNBREAD TAMALE PIE

1 pound ground beef
1 large chopped onion
1/2 cup chopped green pepper
1 can tomato soup
2 cups water

1 teaspoon salt
1/4 teaspoon pepper
1 tablespoon chili powder
1 cup corn

Brown beef, onions, and pepper. Add remaining ingredients and simmer 15 minutes, then place in greased baking dish. Cover with Cornbread Topping.

Cornbread Topping:
3/4 cup cornmeal
1 tablespoon flour
1 tablespoon sugar
1/2 teaspoon salt

1-1/2 teaspoons baking powder
1 egg
1/3 cup milk
1 tablespoon cooking oil

Sift dry ingredients together. Add beaten egg and milk, stirring lightly until combined. Fold in cooking oil. Cover the meat mixture with topping. The topping will disappear but will rise during baking and form a good layer of cornbread.

Bake in 425 degree oven for 20 to 25 minutes or until cornbread is brown.

*J.C. and Ruth Howell: Cindy '63*

# "AFTER HOLIDAY" CASSEROLE

2 cans Cream of Mushroom soup,
    full strength
1 cup Hellman's mayonnaise
1/2 teaspoon curry powder
2-1/2 cups cooked chicken or
    turkey, cut into bite size

2 (8-ounce) cans sliced water
    chestnuts, drained
Croutons or onion rings
Almonds

(Can use left-over chicken or turkey. May be made a day ahead.)

Mix soup, mayonnaise, and curry powder. Add meat and water chestnuts and stir. Place in casserole dish and cover with topping made with croutons and sprinkled with almonds. Bake 30 to 40 minutes at 350 degrees.

*Robert and Betty Berry: Robbie '65; Diann '66*

**Love does not count the cost
Or look for a bargain.**

## CHICKEN BREAST CASSEROLE

2 tablespoons oil
6 chicken breasts, skinned and
   deboned
1/2 cup chopped onion
1/2 cup chopped celery
1 small bell pepper, chopped

1 cup sliced mushrooms
1 can mushroom soup
1 can water
1/2 cup sour cream
Salt and pepper to taste

Pour oil in large skillet. Flour chicken and brown on both sides. Take out and place in casserole dish. Saute onions, celery, pepper, and mushrooms in oil until brown. Mix mushroom soup, water, and sour cream. Add vegetables. Pour over chicken. Bake at 350 degrees for 1 hour. Serve over rice or noodles.

*Cecil and Trilby Gerber: Sandra '50; Butch '52; Jenny '53*

## CHICKEN-BROCCOLI CASSEROLE

2 (10-ounce) packages frozen
   broccoli spears
1/2 cup mayonnaise
1/4 teaspoon lemon juice
1 (10-1/2 ounce) can cream of
   chicken soup, undiluted
2 cups sliced cooked chicken
   (leftovers are good)

1/2 cup fine dried bread crumbs
2 tablespoons oleo, melted
1/4 cup grated sharp cheddar
   cheese
Grease a shallow 1-1/2 quart
   baking dish.

Cook broccoli according to directions. Drain. Blend mayonnaise, lemon juice, and soup. Arrange cooked broccoli in dish. Top with chicken slices and pour sauce evenly over all. Sprinkle with a mixture of bread crumbs and butter. Top with grated cheese. Heat in a 350 degree oven for 25 minutes or until topping is slightly browned.

*Note:* 1/4 teaspoon curry powder may be added to sauce mixture. Blend well. Serves 6.

*Boyd and Delois North: Joy '62; Steve '65*

## CHICKEN CASSEROLE

2 cans Swanson's chicken (white
   meat and drained)
1 small can mushrooms, drained
1 can French style green beans;
   DO NOT DRAIN

1 can Cream of Chicken soup
1 cup cheddar cheese, grated
1/2 cup mayonnaise
1 teaspoon lemon juice
1 can Hungry Jack Flake biscuits

Mix and heat all ingredients, except biscuits. Pour into casserole dish and place 1 can Hungry Jack biscuits on top. Butter tops of biscuits. Bake at 375 degrees for 20 minutes.

*Randy and Reba Stilwell: Shannon '81*

## CHICKEN AND CHIPPED BEEF CASSEROLE

1-1/2 jars chipped beef
3 chicken breasts, halved
Salt and pepper to taste
6 strips bacon
1 can mushrooms, drained

1 can artichoke hearts, drained
1 can mushroom soup, optional
1/2 pint sour cream (or 1 pint, if
   soup omitted)

Grease casserole. Make bed of shredded chipped beef. Salt and pepper each breast half and wrap each one with strip of bacon. Lay chicken breast on beef. Add layer of mushrooms, then layer of artichoke hearts, halved. Mix sour cream and mushroom soup and pour over top of all. Cover tightly and bake in 225 degree oven for 3 hours. Or, you can bake 2-1/2 hours at night and refrigerate, then bake 1/2 hour to heat next morning, or until done.

*N.N. and Adelaide Jones: Bob '50 (recipe of Diana Rowley Jones, Bob's wife)*

## CHICKEN CONTINENTAL

1-1/2 cups cooked, cut-up chicken
1 (4-ounce) can sliced
   mushrooms, drained
1 garlic clove, crushed
2 tablespoons oil
1 (13-1/2 ounce) can chicken broth

1 (9-ounce) package Birdseye
   French cut green beans
1 teaspoon salt
1/2 teaspoon basil leaves
Dash of pepper
1-1/2 cups dry Minute Rice

Saute chicken, mushrooms, and garlic in oil for 2 to 3 minutes. Add remaining ingredients, except rice and bring to a full boil. Stir in rice, remove from heat. Cover and let stand 5 minutes. Makes 4 servings.

*Robert and Lynda Blubaugh: Corey '83*

## CROCK POT CHICKEN

1 package chicken breast (remove
   skin)
Salt and pepper chicken
1 can Cream of Chicken Soup (do
   not add water)
1 teaspoon sage

1/2 teaspoon Accent
1 teaspoon dried onion
1/4 teaspoon garlic salt
1/4 teaspoon oregano
1/4 teaspoon cumin
1/4 teaspoon celery salt

Combine all of above in crock pot and cook 3 to 4 hours on high setting. Serve with rice or noodles.

*Wayne Turley '52 (submitted by his wife, Anna)*

# CHICKEN CRESCENT ROLLS

2 cans crescent rolls
2 to 3 chicken breasts, cooked
   and deboned
1 cup milk

2 cans Cream of Chicken Soup
1 cup grated cheese
1/4 cup butter, melted

Roll chicken in rolls. Make sauce with milk, soup, cheese, and butter. Pour 3 tablespoons of soup mixture in bottom of casserole. Place rolls in dish; pour rest of mixture over rolls. Bake at 350 degrees for 45 minutes or until rolls are brown.

*David and Sharon Walker: Kay Lynn '76*

# CHICKEN AND DUMPLINGS

1 stewing chicken
1 teaspoon salt
Dough:
1 cup sifted flour

1 teaspoon baking powder
1/2 teaspoon salt
2 tablespoons shortening
1/3 cup milk

Boil chicken with plenty water; with 1 teaspoon salt. Debone. Set chicken aside. Mix flour, salt, and baking powder. Cut in shortening until mix resembles coarse crumbs. Add milk and mix until dough follows fork around bowl. Turn out on lightly floured surface and knead 2 or 3 minutes. Roll to 1/8" thickness and cut into 1x4" strips. Bring chicken broth and water to boil. Add dumplings. Cover and simmer 20 minutes. Add chicken and heat. Makes 6 to 8 servings.

*Don and Suzanne Humphrey: Trey '82*

# OLD-FASHIONED CHICKEN AND DUMPLINGS

1 chicken, boiled and deboned
6 cups broth
1 cup milk
2 tablespoons soup base
4 drops yellow food coloring
Pepper to taste
Salt to taste

Dough:
3 cups flour
1 teaspoon salt
5 tablespoons shortening
1 cup milk
2 eggs

Work dough together. Divide and roll out very thin, then cut into narrow strips. Drop into boiling broth. Stir as little as possible.

*Note:* I cut dough with a pizza cutter.

*Calvin and Zella Withers: Linda '55*

# CHICKEN DORITO

1/4 boned chicken or 2 small
cans, chopped
1 can cream of mushroom soup
1 can cream of chicken soup
1 can chopped Rotel tomatoes

Minced onion to taste
Salt and pepper to taste
1 package Doritos
Velveeta cheese

Combine chicken, soups, and Rotel tomatoes. Add minced onions and salt and pepper to taste. Make layer of Doritos in bottom of casserole dish. Pour mixture over Doritos and layer of Velveeta cheese. Cover and heat until bubbly.

*Floyd and Cordell Peacock: Tina '74 (granddaughter)*

# CHICKEN ENCHILADAS

1 chicken, boiled, deboned, and
diced
1 can Pet milk
1 can Cream of Chicken soup

1 can Cream of Mushroom soup
1 can chopped green chilies
1 package tortillas

Prepare chicken; set aside. Mix milk, soups, and green chilies. Put layer of tortillas in bottom of casserole, then a layer of chicken until used up. Pour soup mixture over the layers. Cook in 350 degree oven until hot throughout.

*D.P. and Betty Thomas: Jerry '57; Frances '59*

# CHICKEN ENCHILADAS

1 medium onion, chopped
1 can Cream of Chicken Soup,
undiluted
1 small can Pet milk
1 cup sour cream

1 pound Velveeta cheese
1 can chopped green chilies
1 package tortillas (1 pound)
1 boiled chicken (deboned and
diced)

Saute onion; add soup, milk, sour cream, cheese, and green chilies. Heat until cheese is melted. Take the tortillas, 1 at a time and heat in a small amount of hot oil until tender. Place tortilla in a deep baking dish. Fill each tortilla with chicken, then cover chicken with a large spoon of mixture. Roll them over. Spread the remaining mixture over finished enchiladas and heat 20 minutes in 375 degree oven.

*Olin and Ethel Horton: Johnny '63; Denise '65*

---

**Talk is cheap because supply
always exceeds the demand.**

# CHICKEN ENCHILADAS

1 (2 to 3-pound) chicken, cooked, deboned and chopped
1 large package flour tortillas
2 to 3 cups shredded Monterey Jack cheese

Sauce:
2 cans mushroom soup
1 medium size can chopped green chilies
Mix until smooth (I use blender)

Assemble as follows:

Put tablespoon of sauce on tortilla. Place chopped up chicken in center and top with small amount of cheese. Roll up like enchilada and place seam down in 9x13" pan. Continue until pan is full. Pour remaining sauce over enchilada. Top with remaining chicken and cover with cheese. Bake at 350 degrees for 20 to 30 minutes.

*Morris and Pat Pope: Byron '79; Gwen '83*

# QUICK-FRY CHICKEN

4 boneless chicken breasts, diced
1 bunch chopped green onions
1 teaspoon garlic
1/2 cup teriyaki sauce
Salt and pepper

1 tablespoon oil
1 package Birdseye Japanese vegetables
1 can sliced water chestnuts

Saute chicken, onions, and seasonings in wok or deep frying pan in oil. When chicken is brown, add the rest of the ingredients. Stir-fry for 3 to 4 minutes until vegetables are coated with sauce and seasoning but keep vegetables crisp. DO NOT OVERCOOK. Serve with rice.

*Dan and Tina Newbrough: Heather '84*

# ITALIAN CHICKEN

Desired number of chicken pieces
1 bottle Italian Salad Dressing

1 package Pepperidge Farm Herb Stuffing Mix (easy to find during holiday time — otherwise may be difficult)

Place chicken pieces in bowl and pour bottle of Italian Salad Dressing over parts. Let set about 12 to 24 hours. Turn so all of chicken is marinated. Roll chicken in stuffing mix. Bake in glass dish at 350 degrees — about 1 to 1-1/2 hours.

*Rodney and Jane Noble: Carmen '78*

# LEMON CHICKEN

1 pound skinned and boned
   chicken breasts, cut into strips
1 medium onion, chopped
2 garlic cloves, crushed
2 tablespoons butter or margarine
1 tablespoon cornstarch
1 can (13-3/4 ounce) chicken broth

1 large carrot, sliced diagonally
2 tablespoons fresh lemon juice
1/2 teaspoon grated lemon rind
1/2 teaspoon salt
1 cup snow peas
3 tablespoons chopped parsley
1-1/2 cups dry Minute Rice

Saute chicken, onion, and garlic in butter until chicken is lightly browned — about 5 minutes. Stir in cornstarch and cook 1 minute. Add broth, carrot, lemon juice, lemon rind, and salt. Bring to a full boil. Stir in pea pods, parsley, and rice. Cover; remove from heat. Let stand 5 minutes. Fluff with fork. Makes 4 servings.

This recipe has been one of my favorites. Since I moved out of the dorm, I have to cook; with little time on my hands, this is an easy recipe. It is also great to reheat in the microwave.

*Joe and Sue Summers: Debbie '79 (submitted by Debbie)*

# CHICKEN PALERMO

6 deboned chicken breast halves
3 slices Mozzarella cheese
1/4 cup oleo
1/2 cup dry bread crumbs

1/4 cup Parmesan cheese
1 large jar of spaghetti sauce
1 package spaghetti, cooked and
   drained

Pound chicken breasts between plastic wrap to flatten. Cut each slice of cheese into 4 strips. Place 2 strips in middle of each breast half. Fold chicken around cheese, tucking in ends. Secure with toothpicks. Melt butter in large shallow baking dish; combine crumbs and Parmesan. Roll chicken in butter then in crumbs. Place in pan with remaining butter. Bake uncovered 20 to 30 minutes at 400 degrees. Simmer spaghetti sauce 10 minutes; pour hot sauce over chicken and bake 5 minutes longer or until bubbling hot. Serve with spaghetti.

*Charles and Arlene Clark: Malcolm '74*

# PARMESAN CHICKEN

1 cut up chicken or chicken
   breasts
1/2 cup flour
1/2 cup Parmesan cheese
1 teaspoon paprika

1/2 teaspoon garlic powder
1 teaspoon salt
1 egg
1 tablespoon water
1/2 cup oleo, melted

Combine flour, cheese, paprika, garlic powder, and salt. Mix well. Beat egg and water. Dip chicken in egg and water and then roll in flour mixture. Place in baking dish. Pour melted butter over chicken. Bake 1 hour at 350 degrees.

*Kenneth and Nancy Helvey: Valerie '76*

# CHICKEN POT PIE

Pastry for two 9" pie crusts
2 tablespoons butter
2 tablespoons flour
1 teaspoon salt
1/8 teaspoon pepper
1/2 tablespoon minced onion
1 cup chicken broth

1/2 cup light cream
1 small can Veg-All, drained
1 can peas, drained
Optional: chopped celery, carrots,
potatoes
2 cups cooked cubed chicken

Prepare pastry. Fit into 9" pie pan and save enough for top (to cut into strips and crisscrosses). Cook mixture of butter, flour, salt, pepper, onion, and broth over low heat until smooth. (You may need more broth.) Stir in cream and boil 1 minute. Add vegetables and chicken. Pour into crust; place strips on top. Cook in 425 degree oven for 35 minutes or until brown.

*Gary and Sidney Gaston: Whitney '85*

# JAY'S FAVORITE CHICKEN POT PIE

2 cups cubed chicken, cooked
1 can Cream of Chicken soup
1 can Cream of Mushroom soup

1 can chicken broth
1 package frozen mixed
vegetables

Pour into casserole dish sprayed with Pam. Make crust.

Crust:
1 cup flour

1 cup milk
1 stick melted oleo

Mix. Make crust. Spoon crust mixture over chicken mixture until all is covered.

Bake 1 hour at 400 degrees. (This will feed 6 adults or 3 teenagers)

*Glen and Connie Haggard: Jay '80*

# CHICKEN AND RICE

1/2 to 1 stick oleo
1 can Cream of Celery soup
1 can Cream of Chicken soup
1/2 can Onion soup
1 soup can water

1 cup uncooked rice
1 cut up chicken or 4 to 6 chicken
breasts
Salt and pepper for chicken

Preheat oven to 350 degrees. Butter a large baking dish. In a bowl combine all soups and water. Sprinkle rice in bottom of dish. Place pieces of chicken on rice and pour soups over all. Seal with foil and bake 1 hour without removing foil.

*Robert and Shelly McCrary: Amy '84*

## CHICKEN AND RICE

1 hen, cooked and deboned
2 cups rice, uncooked
1/2 cup onion, chopped
1 to 2 bell peppers, chopped
2 cups celery, chopped
2 (No. 2) cans tomato juice

1 can mushroom soup
2 tablespoons Worcestershire
  sauce
Salt and pepper, to taste
Grated cheese

Stew chicken in water; debone. Cook rice in chicken broth until almost done. Saute onions, peppers, and celery. Add tomato juice and mushroom soup. Combine all ingredients except cheese. Cook in slow oven 30 minutes. Grate cheese on top and set in oven until melted.

*Mrs. Peggy Mathis (Virginia) '49*

## BAKED CHICKEN AND RICE

*Microwave*

1 box Uncle Bens Wild Rice
1 can cream of mushroom soup

1 can cream of chicken soup
1 chicken, cut up

Combine all ingredients. Mix well. Place chicken into mixture. Cover. Cook in microwave 15 minutes on high, then for 28 to 30 minutes on simmer. Let stand 8 minutes before serving. Serve.

*James and Lucille Mitchell: Dwain '51; Dudley '54; Montrella '59*

## SCALLOPED CHICKEN

1-1/2 tablespoons oleo
1/3 cup slivered almonds
1 can mushrooms, drained
1 can onion soup
2 tablespoons flour

2 cups milk
1 cup cooked and sliced potatoes
1 cup cooked and diced chicken
1 cup cooked carrots

Saute almonds in oleo until golden. Stir in mushroom pieces and onion soup. Mix and blend with flour and milk. Simmer until thickened. In 1-1/2 quart greased casserole dish, layer potatoes, chicken, and carrots plus 1/2 of sauce. Repeat layers; top with remaining sauce. Bake 30 minutes at 350 degrees.

*Carla Sue Nordeman (Young '54)*

**Don't let the crowd pressure you;
Stand for something or
you'll fall for anything!**

# SPANISH CHICKEN

1 cooked and boned chicken
1 small onion, chopped
1/2 tablespoon chili powder
1 teaspoon salt
1 can Cream of Mushroom Soup
1 can Cream of Chicken Soup

1 small can green chilies
1 can (large) evaporated milk
1 cup chicken broth
2 cups grated cheddar cheese
Tortillas

Debone chicken; saute onion and add chili powder and salt. Heat soups, onion, milk, broth, and chilies in saucepan. Put layer of tortillas in casserole dish. Add layer of chicken to casserole, then layer of soup mixture. Add until all is used. Pour grated cheese on top. Cook at 350 degrees until cheese melts.

*Kenny and Maxine Thompson: Kenny '60*

# CHICKEN 'N SPAGHETTI

1 stewed chicken, deboned
1 package spaghetti
1/2 cup chopped green pepper
1/2 cup chopped celery
1/2 cup chopped onion
3 tablespoons butter

1 can mushroom soup
1 can tomato sauce
1 tablespoon chili powder
1 tablespoon cumino seed
Grated cheese

Stew chicken in plenty of water. Remove chicken from stew pan and cook spaghetti in chicken broth. Debone chicken. Saute pepper, celery, and onion in butter. Add mushroom, tomato sauce, chili powder, and cumino seed. Mix all ingredients except cheese. Mix well and pour into casserole dish. Top with grated cheese. Cook until hot and bubbly. May wait until casserole is almost done before cheese is placed on top. Return to oven and leave until cheese is melted.

*Howell and Mary Furry: Mike '63*

# CHICKEN-STUFFING BAKE

4 to 6 chicken breasts, skinned
1 package "Stove Top" Stuffing
  Mix, coarsely crushed

Salt and pepper to taste
Melted oleo

Crush Mix until it is like coarse meal; add herb seasoning packet. Set aside. Wash and pat chicken breast dry. Salt and pepper. Dip chicken in several tablespoons of melted oleo, coating. Roll in crumb mixture, coating well. Place on broiler pan and cook at 350 degrees until browned and chicken is thoroughly cooked, turning once.

*Note:* Pork chops may be substituted for chicken. Very simple but a delicious dish!

*Ralph and Brenda Hummell: Jill '79*

# CHICKEN SUZANNE
## (SUPER!)

| | |
|---|---|
| 4 to 6 boneless chicken breasts | 1/2 cup sour cream |
| Salt and pepper | 1/2 cup cooking sherry |
| 1 stick oleo, melted | 1 can Cream of Mushroom Soup |

Season chicken with salt and pepper; brown in skillet in oleo. Remove and place in casserole. Mix remaining oleo with other ingredients; pour over chicken. Cover and bake at 350 degrees for 1-1/2 hours. Serve over rice. (This recipe can be increased or doubled; if you like more gravy, increase sour cream, sherry, and soup. So good, you'll want to repeat using it!)

*Teacher's Pet: Raymond Colvin*

# CHICKEN TETRAZZINI

| | |
|---|---|
| 1 (14-ounce) package spaghetti | 3 slices bacon, cooked and |
| 2 teaspoons salt | shredded |
| 1 large chopped onion | 1 (8-ounce) can Mushroom soup |
| 1 green chopped pepper | (or Chicken soup) |
| 1/2 stick oleo | 1 pound grated cheese |
| 1/4 teaspoon pepper | 2 (flats) canned boned chicken or |
| 1 (4-ounce) can pimiento, | 1 hen boiled |
| chopped | |

Cook spaghetti in salt and drain. Saute onions and pepper in oleo until tender. Add all other ingredients except cheese. Mix and place in 9x12" pyrex dish. Cover with foil. Bake 30 to 35 minutes at 350 degrees. Add grated cheese last. Freezes well, but freeze without cheese. Add liquid, if needed.

*Neil and Doris Laminack: Randy '64*

# CHICKEN WITH TOSTADOS

| | |
|---|---|
| 2 cans boned chicken | 1/2 can of water (from mushroom |
| 1 small can green chilies | soup) |
| 1 small onion, chopped fine | Shredded cheese |
| 1 can cream of mushroom soup | Tostados |

Saute onion; add other ingredients, except cheese and Tostados. Mix well. Cook slowly. In baking dish, place layer of tostados covered with shredded cheese. Pour part of mixture over cheese. Add another layer and do same. Cook 10 to 15 minutes in 350 degree oven.

*Mona Lea: Shyla '67*

# CHICKEN IN WINE

4 boned chicken breasts, salted
  lightly
1 can cream of celery soup
1/2 cup sour cream, or more

1/4 cup white wine (preferably
  sauterne)
Curry powder

Salt breasts lightly. Mix soup, sour cream, and wine. Pour over chicken. Bake at 350 degrees for 1 hour. Touch lightly with curry powder after baking.

*Note:* Increase ingredients proportionally if cooking more.

*Harry and Carol Tipton: Gloria '60; Debbie '62*

# EASY GLAZED HAM

1 (10-pound) ham
Whole cloves
2 cups pickled peach juice or
  nectar peach juice

1/2 cup cider vinegar
1 cup honey
1 cup (packed) brown sugar

Remove rind from ham, leaving thin layer of fat. (Or use Wilson's 95% fat free ham.) Score fat; stud with cloves. Place ham, fat side up, in roaster. Blend peach juice and vinegar; pour over ham. Spread honey over top; sprinkle with brown sugar. Bake at 300 degrees for 1 hour. Cover; bake for 3 hours longer or until ham is tender, basting frequently. Serve with yams and apples.

*Ruben and Esme Olvera (sister and brother-in-law): Olga Gonzales '82*

# BARBECUED PORK CHOPS

1/2 cup water
1/4 cup vinegar
2 tablespoons sugar
1 tablespoon mustard
1-1/2 teaspoons salt
1/2 teaspoon pepper
1/4 teaspoon cayenne
1 sliced lemon

1 medium sliced onion
1/2 cup catsup
2 tablespoons Worcestershire
  sauce
1 or 2 teaspoons Liquid Smoke
10 pork chops, center cut (1/2"
  thick)

Mix first 9 ingredients; bring to a boil and simmer 20 minutes. Add the remaining ingredients. Bring sauce to a boil. Pour sauce over the pork chops. Bake 1 hour and 25 minutes. Turn chops once.

*Note:* This dish is good with steamed rice and gravy or sauce made from pork drippings or juices. Serves 10.

*Max and Elaine Goldsmith: Gary '62; Roger '64*

## BUTCH'S PORK CHOPS

6 pork loin chops (1" thick)
1 tablespoon salt
3/4 cups rice, uncooked (DO NOT USE INSTANT RICE)
1 (8-ounce) can tomato sauce

2-1/2 tablespoons Taco Seasoning Mix
1-1/2 cups water
1/2 cup grated cheese
1 large bell pepper, cut into 1/2" rings

Preheat oven to 350 degrees. Brown chops in bacon drippings or shortening and place in baking dish. Sprinkle salt over chops. Pour uncooked rice in openings around chops. Mix tomato sauce, Taco Seasoning Mix, and water; pour over chops. Cover tightly with foil or lid and place in oven. Cook 1-1/2 hours, depending on thickness of chops. Remove from oven; spread cheese over chops and top with bell pepper rings. Cover and put back in oven for 10 more minutes.

*B.F. and Ann Seay: Mike '50; Tommy '54*

## PORK CHOPS

6 pork chops (1" thick)
2 medium-sized onions, thinly sliced
1 tablespoon shortening
1 (6-ounce) can frozen orange juice
1 tablespoon lemon juice

2/3 cup water
2 tablespoons brown sugar
1-1/2 teaspoons ginger
1 teaspoon poultry seasoning
1 teaspoon Accent
1 teaspoon salt

Trim excess fat from chops; brown in shortening 10 minutes. Arrange in baking dish with onions. Blend orange juice, lemon juice, and water; pour over chops. Sprinkle with spices. Cover casserole. Bake 1-1/2 hours at 350 degrees.

*Note:* Mix brown sugar, ginger, poultry seasoning, Accent, and salt in small bowl. Sprinkle over pork chops before baking.

*Jimmy and Frances Wilkins: Jamie '64; Lee Ann '65*

## PORK CHOP DELIGHT

4 pork chops, seasoned
1 can Cream of Chicken soup
1/2 can milk
4 carrots, sliced

4 new potatoes, cut up
Onion
Seasoning, salt and pepper

Place chops in baking dish and season as desired. Pour Cream of Chicken soup and milk over chops. Place vegetables over chops in dish and bake covered for about 1 hour at 350 degrees.

*Amos and Jo Ann Smith: Dana '59 (submitted by Dana Smith Gifford)*

# PORK CHOPS AND KRAUT

4 to 6 pork chops                    1 (No. 2) can kraut
Salt and pepper to taste

Salt and pepper pork chops. Pour kraut into buttered baking dish. Place pork chops on top of kraut. Cook 1 hour in 350 degree oven.

*Melvin and Mary Webb: Dewey '66*

# PORK CHOPS IN MUSHROOM SAUCE

6 pork chops, coated in flour       1/2 teaspoon pepper
  mixture                           1/4 cup oil
1 cup flour                         1 can Cream of Mushroom soup
1/2 teaspoon salt                   1 (4-ounce) can sliced mushrooms
1/2 teaspoon oregano

Coat pork chops in flour and seasonings. Brown in oil. Add mushroom soup and mushrooms. Cover and simmer for 40 minutes. Serve with cooked rice.

*Jimmy and Gail Martin: Nikki '83*

# WORCESTERSHIRE PORK CHOPS

Pork chops (desired number),        Salt and pepper, to taste
  Thick chops work best             Worcestershire sauce

Salt and pepper pork chops; dredge in flour. Brown pork chops in hot Crisco quickly (brown only). DO NOT FRY. Place browned chops on broiler pan. Sprinkle with Worcestershire sauce to taste. Broil under medium heat. Turn chops; sprinkle opposite side with sauce. Return to broiler. Cook until done. Don't overcook.

*Henry and Bea Grinslade: Robby '78; Kelli '81*

# SWEET-SOUR TIDBITS

1 pound pork sausage                3 tablespoons honey
2 (5-ounce) packages smoked         3 tablespoons vinegar
  links (party size)                1 tablespoon soy sauce
1 (20-ounce) can pineapple          2 tablespoons cornstarch
  chunks, drained but reserve       1 (2-ounce) jar maraschino
  juice                               cherries, drained

Shape sausage into 1" balls and brown with smoked links in skillet. Drain fat and reserve 2 tablespoons fat. Drain pineapple chunks and reserve juice. Add honey, vinegar, soy sauce, and cornstarch to pineapple juice. Blend until smooth. Add 2 tablespoons reserved fat and bring to boil, stirring constantly. Add sausage, pineapple chunks, and cherries. Mix well. Cover and simmer 15 minutes.

*George and Barbara Harrill: Tommy '70*
*J.D. and Ethel Collinsworth: Sandra '50*

# CAJUN SHRIMP SCAMP

3 sticks margarine
1 teaspoon minced garlic
1 teaspoon salt
1 teaspoon cayenne pepper
1/2 teaspoon white pepper
1/2 teaspoon black pepper
1/2 teaspoon thyme

1 teaspoon basil
3/4 cup white cooking wine
1 cup chopped green onions
1 pound peeled and deveined
   shrimp
1/2 pound crab meat

In a medium-sized skillet melt margarine; add garlic and all spices. Cook until margarine starts bubbling. Add green onions, wine, crab meat, and shrimp. Cook until shrimp turns pink. Do not overcook. (THIS IS DELICIOUS AND EASY!

*Note:* I use white cooking wine and cut down or eliminate the salt.

*George and Sherry Averyt: Amy McCoy '80*

# CALIFORNIA SEAFOOD CASSEROLE

1/2 cup butter or oleo
1/2 cup flour
1 teaspoon dry mustard
1-1/2 tablespoons grated onion
   (white)
2 teaspoons Worcestershire sauce
3/4 teaspoon paprika
3/4 teaspoon salt
1/8 teaspoon black pepper
4 cups milk

1 (6-ounce) package Gruyere
   cheese, cubed
3/4 cup slivered ripe olives
2 (6-ounce) cans lobster (may use
   frozen or fresh, if desired)
1 (6-1/2 ounce) can crab meat
   (may use fresh)
1 pound fresh or frozen shrimp,
   cooked or 1-3/4 cups canned
   shrimp
1 avocado for garnish

Melt butter in saucepan over low heat; blend in flour, mustard, onion, Worcestershire, paprika, salt and pepper. Gradually add milk, stirring constantly until smooth and thickened. Add cheese and stir until melted. Add olives, lobster, crab meat, and shrimp to cheese sauce. Pour into 3-quart casserole and bake uncovered 25 minutes at 350 degrees. To serve, garnish with sliced avocados. Hot rolls and crisp salad complete the meal.

*Othel and Flora Mae Ogden: Walker '52*

# SALMON LOAF

1 tall can salmon, flaked
2 tablespoons grated onion
1 cup crushed cracker crumbs
2 tablespoons butter, melted

2 eggs
1 cup milk
1/2 teaspoon salt
1/4 teaspoon pepper

Mix in order given. Pour into buttered loaf pan. Bake 350 degrees for 40 to 45 minutes or until firm.

*Herman and Zina Patterson: Garland '55 (submitted by Wanda Snow)*

# CRAB MEAT COBBLER
*(Hot Casserole)*

1/2 cup butter
1/2 cup chopped green pepper
1/2 cup chopped onion
1/2 cup flour
1 teaspoon dry mustard
1/2 teaspoon Accent salt
1 cup milk

1 cup shredded American cheese
1/2 pound Backfin crab meat or
 canned crab
1-1/2 cups drained (No. 2 can)
 tomatoes
2 teaspoons Worcestershire sauce
1/2 teaspoon salt

Melt butter in top of double boiler. Add peppers and onions and cook over boiling water until tender (about 10 minutes).

Blend in flour, mustard, Accent salt, milk, and American cheese. Cook, stirring constantly until very thick. Stir in crabmeat, tomatoes, Worcestershire sauce, and salt. Pour into 2 quart casserole.

Cheese Biscuit Dough:
1 cup flour
2 teaspoons baking powder
1/2 teaspoon salt

1/2 cup shredded American
 cheese
2 tablespoons shortening
1/2 cup milk

Sift flour, baking powder, and salt. Add cheese and cut in shortening until fine. Add milk. Mix only until moistened. Drop by teaspoonfuls on top of crab mixture. Bake 20 to 30 minutes at 450 degrees.

*Eddie and Joyce Brenholtz: David '61*

# SHRIMP JAMBALAYA

1 cup sliced celery
2 cups diced green pepper
2 medium onions, sliced thin
4 tablespoons butter (use half
 now; other later)
2 garlic cloves, minced
1 pound cooked ham, 3/4" thick
 and cubed

2 lbs. shrimp, peeled and
 deveined
1-1/2 teaspoons salt
1/4 teaspoon hot pepper sauce
1/2 teaspoon chili powder
1 teaspoon sugar
2 cans whole tomatoes
3 cups hot cooked rice

Cook celery, green pepper, and onion in half the butter until tender but not brown. Add garlic and ham; cook 5 minutes longer. Add remaining butter, shrimp, salt, hot pepper sauce, chili powder, and sugar. Cook, tossing often with fork until shrimp are pink. Add tomatoes and heat. Stir in rice. Serves 8.

*Olin and Ethel Horton: Johnny '63; Denise '65*

# SALMON PATTIES

1 can salmon, drained (save
    liquid)

1 egg
1 cup cracker crumbs

Pour drained salmon into bowl and shred with fork. Mix egg and cracker crumbs with salmon. Add liquid from salmon. Form into flat cakes about 2-1/2" around. Roll in additional cracker crumbs and fry in fairly deep fat until lightly browned.

Tartar Sauce:
1/2 cup Miracle Whip

1/4 cup sandwich spread
A little milk or lemon juice

Mix Miracle Whip and sandwich spread. Add a little milk or lemon juice to thin.

*Tom and Pat Harsh: Robert '75; John Currie '76*

# WILD RICE AND SHRIMP

1 can cream of mushroom soup
2 tablespoons green pepper
2 tablespoons chopped onion
2 tablespoons melted butter
1 tablespoon lemon juice
1/2 teaspoon Worcestershire sauce

1/2 teaspoon dry mustard,
    optional
1/4 teaspoon pepper
1/2 cup cheddar cheese, cubed
2 cups wild rice, cooked
1/2 to 1 pound cooked (shelled
    and deveined) shrimp

Mix all ingredients and put in greased casserole. Bake 30 to 35 minutes at 350 degrees. Can be made up and put in refrigerator before cooking OR FROZEN and cooked later.

Good served with French bread and salad.

*Ed and Mickie Snook: Leland '74*

# QUICHE

1 unbaked pie crust
1 cup turkey ham
4 ounces grated Swiss cheese (and
    optional diced onions,
    mushrooms, green chilies, etc.)

4 eggs, beaten
3/4 cup evaporated milk
1/8 teaspoon garlic powder
Salt and pepper to taste

Brown pie crust at 425 degrees for 8 minutes. Mix ham and cheese and any other optional ingredients. Place in cooled pie shell. Whip the eggs; add milk and seasonings. Pour on top of ham mixture. Bake at 350 degrees for 45 minutes.

*Harold and Cleta Garms: Staci '71*

# HAMBURGER QUICHE

1 unbaked 9" pie shell
1 pound hamburger meat,
 browned
1/2 cup mayonnaise
1/2 cup milk
2 eggs
1 tablespoon cornstarch

1-1/2 cups shredded cheddar
 cheese (or other kind)
1 jar sliced mushrooms or 1/2 cup
 sliced green onions (or use
 both)
Salt and pepper to taste

Brown meat in skillet. Drain and set aside. Blend next 4 ingredients, then add remaining ingredients. Turn into pastry shell. Bake at 350 degrees for 50 minutes. (You may add other ingredients you like)

*Joseph and Lynn Lynch: Nathan '86*
*J. Roy and Shirley McAdams: Shell '73*

# HAM AND SWISS QUICHE

2 cups cooked smoked ham
1 cup (4-ounce) shredded Swiss
 cheese
1/3 cup onion or green onion,
 chopped

2 cups milk
4 eggs
1 cup Bisquick Mix
1/4 teaspoon salt
1/8 teaspoon pepper

Mince the ham, cheese, and onion in food processor and sprinkle the mixture in the bottom of a greased pie pan or a 9x13" pan. Beat the milk, eggs, Bisquick mix, salt, and pepper in a blender until smooth and pour over the ham mixture. Bake at 400 degrees for 35 to 40 minutes or until golden brown.

*Note:* I use this as a brunch dish because it doubles easily, holds well for late arrivals, and everyone — children and adults — seem to like it. Leftovers can be reheated in the microwave.

*Keith and Marcella Harding: Barbara '65*

# HOUSTON MEAT AND CHEESE QUICHE

1/2 pound ground beef
1/2 cup mayonnaise
1/2 cup milk
2 eggs
2 tablespoons flour

3/4 cup cheddar cheese, grated
3/4 cup Swiss cheese, grated
1/3 cup sliced green onions
Salt and pepper, to taste
1 (9") unbaked pie shell

Brown meat in a medium skillet and set aside. Blend mayonnaise, milk, eggs, and flour until smooth. Stir in meat, cheese, onion, salt and pepper. Turn mixture into unbaked pastry shell. Bake at 350 degrees for 35 to 40 minutes. This freezes well if you have any leftover!

*John and Katherine Kniffen: Kelly Kniffen Johnson '75 (submitted by Kelly)*

# IMPOSSIBLE QUICHE

12 slices bacon, fried crisp and
crumbled
1 cup shredded Swiss cheese
1/3 cup finely chopped onion or 1
can fried onion rings

2 cups milk
1/2 cup Bisquick
4 eggs
1/4 teaspoon salt
1/8 teaspoon pepper

Heat oven to 350 degrees. Lightly grease 9" pie plate. Sprinkle bacon, cheese, and onion evenly over bottom of pie plate. Place remaining ingredients in blender. Cover and blend on high 1 minute. Pour into pie plate. Bake until golden brown and knife inserted in center comes out clean (about 50 to 55 minutes). Let stand 5 minutes before cutting. Serves 6.

I love this with French Onion Soup!

*Joe and Sue Summers: Debbie '79 (submitted by Debbie)*

# MEXICAN QUICHE

1 (9") pie shell
8 slices bacon
1/2 chopped onion
2 beaten eggs
1/4 cup Half and Half milk

1 tablespoon flour
1/4 teaspoon salt
1/8 teaspoon pepper
1/2 cup grated Cheddar cheese

Prick shell; bake at 400 degrees for 3 minutes. Remove; prick again; bake 5 minutes. Cook bacon until crisp and crumble. Cook onions in bacon drippings. Mix all ingredients and pour into pie shell. Bake 45 minutes at 375 degrees or until set. Can be served with jalapeno slices on top. (This is one of my favorite recipes.)

*Bob and Nancy Campbell: Tammy '80; Steve '82*

# SAUSAGE AND CHEESE QUICHE

1 (9") deep dish unbaked pie shell
3/4 pound pork sausage
1 cup Swiss cheese, grated
1/2 cup Cheddar cheese, grated

8 ounces evaporated milk
1/4 cup chopped onion
2 eggs, beaten

Preheat oven to 400 degrees. Prick holes in bottom of pie shell and on sides. Bake shell for 8 minutes. Remove from heat; and turn oven down to 350 degrees. Fry sausage until almost done; chopping it into small pieces. Sprinkle 1/2 of sausage in the bottom of the preheated shell. In a bowl, combine remaining ingredients. Pour over the sausage in the pie shell. Sprinkle the remaining sausage over the top. Bake for 40 to 45 minutes or until set. Let cool for 5 minutes before serving.

*Rose Vickery (Dawn '85)*

*Vegetables*

Reading in the Attic 1928

# Attic Reading — 1928

When I was in the third grade, we bought the house with an attic. This was the house where I lived until I married.

My parents were always very interested in our education and schooling, but bought literature was very limited in our home. I do not ever remember any bedtime stories being read to us; however, I do remember my father telling us certain stories — over and over. Three pieces of family literature stand out in my mind. The Fort Worth Star Telegram came by mail to our house on a regular basis as long as I can remember. Then, there were two important classics that we owned. One was Alfred Lord Tennyson's Complete Works and the other was Milton's Paradise Lost, a huge red-covered book with biblical pictures I could not understand! (I am sure we owned others.)

The big treasure came when we discovered the previous owners of our house had left a library of books lined against the attic wall. There on the floor in a long line were numerous books just waiting to be rediscovered. Books and more books! This was my place to go. With only two small windows at the end of the attic and as hot as it might get, I could spend hours in isolation and perfect quietness, leafing through all sorts of books. Some of my earliest education took place in that attic!

# BAKED BEANS

2 large cans pork and beans
1/2 cup chopped green onion
1/2 cup chopped bell pepper

1/2 cup catsup
1/2 cup brown sugar
1/2 cup bacon, cut into bits

Garlic salt or garlic powder to taste Bake at 300 degrees for 1 hour.

*Vin and Barbara Betenbough: Sherri '86*

# BAKED BEANS

3 cans pork and beans
1/2 cup brown sugar
1 teaspoon oregano
1 teaspoon dry mustard

1 cup green peppers, chopped
1 cup onions, chopped
Black pepper

Mix all ingredients well. Bake at 300 degrees for 1-1/2 hours.

*Darrel and Charlotte Jackson: Valerie '66; Kevin '71*

# CAJUN RED BEANS AND RICE

1 pound red kidney beans,
    washed
1 onion, chopped
1/2 bell pepper, chopped
3 to 4 cloves garlic, chopped
2 or 3 whole bay leaves
1 ham hock, if possible; salt pork
    otherwise

1 to 2 pounds lean, skinless
    smoked sausage, sliced into
    rounds
1/2 cup chopped flat parsley
1/2 cup chopped green onion tops
Salt, black and red pepper to taste
Tabasco Pepper Sauce to taste

Soak beans overnight in cold water; discard this water. Place first 6 ingredients in large kettle and cover with water. Bring to a boil and lower heat to a simmer. Cover kettle; cook beans until tender. (Will not take as long as pinto beans, but 2 to 3 hours.) Add water, if necessary. Remove ham bone and discard fat, but add good, lean pieces of ham back to beans. Remove bay leaves.

In separate pan, boil sausage to remove excess fat; discard water. Add sausage, salt, peppers, and Tabasco Sauce. Cajun red beans are creamy and rich. Serve over fluffy, white long grain rice. Just before serving, add minced parsley and green onion tops. Some Cajun cooks remove a cup of beans and puree them and return to the pot to thicken.

Cornbread or hot garlic French bread is great.

*L.Z. and Mabel Brown: Sherry '53 (given by Sherry Brown Landry)*

## "BIDDY BEANS"

1 purple onion, chopped
1 bell pepper, chopped
1 can Ranch Style beans
1 can Pinto beans
1 can pork and beans

1 can Trappey's Jalapeno beans
3/4 cup catsup
1/2 cup Grandma's molasses
1 pound hot sausage, cooked

Saute onion and pepper. Combine all ingredients. Cook in crockpot 6 to 8 hours.

*George and Winnie Satterwhite: submitted by Polly Satterwhite (Collins) '52*

## CHALUPA BEANS

1 pound pinto beans
1-1/2 pounds pork roast
7 cups water
1/2 cup chopped onions
2 cloves minced garlic
2 tablespoons salt

2 tablespoons chili powder
1 tablespoon oregano
1 tablespoon cumin
1 (4 ounce) jar chopped chilies
1 (2 ounce) jar diced pimientos

Place all above ingredients in heavy kettle. Cover and cook slowly on simmer (about 5-1/2 hours). Serve over corn chips, grated cheddar cheese, chopped avocado, green onions, tomato, and hot sauce (if desired). May serve plain or with rice.

*Newt and Lil Rogers: Steve '65*

## PECOS RIVER BEANS

2 cups pinto beans
1 pound bacon, diced and cooked
   crisp
2 fresh jalapenos, diced

1 medium onion, diced
3 cloves garlic, minced
1 (No. 303) can tomatoes, drained
Salt and pepper to taste

Cook beans and drain; mash, adding bacon and all the bacon grease. Add jalepenos, onion, garlic, tomatoes, salt, and pepper.

*John and Jean Gilliam: Eric '79*

**We may give without loving,
But we cannot love without giving.**

# PUERTO RICO BEANS

2-1/2 cups dried pinto beans, soaked
Salt to taste
Ham hock
Pinch of oregano

1 large bell pepper, chopped
1 large onion, chopped
Garlic cloves, to taste
1/2 teaspoon paprika
1 can tomato sauce

Soak beans overnight or several hours. Cover with water and cook until about half done. Add ham hock and oregano and cook until almost tender. Saute bell pepper, onion, and garlic in small amount of bacon grease with paprika until tender. Add tomato sauce and mix well. Add to beans and simmer about 1 hour. (Adjust amount of green pepper and onion to your taste.)

*Note:* I worked with an R.N. from Puerto Rico who gave me this recipe. It is good and just right for good 'Ole West Texas!

*Oline and Irene Oxford: Roger '60*

# ALMOND BROCCOLI RING

*(A pretty dish for Christmas)*

1 (10-ounce) package chopped broccoli
1 (10-ounce) package broccoli spears
Salt
3 tablespoons oleo
1/2 cup minced green onions, with tops
3 tablespoons flour
1/4 cup chicken broth

1 cup sour cream
3 eggs, lightly beaten
3/4 cup Swiss cheese, grated
1/2 cup slivered almonds, toasted
1 teaspoon salt
1/2 teaspoon pepper
3/4 teaspoon nutmeg, freshly grated
1 pint cherry tomatoes
2 tablespoons oleo

Steam broccoli until tender; salt lightly and drain. Chop fine and set aside. For cream sauce, mix oleo with green onions and saute lightly. Remove from heat; blend in flour and return to heat. Cook over medium heat for 2 minutes, stirring slowly. Remove from heat; add broth and stir. Return to heat and continue cooking until sauce thickens. Lower heat and cook 2 minutes longer. Blend in sour cream and heat thoroughly. Spoon mixture into an oiled 1-quart ring mold or eight 5-ounce custard cups. Place in large baking pan that is half filled with hot water. Bake at 350 degrees about 50 minutes for molds (30 minutes for custard cups).

When done, an inserted knife comes out clean. When ready to serve invert on a serving platter. Saute cherry tomatoes in oleo (about 5 to 6 minutes. Garnish with tomatoes and fresh herbs or parsley.

*J.R. and Maxine Martin: Bobby Kay '62*

# HARVARD BEETS

1 (No. 303) can sliced red beets
1/4 cup sugar
1 tablespoon cornstarch

1/4 teaspoon salt
2 tablespoons vinegar
1 tablespoon butter

Drain beets, reserving 2 tablespoons liquid. Mix sugar, cornstarch, and salt. Add vinegar and beet liquid. Cook, stirring constantly, until thick and clear. Add beets and butter. Heat and serve.

*Kenneth and Myra Sutton: Rhonda '73*

# BROCCOLI CASSEROLE

2 packages frozen chopped
   broccoli
1/2 cup chopped onion
1/2 cup chopped celery
2 to 3 tablespoons butter
2 cups cooked rice
1 can Cream of Chicken soup

1 can Cream of Mushroom soup
1 can sliced water chestnuts,
   drained
1 can sliced mushrooms, drained
1 cup or 1 can Carnation milk
1 jar Cheese Whiz (I use Velveeta)

Saute broccoli, onion, and celery. Cook rice. Add all ingredients except cheese. Stir well. Top with cheese and bake at 350 degrees for 30 to 40 minutes. This freezes well. Delicious!

*Teachers's Pet: Cleone Colvin*

# BROCCOLI AND NOODLE CASSEROLE

1 (6-ounce) package wide noodles
1-3/4 cups frozen broccoli,
   chopped
1 can Cream of Mushroom soup

3/4 cup Cheese Whiz
2/3 cup sliced mushroom
1/4 cup chopped onions
1/4 cup milk

Cook noodles; drain. Cook broccoli by directions and drain well. Mix all other ingredients. Bake in casserole dish at 350 degrees for 25 minutes.

*Nell Parrish: Ima Jean Parrish '50*

# BROCCOLI AND RICE CASSEROLE

1 package frozen chopped
   broccoli
1 cup Minute Rice, cooked
1 can Cream of Mushroom Soup

1 small jar Cheese Whiz
1/2 cup chopped onion
1/2 cup oleo, melted

Either thaw or cook broccoli to separate it. Then mix all ingredients together. Pour into a buttered casserole and bake for 40 minutes at 350 degrees.

*Andee Daniel '79*

# SAUCY BRUSSELS SPROUTS

2 (10-ounce) packages frozen
    brussels sprouts
1/2 cup chopped onions
2 tablespoons butter or oleo
1 tablespoon flour

1 tablespoon brown sugar
1 teaspoon salt
1/2 teaspoon dry mustard
1/2 cup milk
1 cup dairy sour cream

Cook brussels sprouts according to directions; drain. In a saucepan, cook chopped onion in oleo until tender but not brown. Mix in dry ingredients and stir. Stir in milk and cook until thickened and bubbly. Cook and stir 1 to 2 minutes more. Add sour cream. Add the cooked brussels sprouts. Stir gently to combine. Cook until heated through but DO NOT BOIL. Serves 6 to 8.

*Donna Talent (Jerri Talent) '84*

# RED GERMAN CABBAGE

4 pounds red cabbage, sliced thin
2 large onions, sliced
2 tart apples, sliced
Salt to taste
Pepper to taste

1/2 cup water
1/4 cup oil or bacon fat
1 teaspoon caraway seeds,
    optional

Put all ingredients in large cooking or crock pot. Cook on low heat for at least 2-1/2 to 3 hours.

*O.H. and Vera Sanders: James '50; Pearl '53*

# STIR-FRY CABBAGE

3 slices bacon
1 small head cabbage, shredded
1 large onion, chopped
1 large tomato, peeled and
    chopped

1 large green pepper, sliced
3 stalks celery, cut diagonally
    into thin slices

Fry bacon in Wok or large skillet until crisp; remove bacon, reserving drippings in Wok. Set bacon aside. Add vegetables to Wok; stir fry over high heat (350 degrees for 8 to 10 minutes.) Cover; reduce heat and simmer 5 minutes. Sprinkle with crumbled bacon. Serves 6.

*Frank and Carol Bice: Susan '80*

"Stay" is a charming word in a friend's vocabulary.

# KING ARMS TAVERN
# CREAMED CELERY with PECANS

4 cups celery, cut diagonally in
   1/2" pieces
2 tablespoons butter
2 tablespoons all-purpose flour

2 cups milk
1 teaspoon salt
3/4 cup pecan halves
Buttered bread crumbs

Preheat oven to 400 degrees; grease 1-1/2 quart casserole. Boil celery until tender in enough water to cover; drain. Melt butter over medium heat; stir in flour and add milk slowly to make cream sauce, stirring until thick and smooth. Add salt and well-drained celery. Spoon into prepared casserole; top with pecans, and cover with buttered bread crumbs. Bake at 400 degrees for 15 minutes.

*Joe and Carolyn Weatherby: Randy '70*

# CORN CASSEROLE

2 cans Shoe Peg Corn, drained
Sauce:
1/4 cup milk
1/2 stick butter
2 (3-ounce) packages cream
   cheese

Dash of garlic powder
Dash of salt
1/4 can green chilies, if desired
   (mild or hotter, as desired)

Mix milk, butter, and cream cheese in saucepan. Heat on low; slowly stir until blended. Add garlic powder, salt, and chilies, if desired. Add corn to sauce. Bake in greased casserole dish at 350 degrees until "bubbly" or browned, if desired.

*Note:* May top with buttered bread crumbs before baking.

*Jack and Aileen Morris, (grandparents): Zac Miller '84; Morris Miller '86*
*Henry and Bea Grinslade: Robby '78; Kelli '81*

# CORN PUDDING

1 large can creamed corn
2 beaten eggs
2 tablespoons flour
2 tablespoons sugar

2 tablespoons melted butter
1 cup milk
Nutmeg, sprinkled on top

Mix all ingredients except nutmeg. Turn into buttered casserole and sprinkle with nutmeg on top. Bake at 300 degrees for 1-1/2 hours.

*Dick and Nelda Tobias: Terri '66; Richard '68; David '72*

# CORN-ON-THE-COB ROLL
*(Very Good)*

Clean ears of corn. Season with rubbed butter or oleo. Sprinkle with salt. Sprinkle with a little sugar (like you use salt). Wrap first in clean-washed, damp shucks. Wrap them in foil. Place in hot oven (rather hot). Cook 20 to 30 minutes. Good with barbecue!

*Harold and Martria Durbin: James '49*

# CORN AND GREEN CHILIES CASSEROLE
*(Delicious)*

| | |
|---|---|
| 1 medium onion, diced | 1 (15-ounce) can cream-style corn |
| 1 cup celery, diced | 1 cup cheese, grated |
| 4 tablespoons oleo | 1 (4-ounce) can chopped green |
| 1 (15-ounce) can whole kernel | chilies |
| corn | Cheddar cheese, grated |

Saute onions and celery in oleo. Drain whole kernel corn and mix both cans of corn with sauteed onions and celery. Add grated cheese and (1/2 to 1) can of the green chilies. Mix. Pour into shallow pyrex dish (sprayed with Pam). Garnish with grated cheddar cheese. Bake at 350 degrees in open dish for 40 to 45 minutes.

*Kenneth and Myra Sutton: Rhonda '73*

# EGGPLANT CASSEROLE

| | |
|---|---|
| 1 peeled eggplant, diced | 1 cup milk |
| 1/4 teaspoon salt | 1/4 pound Velveeta cheese |
| 1/4 cup melted butter | Bread crumbs |
| 1/4 cup flour | |

Boil eggplant in salted water until partially cooked. Drain. Melt butter; stir in flour and stir until smooth. Stir in milk and cook until thickened. Remove from heat and stir in cheese, stirring until melted. Combine eggplant and cheese sauce. Place in casserole and top with bread crumbs. Bake in 350 degree oven for 20 minutes.

*Preston and Leona Selby: Jackie '58*

---

**Love is the specialty of the House!**

# BAKED CHEESE GRITS

2-1/2 cups milk
3/4 cups raw grits
1/2 cup oleo
1/2 teaspoon salt

1/3 cup grated Parmesan cheese
1 (5-ounce) jar sharp cheese
  spread

Bring milk to a boil; add grits and cook until thick (about 10 minutes). Stir often. Stir in oleo, salt, and cheeses. Spoon into lightly greased 1 quart casserole. Bake at 325 degrees for 20 minutes. 6 to 8 servings.

*S.P. and Bernice Echols: Delilah '51*

# CHEESE GRITS

1-1/2 cups dry grits
6 cups hot water
1 stick oleo
1 pound grated American cheese
3 eggs, beaten

1 teaspoon salt
1 teaspoon savory salt
1 teaspoon celery salt
1 teaspoon onion salt
1 teaspoon garlic salt

Add grits to boiling water and cook until thick. Mix remaining ingredients and add to grits. Grease a 9x13" baking dish with oil which has 3 to 5 dashes of Tabasco or Worcestershire stirred in. (Stir in amount to your taste or omit.) Bake at 350 degrees for 1 hour. Serves 12.

*Bob, Sr. and Ann Zugg: Bobby '73*
*Bill and Betty Gordon: Lynn '62; Mike '64*

# GARLIC CHEESE GRITS

1 cup quick grits
4 cups water
1 teaspoon salt
1 stick oleo

1 roll garlic cheese (or jalapeno)
2 eggs
American cheese, grated
Paprika

Boil grits in salted water for 5 minutes. Add oleo and garlic cheese. Beat eggs in cup; add enough water to make 1 cup. Add eggs to grits. Put in buttered casserole dish. Top with grated cheese, sprinkled with paprika. Bake 30 to 40 minutes at 350 degrees.

*Floyd and Pat Garrot: Mike '69*

It is far better to follow well than to lead poorly.

# HOMINY CASSEROLE

| | |
|---|---|
| 1 can Cream of Mushroom Soup | 1 teaspoon black pepper (to taste) |
| 1/2 cup Half and Half milk | 1 (No. 2-1/2) can hominy |
| 1/4 teaspoon cayenne pepper | 1/2 pound slivered almonds, |
| 1 teaspoon Worcestershire sauce | toasted |
| 1 teaspoon celery seed | Buttered bread crumbs |

Mix first 6 ingredients in 3-quart baking dish, until well blended and smooth. Add hominy and almonds. Bake at 350 degrees for 30 to 40 minutes. Halfway through, top with buttered bread crumbs. DIFFERENT!

*J.D. and Cozette Sanders: Debbie Sanders Ryals: '60 (submitted by Debbie)*

# OKRA GUMBO

| | |
|---|---|
| 2 tablespoons oil | 1 can stewed tomatoes, (large) |
| 1 medium onion, chopped | 2 small cans tomato sauce |
| 2 boxes, cut frozen okra, thawed | Salt and pepper to taste |
| (fresh okra may be used, also) | |

Saute onions and okra in oil until tender. Add tomatoes and tomato sauce. Simmer on low 20 minutes.

*Variations:* Add 2 teaspoons Gumbo File and 1 package of popcorn shrimp, washed and drained.

*Paul and Pat Wiggington: Joel '70*

# ONION RINGS

| | |
|---|---|
| 2 heaping tablespoons flour | Enough beer to make a thick |
| 2 heaping tablespoons cornstarch | paste |
| 1/2 teaspoon paprika | 1 large sliced onion |

Dip onion rings in batter; then dip in deep hot fat.

*Note:* This was the method used by a restaurant to make onion rings light and fluffy.

*Howard and Doris Bechtold: Gay Lynn '68*

# POTATOES AND GREEN CHILIES

| | |
|---|---|
| 6 potatoes, sliced thin | 1 large can chopped green chilies |
| Salt | 1/2 pound Jack cheese, broken |
| 1 pint sour cream | into pieces |

Mix all together and place in casserole. Bake 30 minutes at 350 degrees.

*Neil and Rhuine McDonald: Lisa '69*

## CROCK POT HAM AND POTATOES

4 medium potatoes, sliced
1 large onion, sliced

1 cup ham chunks or slices
1 can Cream of Celery Soup

Layer all ingredients in crock pot except soup. Spread soup, undiluted, on top of layers, covering all potatoes. Cook slow all day while at work and supper is ready whenever you get home! Makes a thick gravy and is really good.

*Sheila Ross Nelson: David Ross '78*

## HASH BROWN POTATO CASSEROLE

1 (2-pound) package frozen hash
  browns, thawed
1/2 cup oleo, melted
1/2 cup chopped onion
1 cup sour cream
2 cups grated cheddar cheese

1 can Cream of Chicken soup
1 teaspoon salt
1/4 teaspoon pepper
Topping:
2 cups crushed cornflakes
1/4 cup melted butter

Mix all ingredients; put in casserole dish. Top with mixture of cornflakes and butter. Bake at 350 degrees for 45 to 50 minutes. (Longer if hash browns are still frozen.)

*Note:* May bake casserole for 30 minutes, mix topping, and bake an additional 15 minutes.

*Larry and Debbie Gibson: Laura '86*
*Leo and Esther Osterout: Susan '65*

## SPUDS A'LA ELEGANT

1 (8-ounce) package softened
  cream cheese
4 cups hot mashed potatoes
1 beaten egg

1/3 cup finely chopped onion
1/4 cup chopped pimiento
1 teaspoon salt
Dash of pepper

Blend cream cheese and mashed potatoes. Add remaining ingredients. Bake in 1-quart casserole for 45 minutes at 350 degrees.

*Fred and Joyce Weir: Charlotte '68*

## SCALLOPED POTATOES

6 medium-sized potatoes
1 large or 2 medium-sized onions
1 jar Cheese Whiz

Grated cheese
Ritz crackers, crushed

Boil potatoes with skins on. Slice onions and boil them in another pan. Drain potatoes and slice them. Drain onions. Line buttered casserole dish with a layer of potatoes, onions, cheese whiz; potatoes, etc. until the first 3 ingredients are all in the dish. Top with grated cheese. Place Ritz crackers around the edge and bake at 350 degrees for 30 minutes or until the cheese is melted.

*Bob and Margaret Bremerman: John Paul '69; Ralph '74*

# SCALLOPED POTATOES AND HAM

| | |
|---|---|
| 1/2 cup oleo | 3 cups ham, cubed |
| 1/2 cup flour | 1 large green pepper, chopped |
| 2 teaspoons salt | 1 large onion, chopped |
| 1/4 teaspoon pepper | 1/2 cup cheese, grated |
| 3 cups milk | 5 cups potatoes, sliced thin |

Melt oleo in large pan over low heat; blend in flour, salt, and pepper. Cook, stirring constantly 1 minute. Remove; stir in milk; return to heat and cook until thick and bubbly. Fold in ham, peppers, onion, and cheese. Pour mixture over potatoes in large bowl. Stir gently, then pour into buttered dish. Cover with foil. Bake at 350 degrees for 30 minutes. Uncover and bake 1 hour. Let stand 10 minutes.

*Carla Sue Nordeman (Young) '54*

# TASTY POTATOES

| | |
|---|---|
| 9 medium potatoes | 1/2 teaspoon garlic salt |
| 1 (8-ounce) package cream cheese | Butter |
| 1-1/2 cups sour cream | Paprika |

Peel potatoes, cook in boiling water. Drain and beat with electric mixer. Add creamed cheese, sour cream, and garlic salt. Place in greased casserole and dot with butter; sprinkle with paprika. Bake, uncovered, for 30 minutes at 325 degrees.

*Billy and Jane Lucas: Ricky '82; Randa '84*

# SWEET POTATOES

| | |
|---|---|
| 1 (20-ounce) can pineapple chunks, drained (reserve 1/2 of juice) | 1/2 cup oleo or butter |
| | 1/2 cup brown sugar, packed |
| | 1/4 teaspoon nutmeg |
| 1 (20-ounce) can sweet potatoes | 1/2 cup chopped nuts |

Drain pineapples and sweet potatoes. Cut pineapple into bite size pieces; combine and place in baking dish. Melt butter; add rest of ingredients plus 1/2 of pineapple juice. Pour over potatoes and pineapples. Bake 25 minutes in 350 degree oven.

*Oran and Louis Price: Judy '54*

The art of being wise
is the art of knowing what to overlook.

## SWEET POTATO CASSEROLE

3 cups sweet potatoes, cooked
   and mashed
1-1/2 sticks margarine
1 cup sugar
2 eggs, beaten
2/3 cup milk

1 teaspoon vanilla
Topping:
1 cup brown sugar
1/3 cup margarine
1/2 cup flour
1 cup chopped pecans

Mix sweet potatoes, margarine, sugar, eggs, milk, and vanilla and pour into a greased baking dish. Mix topping and sprinkle on top. Bake at 325 degrees for 25 minutes.

*Robert and Shelly McCrary: Amy '84*

## SWEET POTATO CRUNCH

3 cups mashed cooked sweet
   potatoes
1-1/4 cups sugar
1/2 cup melted margarine or
   butter

2 beaten eggs
1-1/2 teaspoons vanilla
1/4 cup milk
Topping

Combine all ingredients. Mix well. Pour into a 2-quart casserole; cover with topping. Bake at 350 degrees for 35 minutes. Serves 8.

Topping:
1/2 cup brown sugar
2/3 cup chopped pecans

1/4 cup flour
3 tablespoons melted butter or
   margarine.

Combine all ingredients. Mix well. Sprinkle on casserole top before baking.

*Jonathon and Sharon Christian: Ivy '77*

## CHINESE FRIED RICE

4 strips bacon, finely cut
2 eggs, slightly beaten
2 cups cooked rice
1/4 cup pork or beef, boiled
1 tablespoon soy sauce

1/4 cup cooked ham
1/4 cup shrimp, optional
1 tablespoon onion, finely
   chopped
Salt and pepper to taste

Fry bacon until slightly brown. Remove from skillet and fry eggs in bacon fat. Set aside. Add cooked rice and fry for 5 minutes. Mix thoroughly. Add all other ingredients, cooked bacon, and seasonings. Garnish with scrambled eggs, ham, and green onions.

*(Dr. Armand Wiltz) and (Dr. Lellani Wiltz): Marie '85*

# DIRTY RICE

| | |
|---|---|
| 1/2 pound ground sausage | 4 cups cooked rice |
| 1/3 cup diced onion | Chili powder |
| 1/3 cup diced bell pepper | Paprika |
| 1/3 cup diced celery | Salt and pepper |

Brown sausage; reserve drippings. Saute vegetables in drippings. In casserole dish add rice, sausage, and vegetable mixture. Season to taste with chili powder, paprika, salt, and pepper. Bake covered at 325 degrees for 20 to 25 minutes or until piping hot. (This is delicious with baked chicken.)

*George and Sherry Averyt: Amy McCoy '80*

# RICE DISH

| | |
|---|---|
| 1 stick oleo | 2 cans chicken with rice soup |
| 1 small jar pimientos, chopped | 1 cup rice |
| 1 small bell pepper, chopped | 1 cup water |
| 1 small jar mushrooms, chopped | 1 teaspoon salt |
| 1/2 onion, chopped | |

Melt oleo in pan; add chopped vegetables; saute until tender. In casserole dish, place soup, rice, water, and salt. Mix well. Add vegetables. Stir well. Bake at 350 degrees for 45 minutes or until done.

*Roland and Josie Rose: Laura '76*

# FRIED RICE

| | |
|---|---|
| 2 cups rice | Meats* |
| 3/4 pound bacon, cut into small | Dash of Accent |
| pieces | Pepper |
| 2 medium to large onions, diced | 2 eggs |
| fine | Soy sauce |
| 3 garlic pods, crushed, | |

Cook rice and let cool. In large deep skillet fry bacon. When done, add finely diced onions, crushed garlic, and then add meat, Accent, and pepper. Break eggs into meat mixture and stir fry until done. Add rice and soy sauce to taste. (Start with 2 tablespoons.)

*This recipe is good to use up leftover meats. Use any of the following or combination as desired: pork roast, diced; boiled chicken, diced; ham, diced; shrimp; crab legs.

My favorite combination is ham, shrimp, and crab legs.

*Jim and Charlene Jackson: "Skeeter" '70*

# RICE DISH

| | |
|---|---|
| 2 pounds stew meat | 1 (16-ounce) can tomato sauce |
| 1 cup onions, chopped | 1 teaspoon each of salt, pepper, |
| 1 cup bell peppers, chopped | and garlic |
| 2 (16-ounce) cans stewed tomatoes | 2 cups rice, cooked |

Cook stew meat until tender (in water). In a 10" skillet add enough oil to saute onions and bell peppers until tender. Drain. Add tomatoes and tomato sauce; add seasonings. Simmer 10 minutes. Mix all together and serve over cooked rice.

*Garland and Diane Fox: Bobby Westbrook '84*

# FRIED RICE

| | |
|---|---|
| 1/2 cup cooked ham | Garlic salt |
| 2 cups cooked rice | 5 chopped green onions, sauted |
| Salt and pepper to taste | 2 eggs, scrambled |

Chop meat into small chunks and fry. Fry rice slightly and season to taste. Saute onions; scramble eggs and break into small pieces. Mix altogether and serve. (5 strips of fried bacon can be substituted for the ham.)

*Lloyd and Margaret Faye Morgan: Susan '63; Nancy '64; Marsha '66*

# RICE AND BROCCOLI CASSEROLE

(Asparagus instead of broccoli is delicious — use 1 can of asparagus.)

| | |
|---|---|
| 1 cup rice, cooked | 1 can cream of mushroom soup, |
| 1 package chopped broccoli, | not diluted |
| cooked | 1 can cream of chicken soup, not |
| 2 teaspoons cooking oil | diluted |
| 1/2 cup onion, chopped | 1 small jar Cheese Whiz |
| 1/2 cup celery chopped | |

Cook rice; cook broccoli. Saute onions and celery in oil; add cooked broccoli. Add soups and Cheese Whiz. Make nest of rice in casserole dish. Pour in filling and sprinkle with paprika. Bake in oven at 375 degrees for 20 minutes. Wonderful!

*Kenneth and Cleo Cook: Carey '51*

---

**Criticism is the one thing that most of us think is
More blessed to give than to receive.**

# RICE PILAF

(The following is from my wife's aunt, Frances Holliday, of Houston, Texas.)

1 stick butter
4 green onions, including tops,
   finely chopped
1/2 pound fresh mushrooms,
   sliced
1 cup raw rice
1/4 teaspoon oregano
1 can beef consomme
1 cup water

Saute sliced mushroom and onions in butter. Add rice, oregano, consomme, and water. Pour into casserole; cover tightly with foil. Bake in 350 degree oven for 1 hour and 15 minutes.

*Othel and Flora Mae Ogden: Walker '52 (submitted by Walker)*

# SPINACH DELIGHT

1 clove fresh garlic, minced or
   pressed
1/4 small onion, quartered and
   sliced thin
1/4 pound fresh mushrooms,
   sliced thin
1 pound fresh spinach
Salt and pepper to taste
1 teaspoon lemon juice

Saute garlic, onions, and mushrooms in hot cast iron skillet. While this is being done, wash spinach and while wet, cut spinach into hot skillet. Add salt and pepper and lemon juice. Stir or toss. Cover and cook 8 minutes. People who hate spinach, love this dish!

*Herman and Joyce Penaluna: Steve '76*

# SUPER SPINACH CASSEROLE

*(This is my very favorite casserole.)*

2 packages frozen chopped
   spinach, drained
1 (8-ounce) cream cheese
1 stick butter or oleo
1 can artichoke hearts, drained
   and sliced
1 can water chestnuts, drained
   and sliced
1 can mushroom pieces, drained
1 can French fried onion rings

Cook spinach; drain and add cream cheese and butter. Stir until melted. Layer a greased casserole with layers of artichoke hearts, water chestnuts, and mushrooms. Spread spinach mixture over all. Sprinkle onion rings on top. Heat at 350 degrees until thoroughly heated.

*James and Sue Ulmer: Lois '61*

# SPINACH SOUFFLE

2 packages frozen chopped
   spinach
1 stick oleo
3 tablespoons flour

1 (16-ounce) carton cottage cheese
1/3 pound cheddar cheese, grated
3 eggs
Salt and pepper

Cook spinach; drain well. Set casserole dish in oven with oleo until it is melted. Add flour and blend well. Cool. Add remaining ingredients and bake 1 hour at 350 degrees.

*Patrick and Pearl Munn: Laura '75*

# SQUASH CASSEROLE

6 to 8 yellow squash, cooked
   until barely tender
1 tablespoon oleo
Salt and pepper to taste

1 small can chopped green chilies
Grated cheese
4 to 5 eggs, beaten

Cook squash until barely tender (don't overcook). Drain and season with oleo, salt, and pepper to taste. Add green chilies. Layer the squash and chilies with grated cheese in a casserole dish.

Beat eggs and pour over layered squash and cheese. Garnish with grated cheddar cheese. Bake at 350 degrees for approximately 45 minutes.

*Kenneth and Myra Sutton: Rhonda '73*

# ANGIE'S SQUASH CASSEROLE

2 pounds squash, boiled,
   drained, mashed, and set
   aside
1 large chopped onion
1 large chopped bell pepper
1 cup chopped celery
1 stick butter
1 cup mayonnaise

2 eggs
1 cup Longhorn cheese, grated
1 can sliced water chestnuts
1 small jar chopped pimientos,
   optional
1-1/2 sticks Ritz crackers
1 stick melted butter

Cook squash and set aside. Saute onions, bell pepper, and celery in butter. Combine with squash. Blend in mayonnaise, eggs, cheese, and water chestnuts. Pour mixture into lightly buttered casserole dish. Combine Ritz crackers with melted butter. Cover casserole with cracker mixture. Bake at 325 degrees for 30 minutes, or until lightly brown. Let set for a few minutes before serving. So good!

*Gary and Sidney Gaston: Whitney '85*

# SPANISH SQUASH

5 cups sliced yellow or white
squash
1 onion, cut wedge-shaped
1 sliced bell pepper

1 chili pepper, optional
2 tablespoons oil
2 cans Cream of Mushroom Soup
1 cup grated cheese

Saute first 4 ingredients in oil until tender. Add soup. Pour in casserole. Top with cheese. Bake 20 to 30 minutes at 350 degrees.

*Phil and Lena Smith: Chad '84*

# TATER TOT CASSEROLE

1 bag tater tots
1 medium onion, chopped
Butter, amount desired

1 can Cream of Chicken OR
Cream of Mushroom soup
1 small can evaporated milk
Grated cheese

Cover the bottom of an oblong casserole dish with tater tots; spread onion over tater tots. Add butter to the top of onions. Mix soup and evaporated milk. Pour over the dish. Sprinkle cheese over the top and bake 30 minutes at 350 degrees.

*Edd and Harlene Farmer: Vivian '68*

# CRESCENT VEGETABLE SQUARES

2 cans (8 ounces each) crescent
dinner rolls
2 (8-ounce) packages softened
cream cheese
1 cup mayonnaise (do not use
salad dressing)
1 (1-ounce) package Hidden
Valley Original Party Dip
Mix
3/4 cup grated Cheddar cheese

3/4 cup finely chopped
cauliflower
3/4 cup chopped broccoli
3/4 cup chopped carrots
3/4 cup chopped green onions
3/4 cup chopped green peppers
OR other vegetables
Diced, seeded tomatoes for
garnish

Preheat oven to 375 degrees. Place crescent roll dough in bottom of an ungreased 15x10" jelly roll pan. Press to seal edges together. Bake 8 to 10 minutes until golden brown. Set aside to cool. Combine softened cream cheese, mayonnaise, and dip mix; blend well and spread over cooled crescent roll crust. Top cream cheese layer with grated cheese. Combine all vegetables and sprinkle over cheese. Garnish with tomatoes. (About 25 squares — 2x3" each.)

*Note:* Food processor works nicely for chopping vegetables.

*Dalton and Katie Criswell: Vicki '62*

## GREEN VEGETABLE CASSEROLE

1 package frozen French cut
   green beans
1 package frozen English peas
1 package frozen Baby Lima
   beans

1 green pepper, thinly sliced
1 (8-ounce) package cream cheese
2 tablespoons mayonnaise
Small amount of milk
Parmesan cheese

Cook vegetables separately according to directions. Layer in casserole. Cover with thinly sliced green pepper. Cover with sauce made of cream cheese, mayonnaise, and enough milk to make thin. Sprinkle with Parmesan cheese. Bake at 350 degrees for 10 to 15 minutes (or longer).

*Note:* I often make a double recipe; if so, put sauce between some layers. Use a long flat dish.

*Joseph and Janet Wright: Barbara '62*

## ITALIAN STUFFED ZUCCHINI

6 medium zucchini
1/2 pound ground beef
1/2 cup chopped onion
1/2 cup chopped green pepper
2 tablespoons oregano

1 garlic clove
1 tablespoon oil
1 cup Parmesan
1 cup tomato soup

Wash zucchini and cut in half. Scoop out pulp and chop. Saute the next 5 ingredients in oil. Stir in pulp, 1/2 cup cheese, and 1/2 cup tomato soup. Spoon mixture into shells; pour soup over. Sprinkle with cheese. Bake at 375 degrees for 30 minutes covered. Uncover and bake 5 more minutes.

*Wayne Turley '52 (submitted by his wife, Anna)*

**The most utterly lost of all days is the one
in which you have not once laughed.**

# Desserts

Taking Care of Mother 1926

*Reflections...*

# Taking Care of Mother — 1926

Christmas time and all other times was gathering time for all our kin on my dad's side of the family to come to celebrate and eat. They all appetizingly regarded my mother, Aunt Jenny, as the one who could "fix" such a good meal in such a short time. And indeed she could!

One memorable Christmas found me, as usual, overwhelmed by the bountiful mounds of goodies — cakes, pies, candies, nuts, and fruits, including the annual bushel basket of oranges and grapefruits my uncle always sent from the Texas valley. Anyway, the temptation of hording took over and bit by bit and sometimes more than bits, I cautiously and continuously slipped little portions and big portions into my hidden box behind the hall door. How it grew! How my guilt grew! There in secret lay my squirrel-like gatherings. Did I get by with it? Are you kidding? Shame on SOMEBODY!!! But my gooey answer was no match for the tell tale explanation I mustered up, "My mother had to work so hard in the kitchen she didn't have time to enjoy all the food brought in! I was storing all this up for her!" (She was so busy, I do not recall any consequences — thanks for the company!)

# FRESH APPLE CAKE

1-1/2 cups cooking oil
1 cup white sugar
1 cup brown sugar
4 eggs
3 cups flour
1/2 teaspoon allspice
1/2 teaspoon cinnamon
1/2 teaspoon salt
1 teaspoon soda
3/4 cup buttermilk
2 teaspoons vanilla
1 cup, peeled and finely chopped apples (or more)
1 cup chopped pecans

Combine and mix cooking oil, sugars, and eggs. Mix and add dry ingredients (except soda). Add mixture of soda and buttermilk and remaining ingredients. Bake in greased and floured tube pan at 350 degrees for 1 hour.

*C.E. and Lois Short: Camille '79*

# APPLE OAT CAKE

3 cups raw apples, peeled and chopped
1/2 cup water
1 cup brown sugar
2 cups sifted flour
1 teaspoon baking powder
1 teaspoon soda
1 teaspoon salt
1 teaspoon cinnamon
1/2 teaspoon allspice
2 eggs, beaten
1/4 cup cooking oil
1 cup oats, uncooked
1/2 cup seedless raisins
1/2 cup chopped nuts

Combine apples, water, and 1/2 cup of the brown sugar. Cook until apples are almost tender (about 5 minutes). Cool.

Sift dry ingredients and add the other 1/2 cup brown sugar, cinnamon, and allspice. Add apple mixture, eggs, and shortening to dry ingredients. Stir just until dry ingredients are moistened. Add oats, raisins, and nuts. Pour into greased tube pan. Bake at 350 degrees for about 40 minutes. Cool in pan 10 minutes before removing.

*Kenneth and Barbara Williamson: Kay '62*

The most important things in life
aren't things.

# FRESH APPLE CAKE

4 cups peeled and diced apples
2 cups sugar
1 cup chopped pecans
3 cups sifted flour
1/2 teaspoon cinnamon
1/2 teaspoon nutmeg

1/2 teaspoon salt
2 teaspoons soda
1 cup vegetable oil
2 eggs, well beaten
1 teaspoon vanilla

Mix apples, sugar, and nuts in large mixing bowl. Let stand 1 hour. Stir often so mixture will make its own juice. Combine dry ingredients and add to apples. Add oil, eggs, and vanilla. Stir ingredients together by hand. DO NOT USE MIXER! Pour batter into greased and floured 10" tube pan. Bake 1 hour and 15 minutes at 350 degrees.

*Clovis and Mary O'Bannon: Mark '72*
*Johnny and Cricket Adams: Suzie '71*

# APPLESAUCE CAKE

*(A favorite holiday gift)*

1 cup shortening or oleo
2 cups sugar
2 eggs
2 cups applesauce
1 cup chopped pecans
1 cup raisins

3 cups flour
1-3/4 teaspoons soda
1 teaspoon cinnamon
1 teaspoon nutmeg
1 teaspoon vanilla

Cream shortening, sugar, and eggs until light and fluffy. Add applesauce and mix. Sprinkle 1/4 cup of the measured flour over nuts and raisins; coat them well and add to mixture. Sift and add all dry ingredients. Add vanilla and beat well. Bake in greased and floured loaf pan for 2 hours at 325 degrees. Cool in pan.

*Note:* May be cooked in 3 (1-pound) coffee can, or 2 loaf pans. Freezes well.

*T.A. and Minnie Payne: *Elizabeth '54; Janice '56*

# APRICOT NECTAR CAKE

1 Yellow Cake Mix
3/4 cup apricot nectar
3/4 cup Wesson oil
1 small package Lemon Jello, dry

4 eggs
1-1/2 teaspoons lemon extract,
   optional

Combine and mix well. Pour into greased and floured Bundt pan. Bake at 350 degrees for 45 to 50 minutes.

Icing:
1-1/2 cups powdered sugar

Lemon juice to desired
   consistency to spread

Mix sugar and lemon juice to spread. Ice hot cake.

*Charles and Claudine McCormick: Rebecca '68*

# BANANA NUT CAKE

1-1/2 cups sugar
1/2 cup brown sugar
3/4 cup shortening
3 eggs, beaten
2-1/4 cups flour
1-1/2 teaspoons baking powder

3/4 teaspoon soda
6 tablespoons buttermilk (1/2 cup scant)
3 mashed ripe bananas
1 teaspoon vanilla
1-1/2 cups chopped nuts

Cream sugar, brown sugar, and shortening. Add eggs, one at a time. Sift dry ingredients; add gradually to first mixture. Add buttermilk, bananas, vanilla, and chopped nuts.

Mix for 2 minutes. Bake in greased and floured tube pan at 350 degrees until done.

Icing:
1/2 box brown sugar
1/4 cup cream

1 stick oleo
6 marshmallows
Powdered sugar

Cook in saucepan about 10 minutes. Beat and add powdered sugar for desired consistency.

*Allen and Eddie Beard: Jeff '69*

# BLACKBERRY JAM CAKE

1 cup butter, softened
2 cups sugar
6 eggs
1 cup sour cream or 1 cup buttermilk
1 teaspoon soda

3 cups flour
1 teaspoon cinnamon
1 teaspoon allspice
1 teaspoon cloves
1-1/2 to 2 cups blackberry jam
2 cups chopped pecans

Cream butter and sugar. Beat in eggs one at a time. Mix soda with sour cream or buttermilk. Stir into sugar mixture. Mix and stir in dry ingredients. Add jam, mixing well. Add nuts. Bake at 300 degrees for 1-1/2 to 2 hours in greased and floured tube pan. Cool. Remove from pan.

*Note:* May be baked in 3 (9") cake pans at 350 degrees for 45 minutes. Cool. Frost with Caramel Icing.

Caramel Icing:
3 tablespoons sugar
2 cups sugar

1 cup heavy cream or condensed milk
1/2 cup oleo
1 tablespoon vanilla

In heavy skillet, slowly brown the 3 tablespoons of sugar. In a large saucepan, combine sugar, milk, and butter; bring to a boil. Reduce heat. Add browned sugar; cook on medium heat until mixture forms a firm ball in cold water. Remove from heat and cool. Add vanilla and beat until thick enough to spread easily. Add a bit of cream if icing becomes too hard while spreading.

*Danny and LaDonna Ragsdale: Lance '80*

# BANANA NUT CAKE

1/2 cup shortening
1-1/2 cups sugar
2 eggs, beaten
1 cup mashed bananas (2 or 3)
1 teaspoon soda

1/4 cup buttermilk, mixed with
   soda
1/2 teaspoon salt
2 cups flour
1 teaspoon vanilla
1 cup chopped pecans

Cream shortening and sugar. Add eggs one at a time alternately with bananas. Add flour mixture alternately with buttermilk. Add nuts. Bake in greased and floured sheet pan for 30 to 40 minutes at 350 degrees.

*Note:* Makes good cupcakes.

*Louisa Calderon: Carlos '58*
*Paul and Phyllis Jordan: Richard '61*
*Jodie and Estelle Carruth: Ellen Ruth '56; Dickie '68*

# BANANA SPLIT CAKE

Crust:
2 cups Graham Crackers, crushed
1 stick oleo, melted
Mix and press into 9x13" pan.
   Bake about 5 minutes. Cool.

Filling:
2 sticks oleo
1 box powdered sugar
2 eggs
1 teaspoon vanilla
1 teaspoon butter flavoring

Mix and beat at high speed with mixer for about 15 minutes. Do not under-beat. Spread over chilled crust.

Topping:
2 small cans crushed pineapple,
   drained

3 to 4 bananas, split lengthwise
1 large container Cool Whip

Spread in layers over filling. Sprinkle with nuts and drizzle with Chocolate Syrup Topping.

Chocolate Syrup Topping:
3/4 cup sugar
1/2 cup cocoa

1/2 cup hot water
1 teaspoon vanilla
Maraschino cherries

Bring sugar, cocoa, and water to boil. Boil 1-1/2 minutes. Add vanilla. Mix. Drizzle over cake. Dot with cherries.

*Note:* This topping is Mom's syrup that she uses as a sauce on other desserts. Cool and store in refrigerator.

*Les and Peggy Hood: Kelly '71*

# CARROT CAKE

1 cup flour
1 cup sugar
1 teaspoon baking soda
1 teaspoon baking powder
1/2 teaspoon salt
1 teaspoon cinnamon

2 eggs
3/4 cup oil
1 teaspoon vanilla
1-1/2 cups tightly packed,
  shredded, pared carrots
1 cup chopped pecans

Line bottom of loaf pan (8-1/2 x 4-1/2 x 2-1/2") with wax paper. Grease paper and sides of pan. Stir together flour, sugar, baking soda, baking powder, salt, and cinnamon. In medium bowl beat eggs enough to blend yolks and whites; add oil and vanilla. Beat to blend. Add flour mixture; stir until smooth and stir in carrots and pecans. Bake at 325 degrees for 1 hour. Let stand for 10 minutes to loosen. Turn right side up on rack and cool completely before frosting.

Frosting:
1/4 cup margarine
1 (4-ounce) package cream cheese

1 teaspoon vanilla
1-3/4 cups powdered sugar

Beat until blended margarine, cream cheese, and vanilla. Gradually beat in powdered sugar. Frost cooled cake.

*Jack and Carol Carlson: Rebecca '79*

# CARROT CAKE

1-1/2 cups Wesson oil
2 cups sugar
4 eggs
2 cups grated carrots
1 small can crushed pineapple
1 cup chopped nuts

2-1/2 cups flour
1 teaspoon soda
2 teaspoons cinnamon
1/2 teaspoon salt
1 teaspoon vanilla

Blend together oil, sugar, and eggs. Add carrots, pineapple, and nuts. Fold in dry ingredients and vanilla and bake in greased pan at 350 degrees for 40 to 50 minutes. Cool. Ice.

Icing:
1 (8-ounce) package cream cheese
1 stick oleo

1 pound powdered sugar
1 teaspoon vanilla

Blend cream cheese and oleo. Add powdered sugar and vanilla.

*Note:* May be baked in layers at 350 degrees.

*Burl and Nita Guy: Stacy '78*

# CHEESE CAKE

Graham Cracker Crust:
30 to 35 Graham crackers, crushed

1 stick oleo, softened

Mix crackers and oleo to make crust. Press 3/4 into bottom of 8x12" pan. (Reserve 1/4 crust for topping.)

Cake:
1 package lemon jello
1 cup hot water
1 tall can Pet milk, chilled

Juice of 1 lemon
1 cup sugar
1 (8-ounce) package cream cheese
2 tablespoons vanilla

Dissolve jello in hot water; cool. Whip milk until stiff; add lemon juice. Cream sugar with cream cheese and add to jello mixture. Mix milk, jello mixture, and vanilla. Pour cheese mixture over crust and cover with rest of Graham Cracker crumbs.

*Connie and Esther Woullard: Sally '62*

# CHEESE CAKE

Crust:
3/4 cup Graham cracker crumbs

2 teaspoons sugar
3 tablespoons margarine, melted

Mix together and spread in bottom of spring form pan.

Cake:
4 eggs, separated
3/4 cup sugar

2 teaspoons vanilla
3 (8-ounce) packages cream cheese, softened

At medium speed combine egg yolks and sugar until creamy. Add chunks of softened cream cheese; mix until smooth. Add vanilla and mix. Add egg whites (not beaten) and beat until creamy at medium speed. Pour into pan. Bake at 350 degrees for 30 to 35 minutes. Cool 15 minutes.

Topping:
1 pint sour cream

2 teaspoons vanilla
1/3 cup sugar

Mix together and whip at low speed until blended. Pour over the top of cake and bake at 400 degrees for 10 minutes.

Chill for 3 hours or more before serving. Top with favorite filling: cherry or strawberry.

*Jay and Johnna Waldrop: Janae '86*

**Laughter is a tranquilizer with no side effects.**

# CHERRY CHEESE CAKE

1 large Angel Food Cake
3 cups powdered sugar
1 (8-ounce) cream cheese, room
    temperature

2 packages Dream Whip
1 or 2 Cherry Pie Filling
Rum flavoring
Butter flavoring

Crumble Angel Food Cake in long pyrex dish. Cream powdered sugar and cream cheese. Beat Dream Whip and add to cream cheese mixture. Spread over cake and push down. Chill one to two hours. Pour one or two Cherry Pie Fillings over top of mixture. Let set overnight.

*Note:* Add a bit of rum and butter flavoring to pie fillings.

*Ross and Marie Crabtree: Larry '56; Donna '61*

# CHOCOLATE CAKE
## *(This is one good cake!)*

1 box chocolate cake mix (any
    kind)
2 eggs, beaten

1 can Cherry OR Blueberry Pie
    Filling

Combine and mix the above. Blend well. Pour into a greased and floured sheet pan. Bake 30 to 40 minutes at 350 degrees.

Icing:
1 cup sugar
1/2 stick oleo

1/2 cup milk
1 cup chocolate chips
1 cup nuts

Combine sugar, oleo, and milk. Boil 1 minute and add chocolate chips. Stir until melted. Add nuts. Spread icing on cake.

*Frankie Garrett: DeDe '72*

# CHOCOLATE UPSIDE-DOWN CAKE

1 cup flour
3/4 cup sugar
2 tablespoons cocoa
2 teaspoons baking powder
1/4 teaspoon salt

1/2 cup milk
2 tablespoons melted butter
1 teaspoon vanilla
1/2 cup chopped pecans

Mix in large bowl the first 5 ingredients. Add remaining ingredients and mix well. Pour into well-greased oblong pan (about 8x11"). Pour topping over batter. Bake in 350 degree oven for 1 hour.

Topping:
1/2 cup sugar
1/2 cup brown sugar

2 tablespoons cocoa
1 cup hot water

Mix sugars and cocoa and sprinkle over batter. Slowly pour hot water over the whole cake. Bake. Serve with whipped cream or ice cream.

*Note:* No eggs in this cake.

*Ed and Berthold Balkum: Cathy '62*

# CHOCOLATE SHEET CAKE

2 cups sifted flour
2 cups sugar
2 sticks oleo or butter
1 cup water
4 tablespoons cocoa
2 well-beaten eggs

1 teaspoon soda, mixed in
  buttermilk
1/2 cup buttermilk
1 teaspoon vanilla
1/2 teaspoon salt
1/2 teaspoon cinnamon

Sift flour and sugar in large mixing bowl; set aside. In a saucepan bring to a boil butter, water, and cocoa. Pour over flour and sugar mixture. Beat well. Add eggs and remaining ingredients. Bake in greased and floured 9x13" pan for 20 minutes at 400 degrees.

*Note:* May use 1 stick oleo and 1/2 cup Crisco instead of 2 sticks oleo.

Icing:
1 stick oleo
4 tablespoons cocoa
6 tablespoons evaporated milk
1 box powdered sugar, sifted

1 teaspoon vanilla
1 cup chopped nuts
1 cup coconut, optional (with
  some recipes)

Bring to boil oleo, cocoa, and evaporated milk. Remove from heat and beat in powdered sugar, vanilla, and nuts. Pour and spread on hot cake. YUM! YUM!

*Virgil and Bert Coffee: Larry '58*
*Odis and Edith Carruth: Joveta '50*
*Connie and Esther Woullard: Sally '62*
*Roy and Frances Buckner: Debbie '63; Spencer '65*
*Forrest and Vida Scott: Stanley '64; Larry '66; Carl '69*
*G.C. and Nadine Black: Gerome '65; Trudee '67*
*Buford and Jackie Andrews: Johnny '66*
*Donald and Barbara Barber: Donita '67*
*Fred and Joyce Weir: Charlotte '68*
*Gordon and Sharon O'Dell: Debbie '68; Kim '70*
*Howard and Joyce Bechtold: Gay Lynn '68*
*Henry and Beth Mohr: Charles '75*
*Robert and Lana Moon: Greg '80*
*Jeannie Willis Crain '56*
*Raymond and Mary Willis: Jeannie '56*
*Bubba and Patsy Hoermann: Tim '70*
*E.W. and Eloise McDowell: Hugh '61*

**Before you borrow money from a friend,
decide which you need more.**

# COCA-COLA CAKE

| | |
|---|---|
| 2 cups flour | 1 teaspoon soda |
| 2 cups sugar | 2 eggs |
| 2 sticks oleo | 1 teaspoon vanilla |
| 3 tablespoons cocoa | 1/4 teaspoon salt |
| 1 cup coke | 1-1/2 cups miniature |
| 1/2 cup buttermilk | marshmallows |

Sift flour and sugar in bowl. Heat oleo, cocoa, and coke to boiling point, then add to flour mixture. Add buttermilk, soda, eggs, vanilla, salt, and marshmallows. Batter will be thin and marshmallows will float on top. Pour into greased and floured oblong pan. Bake at 350 degrees for 30 to 35 minutes.

| | |
|---|---|
| **Icing:** | 1 box powdered sugar |
| 1/2 cup butter | 1 cup chopped pecans |
| 3 tablespoons cocoa | 1 teaspoon vanilla |
| 1/3 cup coke | |

Combine first 3 ingredients and heat to boiling. Pour over sugar. Stir in remaining ingredients and ice cake while hot.

*Note:* Toasted pecans may be used. (Toast while oven is heating.)

*Jim and Nell Brown: Tom '64; Susan '66*

# FUDGE CAKE

| | |
|---|---|
| 2 sticks oleo | 4 tablespoons cocoa |
| 2 cups sugar | 1 teaspoon vanilla |
| 4 eggs | 1 cup pecans, chopped |
| 1-1/2 cups flour | |

Combine and mix well. Bake at 350 degrees in greased and floured sheet pan.

| | |
|---|---|
| **Icing:** | 1 box powdered sugar |
| 1 container marshmallow cream | 8 tablespoons Pet milk |
| 1/2 cup cocoa | 4 tablespoons butter |

Spread marshmallow cream over hot cake. Mix other icing ingredients. Bring to a boil. Stir. Drop on cake and swirl.

*Zel Roberts Matt '68*

Every prize has its price.

# FUDGE CAKE

*(Our favorite family recipe — Yummy!)*

2 sticks oleo
2 cups sugar
2 cups flour, scant
2 tablespoons (heaping) cocoa

Pinch of salt
1 teaspoon vanilla
6 eggs

Melt oleo in a pan or bowl large enough to mix the batter. Add remaining ingredients in order. Mix well and pour into heavy pan or iron skillet. Bake at 325 degrees for 15 to 20 minutes, NO LONGER; DO NOT OVERCOOK. The cake should be baked only about 2" from the edge of the pan. The center will be chocolate sauce, which you spoon on the top of the baked part.

*Harry and Carol Tipton: Gloria '60; Debbie '62*

# HOT FUDGE SUNDAE CAKE

1 cup flour
3/4 cup sugar
2 tablespoons cocoa
2 teaspoons baking powder
1/4 teaspoon salt
1/2 cup milk
2 tablespoons oil

1 teaspoon vanilla
Topping: (Sauce)
1 cup brown sugar, packed
1/4 cup cocoa
1-3/4 cups hot tap water
(Ice Cream)

In ungreased 9x9x2" square pan, stir together flour, sugar, cocoa, baking powder, and salt. Mix in milk, oil, and vanilla with a fork until smooth. Spread evenly over pan. Sprinkle with mixture of brown sugar and cocoa. Pour HOT water over batter. Bake in 350 degree oven for 40 minutes. Let stand 15 minutes. Cut into squares and spoon into dessert dishes (invert into dish). Top with ice cream and spoon the sauce over top. (Makes its own sauce.) Serves 9.

*Henry and Evelyn Singleterry: Susan '69*

**One reason for doing the right thing today —
is tomorrow.**

# HERSHEY BAR CAKE

6 or 7 Hershey bars
1 (5-1/2 ounce) can chocolate syrup
2 sticks oleo
2 cups sugar
4 eggs
1 cup buttermilk

1/2 teaspoon soda
2-1/2 cups flour
1/4 teaspoon salt
2 teaspoons vanilla
1 cup chopped pecans, optional
Powdered sugar

Melt Hershey bars and chocolate syrup in top of double boiler. Cool. Cream oleo and sugar. Add eggs one at a time, beating thoroughly after each egg. Beat in melted chocolate mixture. Add alternately buttermilk (mixed with soda) and dry ingredients. Add vanilla and pecans. Pour into a greased and floured tube pan, NOT A BUNDT PAN. Bake 1-1/2 hours in 325 degree oven. Remove from pan after 15 minutes. Dust with powdered sugar.

*Note:* Most recipes I received dusted with powdered sugar, however, Fudge Icing was a variation instead of the powdered sugar.

**Fudge Icing:**
2 cups sugar
3/4 cup Pet milk
10 large marshmallows
1 stick butter or oleo

1 (6-ounce) package chocolate chips
1 teaspoon vanilla
1 cup chopped pecans

Mix sugar, milk, and marshmallows and bring to a boil. Boil until well blended. Add butter and chocolate chips. Add vanilla and pecans. Blend and spread over cake.

*Donald and Barbara Barber: Donita '67*
*Raymond and Lorene Tucker: Ralph '53*
*Wiley and Helen Bownds: Cheryl '67*

# SOUR CREAM CHOCOLATE CAKE

1 cup boiling water
1 teaspoon soda
1/2 cup cocoa
2 cups sugar
1 cup sour cream

2 eggs
2 cups flour
1/4 teaspoon salt
1 teaspoon vanilla

Pour boiling water over soda and cocoa; stir. Cream sugar and sour cream. Add eggs, then sifted dry ingredients. Add vanilla and boiling water mixture. Bake 375 degrees for 35 minutes in greased and floured sheet pan.

**Icing:**
1 stick oleo
4 tablespoons cocoa
6 tablespoons milk

1 teaspoon vanilla
2 cups powdered sugar (or more)
1/4 teaspoon salt
Nuts, optional

Melt butter and cocoa in milk. Remove and add vanilla, powdered sugar, salt, and nuts.

*Jimmie and Jean Evans: Vicki '67*

# MISSISSIPPI MUD CAKE

2 sticks oleo
2 cups sugar
1/3 cup cocoa
4 eggs
1 teaspoon vanilla
1-1/2 cups flour
1/4 teaspoon salt
1-1/2 cups coconut
1-1/2 cups chopped pecans
1 (8-ounce) jar marshmallow
   creme

Cream oleo, sugar, and cocoa. Add eggs and vanilla. Add flour, salt, coconut, and nuts to creamed mixture. Blend well. Bake in floured and greased 9x13" pan at 350 degrees for 30 minutes. When done, spread with marshmallow creme while hot. Cool.

Icing:
1 stick oleo, melted
1/2 cup evaporated milk
1 teaspoon vanilla
1/3 cup cocoa
1 box powdered sugar
1 cup coconut, optional

Melt oleo; add milk and vanilla. Stir in cocoa and sugar until smooth. Spread on top of marshmallow creme. May be sprinkled with more pecans, if desired.

*Lloyd and Marita Lunceford: '69*
*Forrest and Vida Scott: Stanley '64; Larry '66; Carl '69*

# RAVE REVIEW COCONUT CAKE

1 package Yellow Cake Mix
1 small package Instant Vanilla
   Pudding Mix
1-1/2 cups water
4 eggs
1/4 cup oil
2 cups coconut
1 cup chopped pecans

Blend cake mix, pudding mix, water, eggs, and oil in mixer for 4 minutes at medium speed. Stir in coconut and pecans. Pour into 3 greased and floured 9" pan. Bake at 350 degrees for 35 minutes. Cool in pans 15 minutes; remove, fill, and frost.

Frosting:
4 tablespoons oleo
2 cups coconut
1 (8-ounce) package cream
   cheese, softened
2 teaspoons milk
3-1/2 cups powdered sugar, sifted
1/2 teaspoon vanilla

Melt 2 of the (4) tablespoons of oleo in skillet. Add coconut; stir constantly over low heat until golden brown. Spread coconut on paper towel to cool. Cream 2 tablespoons of butter with cream cheese. Add milk and sugar alternately, beating well. Add vanilla and stir in 3/4 cup coconut. Spread in between layers and on top and sides of cake. Sprinkle remaining coconut on top and sides.

*James and Margaret Taylor: Michael '71*

# 3-DAY COCONUT CAKE

1 (18-1/2 ounce) Butter Flavored
Cake Mix
2 cups sugar
16 ounce sour cream

12 ounce frozen coconut, thawed
1-1/2 cups frozen whipped
topping

Prepare cake mix as directed. Make 2 (8" layers). Cool. Split layers. Combine sugar, sour cream, and coconut; blend well. Chill. Reserve 1 cup of sour cream mixture for frosting. Spread remainder between layers of cake. Combine reserved mixture with whipped topping. Blend until smooth. Spread on top and sides of cake. Seal in air tight container and refrigerate 3 days.

(Doesn't this sound out of this world?)

*N.E. and Sue Sherrill: Bill '72*

# "DIRT" CAKE

This is a great gag for a party or covered dish dinner. You will need to purchase a medium-sized plastic flower pot, a colored trowel (it looks prettier), and a silk flower. I like to add gummy worms on the very top.

1 package Oreos, crushed
1 (8-ounce) cream cheese,
softened
1/2 stick oleo, softened
1 cup powdered sugar

1 (12-ounce) carton Cool Whip
2 small packages Vanilla Instant
Pudding
3-1/2 cups milk

Crush Oreos. Cream cheese, oleo, and powdered sugar. Mix Cool Whip and pudding mix with milk. Blend milk mixture with cheese mixture. Layer cream mixture with crushed Oreos. Oreo layer should be on top. Add flowers and worms. Serve and enjoy!

*Dick and Nelda Tobias: Terri '66; Richard '68; David '72*
*Teacher's Pet: Elwana Brewster*

# DUMP CAKE

1 can Cherry Pie Filling
1 (No. 2) can crushed pineapple,
undrained
1 box Yellow Cake Mix

2 sticks butter or oleo
1 can Angel Flake coconut
1 cup chopped pecans

In a greased 9x13" pan, combine Cherry Pie Filling and pineapple. Sprinkle cake mix over the above. Add oleo, sliced; cover as evenly as possible. Top with coconut and pecans. Bake 1 hour at 325 degrees.

*Note:* Coconut and pecans may be added before and after cake mix is used.

*Norman and Maurine Galloway: Sammy '49*

## APPLE DUMP CAKE

1 (20-ounce) can crushed
    pineapple, undrained
1 can Apple Pie Filling

1 box Yellow Cake Mix
1-1/2 sticks oleo, cut into slices
1 cup chopped nuts

In a greased 9x13" pan, layer apples on top of pineapples. Sprinkle cake mix over apples. Slice oleo over cake mix. Sprinkle with nuts. Bake 1 hour at 325 degrees.

*Roy and Shirley Springer: Donna '71; Sharon '74*

## FIG PRESERVE CAKE

2 eggs, beaten
2 cups sugar
1 cup buttermilk
1 cup oil
2 cups flour
1 teaspoon cinnamon
1 teaspoon nutmeg

1 teaspoon soda
1 teaspoon vanilla
1 teaspoon salt
2 cups chopped pecans
2 cups drained fig preserves, cut
    into small pieces.

Beat together eggs, sugar, buttermilk, and oil. Cream in the flour. Add spices, soda, vanilla, salt, and pecans. Fold in figs. Grease and flour a tube or bundt pan. Pour batter into pan and bake in 350 degree oven for 1 hour. Let cake cool in pan.

Sauce:
1/2 cup buttermilk
1/2  cup sugar
1 tablespoon light corn syrup

1/2 cup butter
1/4 cup sherry wine
1 teaspoon almond flavoring

Bring buttermilk, sugar, and corn syrup to a boil, stirring constantly. Remove from heat and add butter, stirring until melted. Add flavoring. Pour sauce over cake while still in pan. Let soak overnight. Turn out the next day.

*Breland and Ann Bridges: Brenda '61*

**Nothing is as hard to do gracefully
as getting down off your high horse!**

# FRUIT COCKTAIL CAKE

| | |
|---|---|
| 2 cups flour | 1 teaspoon soda |
| 1-1/2 cups sugar | 1 teaspoon vanilla |
| 2 eggs, slightly beaten | 2 cups fruit cocktail, undrained |

Mix all ingredients; beat well. Pour into greased and floured 9x13" pan. Bake for 30 to 35 minutes at 350 degrees.

*Variation:* Sprinkle top of batter with mixture of 1/2 cup brown sugar and 1 cup chopped pecans. Bake.

| Icing: | 1 small can Pet milk |
|---|---|
| 1-1/2 cups sugar | 1 teaspoon vanilla |
| 1 stick oleo | |

Mix and bring to a boil; boil 5 minutes. Cut cake when still warm before pouring icing over cake.

*Variation:* Add 1/2 cup chopped pecans and 1 cup coconut to icing before pouring over warm cake. GREAT ON CHOCOLATE CAKE, TOO!

*Millie Henderson: Scott Flanagan '78*
*Jim and Shirley Worley: Doug Ford: '76*

# FRUIT COCKTAIL CAKE

| | |
|---|---|
| 1 package Pillsbury Butter cake mix | 1 can fruit cocktail, undrained |
| | 3 eggs |

Mix all ingredients well. Bake in well-greased and floured bundt pan at 350 degrees for 40 to 50 minutes. Cool completely. Serve with topping.

| Topping: | 2 tablespoons light cream |
|---|---|
| 1 (3-ounce) package cream cheese, softened | 2 tablespoons sugar |

Combine and beat until smooth. Spread on cooled cake.

*Richard and Clarine Brinkley: Dianne '63; Connie '65*

# GREAT CAKE

| | |
|---|---|
| 1 box Duncan Hines Butter flavored cake mix | 1 (7-ounce) carton sour cream |
| 4 eggs | 1 tablespoon vanilla |
| 2/3 cups butter-flavored Wesson oil | 1 tablespoon lemon extract |

Mix all ingredients well. Grease pan with Crisco; sprinkle sugar in pan before adding mix. Bake at 350 degrees for 45 minutes.

*Maurice and Vaughn Tripplehorn: Paul '66*

# HUMMINGBIRD CAKE

3 cups flour
2 cups sugar
1 teaspoon soda
1 teaspoon salt
1 teaspoon cinnamon
1-1/2 cups cooking oil

3 eggs, beaten
1 (8-ounce) can crushed pineapple
2 cups mashed bananas
1 teaspoon butter flavoring
1 cup chopped pecans
Vanilla, optional

Mix dry ingredients; add oil, eggs, and pineapple. Mix by hand. Add remaining ingredients and bake in Bundt pan at 350 degrees for 60 to 65 minutes. Or cook in three 9" cake pans for 25 to 30 minutes. Let cool 1 hour before removing. Remove. Frost with Creamy Cheese Frosting.

Creamy Cheese Frosting:
2 (8-ounce) packages cream
    cheese, softened
1 stick oleo

2 (16-ounce) packages powdered
    sugar
2 teaspoons vanilla

Combine softened cream cheese and oleo until smooth. Add sifted powdered sugar, beating until light and fluffy. Stir in vanilla. Spread.

*Paul and Ruth Newman: Paula '52*

# IRISH POTATO CAKE

2-1/2 cups sugar
1 cup butter
3 eggs
1 cup sweet milk
1 cup cold mashed potatoes
1 cup chopped pecans
1 cup coconut

3 cups flour, sifted
2 teaspoons baking powder
1 teaspoon allspice
1 teaspoon cinnamon
1/2 pound dates, chopped
10 maraschino cherries, cut in half
2 tablespoons vanilla

Mix in order as written. Bake in 3 greased and floured layer pans at 350 degrees for 30 minutes. A large cake!

Icing:
2 cups sugar
1 cup sweet milk
1 cup chopped pecans

1 cup chopped dates
1/2 cup coconut
10 cherries, cut up

Combine and cook until thick. Add cherries last. Spread on cake.

*W.A. "Bill" and Vera Harris: Geneva '55*

Success is never final and failure never fatal.

# ITALIAN CREAM CAKE

1 stick oleo
2 cups sugar
1/2 cup Crisco
5 eggs, separated
1 teaspoon soda
1 cup buttermilk

2 cups flour, sifted
1 teaspoon vanilla
1 small can coconut (3-1/2 ounce)
1 cup chopped pecans, optional
5 egg whites, stiffly beaten

Cream oleo, sugar, and Crisco. Add egg yolks and beat well. Dissolve soda in buttermilk; add alternately with flour. Add vanilla, coconut, and pecans. Fold in stiffly beaten egg whites.

Bake in 3 layers (8" cake pans) at 350 degrees for 25 to 30 minutes. Cool.

Filling:
1 (8-ounce) package cream cheese
1/2 stick oleo
1 box powdered sugar

1 teaspoon vanilla
1/2 to 1 cup chopped pecans
(Use cream to thin)
(Use coconut if desired)

Mix well; Add chopped nuts between layers and on top.

*Ross and Marie Crabtree: Larry '56; Donna '61*

# JAM CAKE

2 cups sugar
2 sticks oleo
4 eggs, separated
1 cup blackberry jam
3 cups flour
1 teaspoon soda

1 teaspoon cinnamon
1 teaspoon cloves
1 teaspoon nutmeg
1 cup buttermilk
1 cup chopped pecans
4 beaten egg whites

Cream sugar and butter. Add egg yolks one at a time and beat. Add jam and beat well. Sift dry ingredients. Add alternately with buttermilk to cream mixture. Add nuts. Beat egg whites until stiff; fold into batter. Bake 1 hour or more at 350 degrees in greased and floured tube pan.

*Jim and Shirley Nabors: Kathy '64; Jay '66*

**Love in the heart isn't put there to stay.**

# LANE CAKE

| | |
|---|---|
| 1 cup butter | 2 teaspoons baking powder |
| 2 cups sugar | 1 cup milk |
| 3-1/4 cups sifted flour | 8 egg whites |
| 1/2 teaspoon salt | 1 teaspoon vanilla |

Cream butter and sugar until very light. Sift flour, salt, and baking powder 3 times and add alternately with milk to creamed mixture. Fold in well-beaten egg whites and vanilla. Bake in 3 well-greased and floured 9" cake pans. Bake at 375 degrees for 20 to 25 minutes.

| | |
|---|---|
| Filling: | 1 cup pecans |
| 8 egg yolks | 1 cup coconut |
| 1-1/4 cups sugar | 1 cup raisins |
| 1/2 cup butter | 1 teaspoon vanilla |

Beat egg yolks, sugar, and butter; place in double boiler and cook until thickened to spreading consistency. Add remaining ingredients and spread over cooled cake.

*Theron and Christine Dockery: Terry '61*

# LEMON DREAM CAKE

| | |
|---|---|
| 1 Duncan Hines Lemon Cake Mix | 4 eggs |
| 1/2 cup cooking oil | 1 cup water |
| 1 lemon Instant Pudding Mix | |

Combine and mix all ingredients. Bake in greased and floured 10" tube pan 45 to 55 minutes at 350 degrees. Cool in pan (right side up) for 15 minutes.

| | |
|---|---|
| Glaze: | 2 tablespoons milk (or 1/2 milk |
| 1 cup powdered sugar | and 1/2 lemon) |

Mix and spread over warm cake.

*Stanley and Ruth Reid: Terri '69; Larry '71; Tammy '74*
*Charles and Dorothy Byrne: Patti '67; Teresa '69; Charles '73*

**Behind every argument is
someone's ignorance.**

# LEMON FRUIT CAKE

1 pound butter
1 pound brown sugar
6 eggs, separated
4 cups flour (divided)
1 teaspoon baking powder
1/4 teaspoon salt
1-1/2 ounce (3 tablespoons)
  lemon extract

1 pound chopped pecans
1 (12-ounce) package candied
  cherries, chopped
1 (12-ounce) package candied
  pineapples, chopped
6 egg whites

Cream butter and sugar. Add egg yolks, one at a time, beating well. Sift 2 cups flour with baking powder and salt. Add alternately with lemon extract, beating well. Dredge nuts and fruits with remaining 2 cups flour. (It is best if fruit is dredged and let set overnight.) Pour batter over fruit mixture. Mix well. Fold in stiffly beaten egg whites. Bake in greased and floured 10" tube pan about 3 hours at 250 degrees or until done.

*Note:* Next day after cake is baked, dip a cloth in a bowl of Mogan David wine and slap over cake. Cut a slice of apple and lay in center of tube cake; lay damp soaked cloth (with wine) in center with apple. Repeat every week or so, just to keep it moist. Can start making these cakes in the fall as soon as it begins to cool. Do not have to place in refrigerator; just wrap in heavy foil and leave out. Make about Thanksgiving for Christmas.

*Note:* One Christmas I made 150 of these for an oil company to give to their employees.

*Variation:* Once a week, unwrap, and brush with pineapple or orange juice. (In place of wine treatment)

*Lloyd and Margaret Ford: Cindy '55*
*Harry and Cora Tate: Mike '50*

# LEMON POPPY SEED CAKE

1 Lemon Cake Mix
1 Lemon Instant Pudding Mix
  (small)
1 cup water

1/2 cup oil
2 tablespoons poppy seed
5 eggs

Mix and pour into 2 greased loaf pans. Bake for 45 minutes at 350 degrees.

*Wayne and Dodie McAdoo: Tonya '83*

The joy you give
is the pleasure you get.

# MANDARIN ORANGE CAKE

1 box Duncan Hines butter cake
  mix
3/4 cup oil

4 eggs
1 (11-ounce) can Mandarin
  oranges

Mix the above ingredients well. Pour into 3 (8") cake pans (greased but not floured). Line bottom with wax paper. Bake at 350 degrees for 20 to 25 minutes. Cool completely and frost with frosting.

Frosting:
1 (9-ounce) carton Cool Whip
1 (20-ounce) can crushed
  pineapple, undrained

1 (11-ounce) can Mandarin
  oranges, drained
1 small box (3-ounce) Vanilla
  Instant Pudding Mix
1 can coconut, optional

Beat all ingredients and spread between layers and on sides and top.

*James and Mary Beth Berry: Jera '76*
*James and Betty Dillard: Johnny Chapman '70*

# MAYONNAISE CAKE

2 cups flour
1 cup sugar
1/4 cup cocoa
1-1/2 teaspoons soda

1/4 teaspoon salt
1 cup water
1 cup mayonnaise
1 teaspoon vanilla

Sift dry ingredients into bowl. Combine water, mayonnaise, and vanilla. Beat about 1 minute with mixer. Pour into dry ingredients and mix well (about 2 minutes). Pour batter into greased and floured 9x13" pan. Bake at 350 degrees for 30 to 35 minutes. Cool.

Icing No. 1 (optional):
2 cups sugar
1/2 cup cocoa

1/2 cup oleo
1/2 cup milk
1 teaspoon vanilla

Mix ingredients and bring to boil. Boil 1 minute. Spread over cooled cake.

Icing No. 2:
1 stick oleo
4 tablespoons cocoa
6 tablespoons canned milk

1 box powdered sugar
1 teaspoon vanilla
1 cup chopped pecans

Combine oleo, cocoa, and milk. Bring to a slow boil. Add sugar, vanilla, and pecans. Ice hot cake.

*Thurman and Grace Carter: Guy '67; Cobbie '68; Katrina '69*
*Charles and Arlene Clark: Malcolm '74*

# MILKY WAY CAKE

6 to 8 regular or 13 fun-size
   Milky Way bars
2 sticks oleo
2 cups sugar
4 eggs
2-1/2 cups flour

1/2 teaspoon salt
1/2 teaspoon soda
1-1/4 cups buttermilk
1 teaspoon vanilla
1 cup chopped pecans

Melt candy and 1 stick oleo. Cream sugar and other stick of oleo. Add eggs and beat well after each addition. Add alternately flour and salt with buttermilk and soda. Add vanilla, melted candy mixture, and nuts. Bake in greased and floured 10" tube pan at 350 degrees for 1 hour and 20 minutes.

*R.J. and Erie Walker: Sue '54*

# MINCEMEAT CAKE

1-1/4 cups brown sugar, firmly
   packed
1/2 cup shortening
2 eggs
2 cups flour
2 teaspoons baking powder

1/2 teaspoon salt
1/2 teaspoon cinnamon
1/4 teaspoon cloves
1/4 teaspoon allspice
1/2 cup milk
1 cup prepared mincemeat

Thoroughly cream sugar and shortening. Beat in eggs. Sift dry ingredients. Add dry ingredients and milk alternately to creamed mixture. Mix well with each addition. Fold in mincemeat. Bake in greased and floured square pan at 350 degrees for 50 to 60 minutes. Cool. Frost with butter icing, if desired.

Butter Icing:
1 stick oleo, melted
3 cups powdered sugar

1 teaspoon vanilla
1-1/2 tablespoons strong coffee

Mix and spread over cake.

*Buck D. and Marion Harrelson: Richard '67*

Cook carefully
Serve lovingly
Eat joyfully!

# NEIMAN MARCUS CAKE

*A popular recipe!*

1 box Lemon OR Yellow Cake
   Mix
1 stick melted oleo
1 teaspoon vanilla
1 egg

1 cup chopped pecans
1 pound powdered sugar
1 (8-ounce) package cream
   cheese, softened
3 eggs

Mix together first 5 ingredients and press into a 9x13" pan. Mix together remaining ingredients and spread over cake mixture. Bake at 350 degrees for 45 to 50 minutes. Cut into squares.

*Charles and Barbara Russell: Joni '72*
*Linda Henderson Parmley: Lisa '74; Greg '75*
*James and Elewese Crain: James '54; Jan '56; Rhonda '59*
*Ricky and Brenda Loving: Jason '86*
*Sara (Stone) Shorter: Jerry Ragland '83*

# OATMEAL CAKE

1-1/2 cups boiling water
1 cup oatmeal
1 stick oleo
1 cup white sugar
1 cup brown sugar
2 eggs, beaten

1-1/3 cups flour
1/2 teaspoon salt
1 teaspoon soda
1 teaspoon cinnamon
1 teaspoon vanilla
1/2 cup nuts, optional

Pour boiling water over oats; let stand 20 minutes. Cream oleo, sugars, and eggs. Mix well. Mix dry ingredients and add to creamed mixture. Add vanilla and mix well. Pour into greased and floured sheet pan and bake at 350 degrees for 30 to 35 minutes.

Icing:
6 tablespoons butter
1/4 cup cream
1/2 cup brown sugar

1/2 teaspoon vanilla
1 cup coconut
1 cup nuts, chopped

Mix butter, cream, and sugar; bring to a boil; boil 2 minutes. Add vanilla, coconut, and nuts. Spread on cake. Place under broiler and brown.

*James and Lois Carlisle: Patti '51*
*B.B. and Brooksie Stephens: Beckie '78*

**A word to the wise is not sufficient**
**if it doesn't make sense.**

# ORANGE FRUIT CAKE

1 cup butter
2 cups sugar
3-1/2 cups flour
1/2 teaspoon salt
4 eggs
1 teaspoon soda

1/2 cup buttermilk
2 tablespoons grated orange peel
1/2 cup coconut
1 cup chopped pecans
1 package chopped dates

Combine butter, sugar, flour, salt, and eggs. Beat until light and fluffy. Add soda to milk and mix the two mixtures. Add remaining ingredients and stir well. Bake in greased and floured Bundt pan at 350 degrees for 1 hour. (May cook in loaf pans.)

*Variation:* Any kind of candied fruit may be added to cake batter.

Glaze:
2 cups powdered sugar

1 cup orange juice
2 tablespoons orange peel

Mix and heat to melt sugar. Dribble over hot cake until saturated. Punch holes with fork into cake so glaze will soak in.

*E.R. and Ruby Wortham: Stayce Williams '83*

# PEACH CAKE

1-1/2 cups sugar
2 eggs
3/4 cup cooking oil
2 cups flour
1/4 teaspoon salt
1 teaspoon soda

1 teaspoon cinnamon
1-1/3 cups chopped peaches, with
  juice
1/2 cup coconut
1/2 cup chopped pecans

Cream sugar, eggs, and oil; stir well. Mix dry ingredients and add to creamed mixture. Add peaches, coconut, and nuts. Bake in greased and floured 2 layered pans at 350 degrees for 25 to 30 minutes. Bake 1 hour for tube pan. Loaf pan: 35 to 40 minutes.

Icing:
1 cup sugar
1 stick oleo
1 cup canned milk

2 eggs, beaten
1/2 cup coconut, optional
1/2 cup nuts
1 teaspoon vanilla

Cook sugar, oleo, milk, and egg until thick. Add coconut, nuts, and vanilla. When cool frost cake.

*Danny and Imogene Thomas: Tammy '74*

---

**Nobody ever listened to reason
on an empty stomach.**

## EASY PINA COLADA CAKE

1 Yellow Cake Mix
1 can Eagle Brand Milk
1 can Casa Cream of Coconut

1 small can crushed pineapple
1 medium carton Cool Whip
1 can coconut

Bake cake according to directions in greased and floured 9x13" pan. Punch holes in top with fork while warm. Mix milk and cream of coconut and pour over cake. Pour can of pineapple over the coconut mixture. Spread Cool Whip over top of cake. Sprinkle can of coconut over the top of Cool Whip.

*Steve and Sherry Marshall: Cory '86*

## PLUM FUN CAKE

1 cup cooking oil
2 cups sugar
3 eggs
2 small jars plum baby food
1/2 teaspoon red food coloring,
   optional
2 cups flour

1/2 teaspoon soda
1/2 teaspoon salt
1 teaspoon cloves
1 teaspoon cinnamon
1 cup chopped nuts
1 teaspoon vanilla

Mix together the first 5 ingredients. Beat well. Combine dry ingredients and add nuts. Add vanilla to creamed mixture along with dry ingredients. Pour into greased and floured Bundt pan and bake at 350 degrees for 50 to 60 minutes.

Glaze:
1 cup powdered sugar

3 tablespoons lemon juice
1 teaspoon lemon rind

Mix and heat until mixture comes to a bubble and is thick. Spread with a pastry brush while cake is hot.

*Bill and Dora Jones: Annette '59,*

**A friend is one who knows all about you
And loves you just the same.**

# POPPY SEED CAKE

1 cup buttermilk
1 tablespoon poppy seed
3 cups sugar
1 cup shortening
6 eggs, separated

3 cups flour
1/4 teaspoon salt
1/4 teaspoon soda
1 teaspoon vanilla
1 teaspoon almond extract

Soak poppy seeds in buttermilk. Cream sugar and shortening; add egg yolks and buttermilk. Sift and mix dry ingredients; add to creamed mixture. Add stiffly beaten egg whites and flavorings. Bake in greased and floured Bundt pan at 325 degrees for 1-1/2 hours. Serve plain or with a glaze.

Glaze:
1/2 cup orange juice
1 teaspoon vanilla

1 teaspoon almond extract
1 teaspoon butter
1-1/2 cups powdered sugar

Let come to a boil and pour over hot cake. Pierce warm cake with fork while glazing.

*Fred and Ora Herrera: Freddie '78*

# PRUNE CAKE

2 cups sugar
3/4 cup butter
5 eggs
2 cups sifted flour
1 teaspoon baking powder
1 teaspoon soda
Pinch of salt

2 teaspoons cinnamon
1 teaspoon allspice
1/2 cup buttermilk
1/2 cup prune juice
2 cups, cooked and mashed
  prunes

Cream sugar and butter in large bowl until smooth. Add one egg at a time, beating well after each addition. Set aside. Sift dry ingredients together 3 times. Add sifted ingredients to creamed mixture, alternately with buttermilk and prune juice. Beat well after each addition. Stir in prunes. Pour into 2 well greased and floured cake pans. Bake at 350 degrees 25 to 30 minutes.

Icing:
1 box powdered sugar
1/2 cup soft butter, or less

2 or 3 tablespoons canned milk
A little prune juice
1 cup mashed prunes

Mix powdered sugar and butter. Add milk and prune juice. Add prunes to form a consistency to spread between layers and on top of cake.

*H.M. and Mary Smith: Winnie '56*

The past is a bucket of ashes.

# PUMPKIN CAKE

3-1/3 to 3-1/2 cups flour
3 cups sugar
2 teaspoons nutmeg
3 teaspoons cinnamon
1 teaspoon salt
2 teaspoons soda

1 cup Crisco oil
4 eggs
2/3 cup water
1 (16-ounce) can pumpkin
1 cup chopped dates
1 cup chopped pecans

Combine and mix all dry ingredients. Add eggs; beat. Add liquid ingredients. Add remaining ingredients. Mix. Pour into greased and floured 9x5" loaf pans. Bake 1 hour at 350 degrees.

*Henry and Ethel Cook: Ray '52; Henry '53*

# PUMPKIN CAKE

2 cups sugar
1-1/2 cups cooking oil
4 eggs
2 cups flour

1 teaspoon salt
2 teaspoons soda
3 teaspoons cinnamon
1-1/2 cups canned pumpkins

Mix sugar and oil. Beat in eggs one at a time. Mix dry ingredients and add. Fold in pumpkins. Beat 1 minute. Pour into greased and floured Bundt pan and bake at 350 degrees for 1 hour.

Icing:
1 stick oleo, room temperature
1 (8-ounce) package cream
 cheese, softened

1 box powdered sugar
1 teaspoon vanilla
1 cup chopped nuts

Cream oleo, cream cheese, and sugar. Add vanilla and nuts. Mix well; spread over cake.

*Floyd and Christine Martin: Ray '54; Gail '59*

# PUNCH BOWL CAKE

1 box Yellow Cake Mix, prepared
2 cans Cherry Pie Filling
4 boxes Instant Vanilla Pudding
 Mix, prepared
1 (16-ounce) can chunk pineapple

4 bananas, sliced
1 (16-ounce) carton Cool Whip
Chopped pecans
Chopped cherries
Coconut

Crumble cooled baked cake. Layer 1/2 of cake cubes in clear punch bowl. Top with 1 can pie filling, 2 boxes pudding, half of pineapple, half of bananas, and half of Cool Whip. Repeat layers, using rest of each ingredient. Garnish with pecans, cherries, and coconut.

*Note:* Best to dip bananas in lemon juice.

*Ed and Harlene Farmer: Vivian '68*

# BUTTERMILK POUND CAKE

3 cups sugar
1 cup shortening
6 eggs, separated
3 cups flour
1/2 teaspoon salt

1/4 teaspoon soda
1 cup buttermilk
2 teaspoons vanilla OR 2
  teaspoons lemon extract
6 egg whites, beaten

Cream sugar and shortening. Add beaten egg yolks; beat. Mix dry ingredients and add alternately with buttermilk and flavorings. Fold beaten egg whites into cake batter. Bake at 350 degrees for 1 hour. Reduce heat to 325 degrees and bake 10 minutes longer.

*Note:* 1 can coconut may be added to batter, if desired.

**Lemon Glaze:**
1-1/2 cups powdered sugar, sifted

4 tablespoons lemon juice
1 teaspoon lemon extract

Mix and beat ingredients while cake is baking and let stand. Pour over warm cake.

*Jim and Shirley Worley: Doug Ford '76*
*James and Wanda Mosley: Shirley '61; Jana '64*

# CHOCOLATE POUND CAKE
## *(Very Good)*

2 sticks oleo
1/2 cup shortening
3 cups sugar
5 eggs, separated
4 tablespoons cocoa
3 cups flour

1/2 teaspoon baking powder
1/2 teaspoon salt
1 cup sweet milk
2 teaspoons vanilla
3 egg whites, beaten
1 cup pecan halves, optional

Cream oleo and shortening; gradually add sugar. Add egg yolks one at a time and beat well after each addition. Mix dry ingredients; add alternately with milk and vanilla. Fold in egg whites. Pour into a greased and floured tube pan. Gently press nuts on top, covering the entire cake. Bake at 350 degrees for 1 hour and 15 minutes. Do not overbake. Good to omit nuts.

*Bin and Pat Goolsby: Douglas '66*
*Tom and Frances Fee: Carol '63*

---

**Happy is the house that shelters a friend.**

# GERMAN CHOCOLATE POUND CAKE

1 package German chocolate,
   softened
2 cups sugar
1 cup shortening
4 eggs
3 cups flour

1/2 teaspoon soda
1 teaspoon salt
1 cup buttermilk
2 teaspoons vanilla
2 teaspoons butter flavoring

Soften chocolate in double boiler. Set aside. Cream sugar, shortening, and eggs. Mix dry ingredients and add to creamed mixture alternately with buttermilk. Add flavorings and German chocolate. Blend well.

Bake in greased and floured tube or Bundt pan at 300 degrees for 1-1/2 hours. Remove from pan. While still hot, place under tightly fitting cover until thoroughly cool. Tastes great without glaze.

Glaze:
1 (4-ounce) package German
   chocolate, softened
1 tablespoon oleo

1 cup powdered sugar
Dash of salt
1/2 teaspoon vanilla

Melt over low heat; spread on cake.

*Boyd and Lillian Field: Eleanor '56*

# NORWEGIAN POUND CAKE

4 eggs
2 cups sugar
1/2 cup brown sugar
1 stick oleo
1/2 cup Crisco
2-1/2 cups flour

1/4 teaspoon salt
1 teaspoon baking powder
1 cup sweet milk
1 can Angel Flake coconut
1 cup pecans
1 teaspoon vanilla

Cream eggs, sugar, and shortening. Mix dry ingredients and add alternately with milk. Fold in coconut, pecans, and vanilla. Bake 1 hour and 15 minutes or 1-1/2 hours at 350 degrees.

*Dean and Alice Crawley: Kelly '71*

The path to a friend's house is never far.

# OLD FASHIONED POUND CAKE

2 sticks butter
2 cups sugar
6 eggs
1 teaspoon vanilla

1 tablespoon lemon juice,
  optional
1/4 teaspoon salt
2 cups flour

Cream butter and sugar; add eggs one at a time; beat. Add flavorings. Sift flour and salt and add. Pour into greased and floured Bundt pan. Place in cold oven; set at 350 degrees and bake 1 hour or until lightly brown.

*Note:* May bake in hot oven set at 325 degrees and bake 1 hour and 15 minutes.

*Variation:* Add 1 can coconut and omit lemon juice.

*Jess and Opal Lowther: Jimmy '49*

# SOUR CREAM POUND CAKE

2 sticks oleo
3 cups sugar
6 eggs
1 cup sour cream
3 cups flour

1/4 teaspoon soda
1/2 teaspoon salt
1 teaspoon vanilla OR 1 to 2
  teaspoons lemon extract OR
  1/2 teaspoon almond extract

Cream oleo and sugar together. Add eggs one at a time, beating after each addition. Add sour cream and beat well. Sift flour, soda, and salt together and add to first mixture (1/2 cup at a time). Beat well. Add one of the listed flavorings and mix. Bake in greased and floured Bundt pan at 325 degrees for 1-1/2 hours.

*Variation:* Separate eggs. Add yolks and beat into mixture. At the last, add stiffly beaten egg whites to batter and bake.

*G.B. and Lois Pilgrim: Ann '51*
*Paul and Phyllis Jordan: Richard '61*

**Small deeds done are better
than great deeds planned!**

# PINEAPPLE POUND CAKE

1 package Butter Recipe Cake
  Mix
1 package Pineapple Instant
  Pudding Mix

3/4 cup warm water
1 stick oleo
1/4 cup oil
6 eggs

Mix cake mix, pudding mix, water, oleo, and oil. Mix well. Add eggs one at a time and beat well. Beat until smooth. Pour into greased and floured Bundt pan. Bake at 350 degrees for 35 to 45 minutes. Remove from oven and glaze.

Glaze:
1 (8-ounce) can crushed
  pineapple, undrained

1 cup powdered sugar
1/4 cup water

Mix pineapple, sugar, and water; heat to spreading consistency. Spread over warm cake.

*James and Carolyn Abney: James '71 ; Sherry '72; Angela '75*

# TEXAS POUND CAKE

6 eggs
3 sticks, butter
1 pound box powdered sugar

1 powdered sugar box of flour
Pinch of salt
1 teaspoon vanilla

Combine and beat eggs and butter. Add 1 box of powdered sugar. Fill empty sugar box with flour and add to creamed mixture. Add salt and vanilla. Mix thoroughly. Pour into greased and floured Angel Food pan and bake at 325 degrees for 1 hour and 25 minutes.

*Charles and Annette Clevenger: Jackie '76*

# RUM CAKE

1 cup pecans, chopped
1 box Duncan Hines Golden
  Butter Cake Mix
1 package Instant Vanilla
  Pudding Mix (3-3/4 ounces)
4 eggs
1/2 cup Bacardi rum

1/2 cup water
1/2 cup cooking oil
Glaze:
1 stick oleo
1 cup sugar
1/4 cup rum
1/4 cup water

Grease and flour a Bundt or tube pan. Sprinkle nuts on bottom of pan. Mix cake and pudding mix; add eggs and liquids. Beat 3 minutes or until thoroughly mixed. Pour into pan and bake at 325 degrees for 50 to 60 minutes. Mix glaze ingredients and boil 3 minutes. Pour hot glaze over cake and leave in pan for 1 hour before removing.

*Bill and Mary Moren: Bryce King '68; Leighton Moren '78*

# SAD CAKE

1 stick oleo
1 box brown sugar
4 eggs, beaten well
2 cups Bisquick

1 cup chopped pecans
1 can coconut
1 teaspoon vanilla

Cream oleo and brown sugar. Add eggs, biscuit mix, pecans, coconut, and vanilla. Bake in greased and floured 9x13" pan, in 350 degrees oven for 30 to 35 minutes. Serve plain or with whipped cream.

*Oran and Louis Price: Judy '54*

# 7-UP CAKE

3 cups sugar
2 sticks oleo
1/2 cup cooking oil
5 eggs

3 cups flour
1 tablespoon butter flavoring
1 teaspoon vanilla
1 (7-ounce) bottle 7-Up

Cream sugar, oleo, and oil. Fold in eggs, one at a time, and beat. Fold in sifted flour, flavorings, and 7-Up. Bake in greased and floured tube pan at 325 degrees for 1 hour and 15 minutes or until done. *Variation:* Use 3 teaspoons lemon flavoring instead of other flavorings.

*Virgil and Bert Coffee: Larry '58*

# BAKELESS SNOWBALL CAKE

2 envelopes Knox gelatin
4 tablespoons water
1 cup boiling water
Juice of 1 lemon
1 cup sugar

1 large can crushed pineapple,
    drained (save)
1 can coconut
3 envelopes Dream Whip
1 large Angel Food Cake

Dissolve gelatin in 4 tablespoons water. Stir into boiling water. Add lemon juice, sugar, and pineapple juice. Chill. Prepare 2 envelopes of Dream Whip. Stir in pineapple and coconut. Blend all together. Break cake into small pieces. Lightly butter an oblong pan; alternate layers start with cake and then mixture. End with mix on top. Whip other package of Dream Whip and spread on top. Top this with coconut and chill overnight. DELICIOUS!

*J.F. and Martha Wright: Ronnie '64*

Out of the abundance of the heart,
the mouth speaketh.
— Matthew 12:34

# SOCK IT TO ME CAKE

1 box Yellow Butter Cake Mix
(Duncan Hines)
1/2 cup sugar
1 cup sour cream
2/3 cup Wesson oil

4 eggs
2 teaspoons cinnamon
2 tablespoons brown sugar
1/2 cup chopped pecans

Combine first 4 ingredients and blend well. Add eggs, one at a time, beating after each addition. Pour 1/2 batter into greased and floured tube pan. Combine filling ingredients and sprinkle over batter. Add remaining batter. Bake in 350 degree oven for 50 to 60 minutes. Cool 10 minutes and remove from pan. Icing, optional.

Icing:
1 cup powdered sugar
2 tablespoons milk

1 teaspoon vanilla
2 tablespoons butter, melted

Mix well and spread over cake.

This is one of the best cakes I've ever baked!

*Mrs. Helen Hudman: Richard '70*

# SODA CRACKER CAKE

3 egg whites
1 cup sugar
1/4 teaspoon cream of tartar

18 crushed crackers
1 teaspoon vanilla
1 cup pecans, chopped

Beat egg whites; add other ingredients. Bake for 30 minutes at 350 degrees.

Topping:
1 small can crushed pineapple

1 carton whipped cream
1 cup coconut

Mix all ingredients and pour on top of cake.

*George and Beatrice Pendleton: Sammy '52*
*(submitted by: Gloria Pendleton, sister-in-law)*

**Mother's run on love, patience, grit, and an occasional night out!**

# STRAWBERRY JELL-O CAKE

| | |
|---|---|
| 1 package White Cake Mix (that calls for eggs) | 1/2 cup water |
| | 3 eggs |
| 1 box strawberry gelatin | 1 small box frozen strawberries |
| 1/2 cup vegetable oil | |

Add gelatin to cake. Add vegetable oil, and water; blend together. Add eggs and 3/4 package of frozen strawberries (saving 1/4 package for icing). Beat as directed on prepared cake mix box. Bake in 300 degree oven in layers or as sheet cake until done.

| Icing: | 1 stick oleo |
|---|---|
| 1 box powdered sugar | 1/4 package strawberries |

Blend together and ice cake.

DELICIOUS!

*Variation:* Bake in greased and floured tube pan at 350 degrees for 50 to 60 minutes.

| Glaze: | Strawberry juice |
|---|---|
| 1 cup powdered sugar | |

Punch holes into hot cake with ice pick or fork. Pour glaze over hot cake. Return to oven 5 minutes. Cool.

*Bill and Marilyn Wheeler: Bryan '68*

# VANILLA WAFER CAKE

| | |
|---|---|
| 2 sticks oleo | 1/2 cup milk |
| 2 cups sugar | 1 (7-ounce) package flaked |
| 6 eggs | coconut |
| 1 (12-ounce) box Vanilla Wafers, crushed | 1 cup chopped pecans |

Cream butter and sugar; gradually add beaten eggs, one at a time to the creamed mixture. Add crushed wafers, coconut, and nuts alternately with milk. Pour batter into greased and floured tube pan and bake at 325 degrees for 1 hour and 15 minutes or until done.

*Stanley and Brenda Morris: Kim '80*
*Julius and Herta Fuhrman (grandparents) David '68*

---

**It is not fair to ask of others what you
are not willing to do yourself.
— Eleanor Roosevelt**

# WACKY CAKE

3 cups flour
2 cups sugar
4 tablespoons cocoa
2 teaspoons soda
1 teaspoon salt

3/4 cups Wesson oil
2 tablespoons vinegar
2 cups cold water
2 teaspoons vanilla

Sift first 5 ingredients into mixing bowl. Add oil, vinegar, cold water, and vanilla. Beat until smooth. Pour into greased and floured 9x13" pan and bake at 350 degrees for 25 to 30 minutes.

*Note:* CAN JUST MIX ALL TOGETHER AND BAKE!

*Marlow and Martha Summitt: Sherri '70*
*G.C. and Nadine Black: Gerome '65; Trudee '67*

# WON'T LAST LONG CAKE

3 cups flour
2 cups sugar
1 teaspoon soda
1 teaspoon salt
1 teaspoon cinnamon
2 cups bananas mashed (4
    medium)

1 small flat can crushed
    pineapple, undrained (in
    heavy syrup)
1-1/3 cup oil
1 teaspoon vanilla
3 beaten eggs
1 cup nuts

Mix first 5 dry ingredients. Add other ingredients in order. Mix well. DO NOT BEAT! Bake 1 hour; 20 minutes at 325 degrees in a greased and floured bundt pan. Grease with Crisco (Pam will not work.)

*Note:* This cake is new and it is real good and moist.

*Wayne and Ola Mitchell: Troy '52; Joyce '59*

# WORKING-GIRL CAKE

1 can crushed pineapple
1 can Cherry Pie filling
1 box Yellow Cake Mix

1-1/2 sticks butter
1-1/2 cups chopped pecans

Pour pineapple in bottom of oblong cake pan. Spoon Cherry Pie filling on top of pineapple. (DO NOT MIX.) Sprinkle dry Yellow Cake mix on top of pie filling. Melt butter and pour over top of cake mix, then add chopped pecans to the top of the cake. Bake at 350 degrees for 45 minutes or until done.

*Jonnie and Linda Miller: Jana '84*

**Malice sucks up the greatest part of its own venom,
and poisons itself.**

# YUMMY CAKE

| | |
|---|---|
| 1 box Yellow Cake Mix | 3/4 cup cooking oil |
| 1 box Pineapple OR Vanilla | 4 well-beaten eggs |
| Instant Pudding Mix | 1 (10-ounce) Lemon-lime soda |

Mix all ingredients except soda water. Add it last and beat well. Bake in greased and floured 9x13" pan at 350 degrees for 40 minutes.

| | |
|---|---|
| **Icing:** | 1 stick oleo |
| 3 eggs, beaten | 1 cup crushed pineapple |
| 1-1/2 cups sugar | 1 small can coconut |
| 2 tablespoons flour | |

Cook eggs, sugar, flour, and oleo over medium heat until thickened. Add pineapple and coconut. Pour over cake while still hot.

*Curtis and Joyce Nix: Carol '68*

# TOLL HOUSE CUPCAKES

| | |
|---|---|
| 1/2 cup oleo | 1 egg |
| 6 tablespoons sugar | 1 cup and 2 tablespoons flour |
| 6 tablespoons brown sugar, | 1/2 teaspoon soda |
| packed | 1/2 teaspoon salt |
| 1/2 teaspoon vanilla | |

Combine in bowl oleo, sugar, brown sugar, and vanilla. Beat until creamy. Beat in egg. Sift dry ingredients. Mix. Spoon into paper lined 2-1/2" cupcake cups, using 1 tablespoon for each. Bake at 350 degrees for 10 to 12 minutes.

| | |
|---|---|
| **Topping:** | 1 (6-ounce) package chocolate |
| 1/2 cup brown sugar, packed | chips |
| 1 egg | 1/2 cup chopped nuts |
| 1/8 teaspoon salt | 1/2 teaspoon vanilla |

Combine in bowl the sugar, egg, and salt. Beat until thick and lemon colored. Stir in chocolate chips, nuts, and vanilla. Mix. Spread on cupcakes while warm.

*Bill and Ruth Wyche: Nancy '58*

Bloom where you are planted.

# YUMMY CHOCOLATE NUT CUPCAKES

4 squares Baker's Semi-Sweet
  Chocolate
2 sticks oleo
1-1/2 cups chopped pecans,
  optional
1/4 teaspoon butter flavoring

1/4 teaspoon salt
1 cup flour
1-3/4 cups sugar
4 eggs
1 teaspoon vanilla

Melt chocolate and oleo. Cool slightly; add pecans and butter flavoring. Mix dry ingredients and add with eggs and vanilla. Mix well but DO NOT BEAT. Bake in greased muffin tins at 325 degrees for about 30 to 40 minutes or until lightly brown. Makes 18 cupcakes.

*Eddie and Betty McNett: Becky '82*

# CHOCOLATE CHIP ICING

1 small can Carnation milk
2 cups sugar
1 stick oleo

1 package chocolate chips
1 tablespoon butter

Combine milk and sugar and place over heat. When bubbles form, cook 5 minutes. Pour over oleo and chocolate chips. Add butter and stir. Spread over cake.

*Luther and Jesse Swift: Nancy '63*

# COCONUT PECAN FROSTING
### *(For Chocolate Cake)*

1 cup evaporated milk
1 cup sugar
3 egg yolks
1 stick oleo

1 teaspoon vanilla
1-1/3 cups coconut
1 cup chopped pecans

Combine milk, sugar, egg yolks, butter, and vanilla in a saucepan. Cook over medium heat, stirring constantly, until mixture thickens, about 12 minutes. Remove from heat. Add coconut and pecans. Beat until cool and spreading consistency. Use on chocolate cakes.

*Lowell Whisenant: '53*

**The only certain happiness in life
is to live for others.**

# HARD SAUCE
### *(for Prune Cake)*

Make in double boiler.

1/2 cup sugar
1 tablespoon cornstarch
1 cup boiling water

Salt
2 tablespoons butter
Vanilla

Mix sugar and cornstarch; add water and pinch of salt. Boil in double boiler until thick and clear. Continue cooking over hot water for 20 minutes. Beat in butter and vanilla. Use hot over PRUNE CAKE or any other cake.

*Note:* Can store in covered jar in refrigerator; take out when ready to use, heat and use hot over cakes.

*Ike and Betty Whitehead: Ginger '64*

# PEANUT BUTTER SAUCE

2/3 cup sugar
3 level tablespoons flour
1-1/2 cups milk

2 tablespoons oleo
2 tablespoons peanut butter
1/2 teaspoon vanilla

Mix sugar and flour. Heat milk to boiling point; add sugar mixture. Cook until thick. Add oleo and peanut butter. Beat well with mixer. Add vanilla. This sauce is good for cake and muffins.

*George and Mozelle Abee: Glynda Clark '56*

# PINEAPPLE CAKE FILLING

1 small can crushed pineapple,
  undrained
1/2 cup sugar

1 to 2 tablespoons flour
1 beaten egg

Mix all ingredients; bring to boil. Thicken. Spread on cake.

*Carl and Thelma Dunaway: Jimmy '59; Patsy '60*

**Along life's way...
take time to smell the flowers.**

# APPLE PIE

6 medium tart apples (or use
 canned apples)
1-1/2 cups sugar
3 tablespoons flour
1/4 teaspoon salt

1/2 teaspoon cinnamon
1 teaspoon vanilla
2 tablespoons butter
1/4 cup sugar
1 double pie crust

Slice and dice peeled apples; mix with sugar thoroughly. Mix and add dry ingredients; add vanilla. Pour into unbaked pie shell and dot with butter. Adjust top crust and flute edges. Brush top with milk or cream and sprinkle with 1/4 cup sugar. Bake 10 minutes at 450 degrees, then reduce to 350 degrees and bake 45 minutes.

*Marlow and Martha Summitt: Sherri '70*

# FRENCH APPLE PIE

Make pastry for 9" pie and place in refrigerator.

6 cooking apples, pared and
 sliced thinly
2/3 cup white sugar
1 teaspoon cinnamon

2 tablespoons flour
Dash of nutmeg
Dash of cloves

Peel apples; mix remaining ingredients and coat apples thoroughly. Mix and arrange in pie shell.

Topping:
1 stick oleo

1/2 cup brown sugar
1 cup flour

Mix butter and sugar. Work in flour for crumb mixture. Sprinkle on apples. Bake 15 minutes at 450 degrees; reduce temperature to 350 degrees and continue baking for 30 minutes.

*Note:* This pie can be made by using 1 can of Comstock pie apples and using 3/4 cup sugar. Follow same directions as above recipe.

*Chauncey and Marguerite Critz: Carolyn '66*

# APPLE SOUR CREAM PIE

1 beaten egg
2/3 cup sugar
1/2 cup brown sugar
1 cup sour cream

1/2 cup raisins
7 medium apples, sliced thin
1 (9") double crust

Combine egg, sugar, brown sugar, and sour cream. Stir in apples and raisins. Turn into unbaked pastry shell; add pastry top. Seal edges and flute. Bake at 400 degrees for 50 minutes or until done, covering with foil during last 15 minutes.

*John and Wanda Lee: David '74*

# APRICOT CREAM PIE

| | |
|---|---|
| 1 baked pie crust | 2 tablespoons butter |
| 1/2 cup sugar | 3 eggs, separated |
| 3 tablespoons cornstarch | 1 tablespoon lemon juice |
| 1/4 teaspoon salt | 1 cup apricot pulp, cooked |
| 1-3/4 cups milk | Meringue |

Mix sugar and cornstarch in top of double boiler. Add salt, milk, and butter and stir over hot water until thick and smooth. Add beaten egg yolks (a little at a time) and lemon juice to double boiler. Cook 3 or 4 minutes. Stir while cooking. Cool and pour into crust. Cover with apricot pulp. Top with meringue and bake until brown.

*O.F. and Edith Hamilton: Linda '61 (submitted by Linda H. Holder)*

# BANANA-BLUEBERRY PIE

*(Furr's)*

| | |
|---|---|
| 1/4 cup sugar | 1 can blueberries |
| 1/4 teaspoon salt | 1 teaspoon lemon juice, optional |
| 1-1/2 tablespoons flour | Whipped cream, sweetened |
| 1/8 teaspoon nutmeg | Sliced bananas |
| 1/8 teaspoon cinnamon | 1 baked pie shell |

Mix dry ingredients in saucepan and add blueberries. Cook until thick; cool. Pour into cool baked pie shell. Before serving, top with sliced bananas and sweetened whipped cream.

*Kenneth and Mary Sacke: Schaun '66; Corbi '70*

# BLUEBERRY CHEESE CAKE/PIE

*(Choice Recipe)*

| | |
|---|---|
| 1 Graham Cracker crust | 1 large can blueberries, drained; |
| 2 (8-ounce) packages cream | reserve juice |
| cheese, softened | 1/4 cup sugar |
| 2 eggs, well beaten | 2 tablespoons flour |
| 1/2 cup sugar | 1 tablespoon lemon juice |
| 1 teaspoon vanilla | 2 cups whipped cream |

Make Graham Cracker crust according to directions. Press into a 9x11" pan. Mix cream cheese, eggs, sugar, and vanilla; pour over crust. Bake 20 minutes at 325 degrees. Drain berries; add juice to sugar, flour, and lemon juice. Cook until thick; cool. Add berries. Pour over the first mixture and place in refrigerator for a few hours. Serve with sweetened whipped cream. Serves 12.

*George and Evelyn Clements: Donna: '62*

# BUTTERFINGER PIE

3 Butterfinger candy bars
1 quart soft vanilla ice cream

1 (9") Graham Cracker crust
Hot fudge sauce

Crush butterfingers; mix well with softened ice cream. Fold mixture into pie crust. Top with fudge sauce. Refrigerate until ready to serve.

*Note:* You may use chocolate crust.

*Jack and Gaynell Gregg: Joey '68*

# BUTTERMILK PIE

3 eggs, well beaten
2 cups sugar (less sweet, 1-1/2 cups)
3 tablespoons flour
1 stick butter or oleo

1 cup buttermilk
1 or 2 teaspoons vanilla
Dash of nutmeg
1 (unbaked) pie shell

*Variation No. 1:* Add 3 tablespoons lemon juice or 1 teaspoon lemon extract along with vanilla.

*Variation No. 2:* Add 1 cup coconut to mixture. Double the recipe and bake two. Eat one and freeze one. DO NOT REFRIGERATE (makes crust soggy). Reduce sugar to 3 cups for 2 pies.

*Walter and Odessa Reamy: Nola Mae '52; Jackie '53*
*Gerald and Shirley McCaskill: Kathlleen '63; Danny '65; David '67*
*Willard and Loudine Turner: Alan '72*
*M.O. and Newell Woolam: Marie '53*

# CANTALOUPE PIE

*(Makes 2 pies)*

2 baked pie shells
2-1/2 to 3 cups diced cantaloupe
6 egg yolks
6 tablespoons flour

1-1/2 cups sugar
2-1/2 cups canned milk
2 teaspoons vanilla
1 stick oleo

Cover diced cantaloupe with water and cook until tender. Drain excess juice off and measure 2-1/2 to 3 cups. Pour into large saucepan add milk and other ingredients (except vanilla and oleo). Cook until thick; add vanilla and oleo. Pour into baked pie shells. Top with meringue (made with egg whites) and brown in moderate oven.

*Teacher's Pet: Gene Young*

---

**In youth we learn; in age we understand.**

# CARAMEL PIE

| | |
|---|---|
| 1 cup sugar | 4 tablespoons flour |
| 3 eggs | 1 teaspoon vanilla |
| 1-1/2 cups milk | 1 cup pecans, chopped |

Brown or caramelize 1/2 cup of the sugar; add enough oleo and water to melt (just a very small amount). Mix remaining ingredients. Stir and cook over medium heat until consistency to pour into baked pie shell. Makes 2 small pies.

*Teacher's Pet: Aunt Lora*

# CHERRY PIE
## *(Double Crust)*

| | |
|---|---|
| 1 (9") pie shell | 3-1/2 cups (2-pound can) red sour |
| 1 cup sugar | pitted cherries, drained |
| 1/4 cup flour | 3/4 cup cherry juice |
| | 1/2 teaspoon almond extract |

Mix sugar and flour in saucepan. Stir in cherries, juice, and extract. Cook over medium heat, stirring constantly until mixture boils and thickens. Pour into pie shell; place top crust over filling. Trim and seal. Prick to allow escape of steam. Bake in 400 degree oven for about 30 minutes or until crust is nicely brown.

*Note:* Take same recipe and substitute 1 (No. 2) can of crushed pineapple and thicken.

*Lee Roy and Marie Ward: Bobbie Lee '59*

# CHERRY CREAM CHEESE PIE

| | |
|---|---|
| 1 Graham Cracker crust | 1/3 cup lemon juice |
| 1 (8-ounce) package cream | 1 teaspoon vanilla |
| cheese, softened | 1 can Cherry Pie Filling, chilled |
| 1 can Eagle Brand Milk | 1 cup chopped pecans, optional |

Beat cream cheese until fluffy. Gradually add milk and stir until well blended. Add lemon juice and vanilla. Blend well. Pour into prepared pie crust and chill 2 or 3 hours. Before serving, garnish with Cherry Pie Filling or cherry glaze.

| | |
|---|---|
| Glaze: | 2 tablespoons cornstarch |
| 1 cup drained pitted sour cherries | 1 cup cherry juice |
| 2 tablespoons sugar (I use more) | |

Mix and cook until clear. Spread over creamed mixture.

*V.C. (Buddy) and Dorothy Melton: Evans '58*

# CHERRY NUT PIE

1 can Eagle Brand Milk
Juice of 2 lemons
1 can red pie cherries, drained
2 cups chopped pecans

1/2 pint whipping cream,
   whipped
Few drops red food coloring,
   optional
2 Graham Cracker crusts

Mix and stir Eagle Brand milk and lemon juice until it thickens. Add drained cherries and pecans. Fold in whipped cream. Pour into baked pie shell. Chill several hours.

*Cecil and Willa Hawthorne: Barbara '64*

# BOBBY'S CHOCOLATE PIE

1 cup sugar
4 tablespoons flour
1/4 teaspoon salt
1/3 cup cocoa

2 cups milk
3 eggs, separated
1 tablespoon butter
1 teaspoon vanilla

Mix sugar, flour, salt, and cocoa. Add half (1 cup) milk and mix well. Add rest of milk and cook until thick. Add a little of this mixture to beaten egg yolks a little at a time. Cook about 1 minute longer. Add butter and vanilla. Stir into baked pie shell. Cool; top with egg white meringue.

*Note:* This is really a delicious pie! Filling can be cooked in microwave. Cook and check for desired consistency.

*Johnie and Ruby Ransom: Bobby Joe '54*

# CHOCOLATE CHESS PIE

1 unbaked pie shell
1/2 stick oleo
1-1/2 cups sugar
1 tablespoon flour

1/3 cup cocoa
2 eggs, beaten
1 cup milk
1 teaspoon vanilla

Mix well and pour into pie shell. Bake 35 to 40 minutes at 350 degrees.

*Maurice and Marie Simmons: Jill '65*

**God does not listen to the prayers of the proud.**
**— Hebrew Proverb**

# CHOCOLATE CHIFFON PIE
## (Furr's)

| | |
|---|---|
| 2 baked pie shells | 3/4 cup sugar |
| 3/4 cup sugar | 1 teaspoon vanilla |
| 1/4 cup cocoa | 4 tablespoons cornstarch |
| 1/8 teaspoon salt | 1/4 cup cold water |
| 1-1/2 cups hot water | Whipped cream |
| 1/2 cup egg whites, beaten | Chopped pecans |

Mix first 4 ingredients. While hot, pour over stiffly beaten egg whites that have been beaten with sugar and vanilla. Beat just long enough to mix. Bring to boil and add cornstarch and water. Boil longer until thick. Finish by hand. Pour into baked pie shells and top with whipped cream and chopped pecans.

*Kenneth (Ken) and Mary Sacke: Schaun '66; Corbi '70*

# CHOCOLATE FUDGE PIE

| | |
|---|---|
| 1 stick margarine | 3 tablespoons flour |
| 2 squares Baker's unsweetened | 1 teaspoon vanilla |
| chocolate | 1 cup chopped nuts (more or less |
| 1 cup sugar | to suit your taste) |
| 3 eggs | |

Melt margarine and chocolate together. Add sugar and mix well. Add 1 beaten egg at a time and mix. Add flour and mix well. Add vanilla and nuts. Put in greased and floured 8" pie pan and bake at 325 degrees for 30 to 35 minutes. Top should be dry and shiny and cracked, but don't let it brown too much on bottom and sides. Serve by itself, with ice cream, or with whipped cream.

*Bob and Barbara Knight: Dee Ann '68*

# DUSTY'S MICRO-CHOCOLATE PIE

| | |
|---|---|
| 1 cup sugar | 2 cups milk |
| 2 tablespoons cocoa | 1 teaspoon vanilla |
| 4 tablespoons flour | 1 tablespoon butter |
| 2 egg yolks | |

Mix sugar, cocoa, and flour. Add the rest with mixer. Continue to mix until lumps are gone. Place in microwave for 7 minutes on high. Stir every 2 minutes. Pour into baked pie shell and top with meringue made with 2 egg whites and sugar. Or may top with Cool Whip. Enjoy!

*Ronnie and Janette Rider: Dusty '85*

# BLUE RIBBON
# COCONUT CREAM PIE

| | |
|---|---|
| 1 cup sugar | 3/4 cups chopped dates |
| 1/3 cup flour | 1/2 cup coconut |
| 1/3 teaspoon salt | 1 (9") pie crust |
| 2 cups milk | Meringue: |
| 3 egg yolks, slightly beaten | 3 egg whites |
| 1 tablespoon butter | 1/4 teaspoon cream of tartar |
| 1 teaspoon vanilla | 6 tablespoons sugar |

Combine sugar, flour, and salt. Gradually stir in milk. Cook and stir over medium heat until mixture thickens. Stir a small amount of hot mixture into egg yolks; return to hot mixture; cook 2 minutes longer. Remove from heat. Add butter, vanilla, dates, and coconut. Stir until well blended. Pour into baked pie crust. Top with meringue.

To make meringue, beat egg whites with cream of tartar until soft peaks form. Gradually add sugar, beating until stiff peaks form and sugar is dissolved. Spread on top of pie, taking care to seal edges. Bake about 12 to 15 minutes in a 350 degree oven or until meringue is a golden brown.

*Note:* This pie tastes great in a pecan crust! (Pie crust follows.)

*Emory and Suzanne Smith: Christy '78*

# PECAN PIE CRUST

| | |
|---|---|
| 1/2 cup butter or margarine | 1 cup flour |
| 1/4 cup brown sugar | 1/2 cup chopped pecans |

Preheat oven to 450 degrees. Cream butter and sugar. Add flour and pecans. Spread in 9x13" pan. Bake 15 minutes. Take from oven and stir into a crumbly mixture. Press crumbs against bottom and sides of 9" pan.

*Emory and Suzanne Smith: Christy '78*

Sunshine and smiles
don't care whose life they brighten.

# EASY COBBLER PIE

Filling:
1 large can fruit

1 cup water
Sugar to taste

Put fruit on to cook with plenty of juice. Let come to a boil.

Crust:
1 stick oleo
1 cup flour
1 cup sugar

1/4 teaspoon salt
1 teaspoon cinnamon
1/2 cup milk
1 teaspoon baking powder

Melt oleo in baking dish. Mix above ingredients to make a cake-like batter. Spread over oleo. Pour fruit over batter. Bake at 350 degrees for 45 minutes. Crust will come to top and brown. It's delicious and can be used with any kind of fruit.

*T.E. and Ruby Reynolds: Betty '54*
*Jimmy Faye Todd (Sullivan): '49*

# CHOCOLATE MOUSSE PIE

1/2 cup butter or oleo
3/4 cup sugar
2 eggs

2 (1-ounce) squares unsweetened
chocolate, melted and cooled
1 (4-1/2 ounce) carton Cool Whip
1 Graham Cracker pie shell

Cream oleo and sugar until fluffy. Add eggs one at a time, beating 5 minutes after each addition. Add chocolate and mix. Fold in Cool Whip and spoon into Graham Cracker crust. Top with chocolate shavings. Serve frozen.

*Donald and Dee Cox: Cary '85*

# FRENCH COCONUT PIE

1 unbaked pie shell
3 eggs, beaten
1-1/2 cups sugar
1 stick oleo (scant)

1 teaspoon vanilla
1 tablespoon vinegar
1 can coconut

Beat eggs very little; add remaining ingredients and pour into unbaked pie shell. Bake at 350 degrees for about 1 hour.

*Note:* Brush a little egg white on the unbaked pie shell and bake at 400 degrees for about 1 minute. This prevents soggy crusts.

*Johnie and Ruby Ransom: Bobby Joe '54*

It is not only fine feathers
that make fine peacocks.

## ICE BOX COCONUT PIE

1 (8") Graham Cracker crust
1 (3-ounce) package cream
   cheese, softened
2 tablespoons sugar
1/2 cup milk

1-1/3 cups coconut
1 (8-ounce) carton Cool Whip
2 teaspoons lemon extract OR 1
   teaspoon vanilla

Combine cream cheese, sugar, milk, and coconut in electric blender. Blend on medium speed for 30 seconds. Fold into whipped topping and add extract. Spoon into crust and freeze until firm (about 4 hours). Sprinkle with additional toasted coconut. Let set at room temperature 5 minutes before cutting.

*Bill and Vida Pinkston: Janis '64; Billy '67*

## CREAM PIES

1/3 cup + 1 tablespoon flour
2/3 cup sugar
1/4 teaspoon salt
2 cups milk (I substitute 1/2 cup
   Pet for 1/2 cup milk for richer
   filling.)

3 egg yolks, slightly beaten
3 tablespoons butter
1 tablespoon vanilla
Meringue (see recipe)
1 (9") baked pie shell

Mix flour, sugar, and salt; gradually add 1-1/2 cups scalded milk and cook on low heat until thick, stirring constantly. (This can be cooked in microwave too, just stir as needed.) Beat 3 egg yolks in 2 cup measure; add remaining 1/2 cup milk and gradually add to the hot mixture. Return to low heat and boil 2 minutes, or to desired thickness. Add butter and vanilla and cool while making meringue.

**Meringue:**
3 egg whites

**9 tablespoons sugar**

Beat egg whites until very stiff; add 9 tablespoons sugar (adding 1 tablespoon at a time) and continue beating. Pour filling into 9" baked pie shell; spread with meringue. Bake in 300 degree oven (very low heat) for 30 to 45 minutes, or until golden brown. Cool on rack.

**Variations of Cream Pie:**

*Chocolate:* Increase sugar to 1 cup; melt two (2) 1 ounce squares Hersheys unsweetened chocolate in the scalded milk. It will melt on low heat without being grated.

*Coconut:* Add 1 cup moist shredded coconut to cooled filling. Sprinkle 1/2 cup coconut over meringue before browning and reduce oven temperature.

*Pineapple:* Add 1/2 cup well-drained crushed pineapple to cooled filling.

*William (Bill) and Sammie Jo Manes: Glenna '60; Paula '64*

# CUSTARD PIE

*Note:* Make homemade regular pie dough and cover pie pan thin. (Some regular bought pie crusts are too stiff.)

2 eggs, beaten well
1 pint milk; maybe a little more

1-1/2 teaspoons vanilla
1/2 to 1 cup sugar (to suit taste)

Beat eggs; add milk, vanilla, and sugar. Put mixture in the uncooked pie shell. Cook slowly until thick and done, and that's your real homemade custard pie.

*James and Flo Whitcomb: Janet '53*

# EMPANADAS

2 pounds Gold Medal Flour
1 pound Crisco

1 can beer
Cinnamon and sugar mixture

Cut flour and Crisco; add beer to make dough. Roll dough out and cut into circles with cutter (or make the size you choose). Fill one half side of circle with preserves; fold over to make a half circle. Crimp edges together with fork. Bake at 350 degrees for about 20 minutes on cookie sheet. Coat in cinnamon and sugar mixture while hot. (Good for parties.) Crisp and flaky.

*Henry (Shorty) and Petra (Mary) Luna: Celia '55 (submitted by Celia Luna Fuente)*

# FRUIT PIES

*(Makes 3)*

3 Graham Cracker crusts
1 can Pineapple Pie Filling
1 can Cherry Pie Filling

1 small box orange Jello*
1 cup chopped pecans
3 or 4 sliced bananas

Mix and heat pie mixes. Add jello and set aside to cool. Add pecans and sliced bananas. Mix all together. Pour into baked pie shells or Graham Cracker crusts.

*Note:* May use large orange jello and 4 or 5 bananas.

**Graham Cracker Crusts:**

(One box of Graham Cracker crumbs is just enough for the 3 pies.)

1 box Graham Cracker crumbs
3/4 cup soft butter

3/4 cup sugar

Mix well and press in pie pans.

*Walter and Millie Miller: Tommy '62; Jimmy '66*
*T.O. and Lorene Tyner: Paula '53*

## GERMAN SWEET CHOCOLATE PIE

1 (4-ounce) package German
   sweet chocolate
1/4 cup butter
1-2/3 cups (14-ounce can)
   evaporated milk
1-1/2 cups sugar

3 tablespoons cornstarch
1/8 teaspoon salt
2 eggs, beaten
1 teaspoon vanilla
1-1/2 cups coconut
1/2 cup chopped pecans

Melt chocolate and butter over low heat, stirring until blended. Remove from heat; gradually blend in milk. Mix sugar, cornstarch, and salt thoroughly. Beat in eggs and vanilla. Pour into pie shell. Combine coconut and nuts; sprinkle over filling. Bake at 375 degrees for 45 minutes. Filling will be soft, but will set when cooled. Cool at least 4 hours before cutting. Makes 1 (10") pie or 2 (8").

*James and Toloah Bray: Linda '61*
*Luther and Jesse Swift: Nancy '63*

## HAWAIIAN PIE

### (Very Simple)

3 eggs
1-1/2 cups sugar
1 stick oleo

1 small can crushed pineapple
1 can coconut
2 tablespoons flour

Mix and pour into unbaked pie shell. Bake at 350 degrees for 1 hour.

*L. R. and Rita Hill: Donna '78*

## HERSHEY PIE

1 pie shell, make with pecans in
   crust
18 regular size marshmallows
5 plain Hershey bars

1/2 cup milk
1/2 pint whipping cream,
   whipped

Melt marshmallows, Hersheys, and milk. Cool — VERY COOL — until gooey thick. Add whipped cream and pour into cool pie shell. Freeze and when ready to serve, thaw short time and top with whipped cream.

*Tom and Alice Hood: Pam '52*

He that lieth down with dogs
shall rise up with fleas.
— **Poor Richard's Almanac**

# LEMON PIE
## *(Excellent)*

2 cups sugar
2 heaping tablespoons flour
2 heaping tablespoons cornstarch

4 egg yolks, with a little water
1 tablespoon butter
Juice of 2 or 3 lemons

Mix sugar, flour, cornstarch, and egg yolks. Mix well; cook in double boiler until thick. Add butter and lemon juice after pie filling is done. Beat well. Pour into 9" baked pie shell. Make meringue from well beaten egg whites.

*Mrs. George Abee (Mozelle) Glynda Clark '56*

# LEMON BLENDER PIE

1 large (8-ounce) package cream
    cheese, room temperature
1 can Eagle Brand Milk

1/2 cup lemon juice
1 teaspoon vanilla
1 can Cherry Pie filling

Pour first 4 ingredients into blender. Blend.
Pour into Graham Cracker crust. Cover with Cherry Pie filling.

*Earl and Janice Slayton: Jack '56*

# LEMON CHESS PIE

2 cups sugar
1 tablespoon flour
1 tablespoon cornmeal
4 eggs, beaten
1/4 cup sweet milk

1/4 cup melted oleo
1/4 cup lemon juice
3 tablespoons grated lemon rind,
    optional

Sift sugar, flour, and cornmeal. Add remaining ingredients. Beat until smooth. Pour into unbaked pie shell and bake in 350 degree oven until set and lightly browned (about 35 to 40 minutes).

*James and Nell Reeves: Joyce '53*

**Trying times are times for trying!**

# LEMON MERINGUE PIE
## (Very Good)

2 cups hot water
6 tablespoons cornstarch
1/4 teaspoon salt
1 cup sugar
3 egg yolks

1/2 cup lemon juice (or less)
1 teaspoon lemon rind
2 tablespoons butter
Meringue

Mix water, cornstarch, salt, and 1/2 cup of the sugar. Cook in double boiler until thick, stirring well. Beat egg yolks with other 1/2 cup of sugar. Pour 1/2 of cornstarch mixture into egg and sugar mixture; stir well. Return to heat and cook 2 minutes longer, stirring. Add lemon juice, lemon rind, and butter. Stir well and let cool, NOT stirring. Spoon into baked pie shell and top with meringue.

**Meringue:**
3 egg whites

6 tablespoons sugar

Beat egg whites until stiff, adding 6 tablespoons sugar gradually as you beat whites. Spread over pie. Brown in moderate oven until meringue is slightly browned. This is good!

*Ike and Betty Whitehead: Ginger '64*

# MILLIONAIRE PIE

1 baked and cooled pie crust
1 cup powdered sugar
1/2 stick oleo, softened
1 egg
1/2 teaspoon vanilla
1/4 teaspoon salt
2 cups whipped topping (Pet Whip or other)

1 (8-ounce) can crushed pineapple, drained
1/2 cup chopped pecans
1 tablespoon milk
1/4 cup Maraschino cherries, chopped (optional)

Cream sugar and softened oleo. Add egg, vanilla, and salt. Beat until smooth and creamy. Spread mixture into baked pie shell. Chill. Combine whipped topping, pineapple, pecans, milk, and cherries until blended. Spread over chilled filling. Chill. Double for 2 pies.

*Jerry and Sue Fox: Sharry '80; Stacy '82*

**Too much rest is rust.**

# MISSISSIPPI MUD PIE

1-1/2 cups sifted powdered sugar
1/3 cup butter
1/2 cup cream
3 envelopes (3-ounce) NESTLE
  CHOCO BAKE unsweetened
  baking chocolate flavor
3 tablespoons light corn syrup

1/4 teaspoon salt
1 teaspoon vanilla
1 deep dish pie shell, baked
1 cup chopped pecans, divided
3 cups coffee ice cream, softened;
  divided
Whipped cream

In saucepan, combine first 6 ingredients. Stir constantly over low heat until mixture is smooth. Stir in vanilla. Cool to room temperature. Spread 1/2 cup sauce on bottom of pie shell. Sprinkle with 1/4 cup nuts. Freeze 10 minutes. Spread 1 cup ice cream (softened) over sauce/nut layer. Freeze 20 minutes. Repeat this procedure twice more. Garnish with whipped cream. Drizzle remaining sauce on top; sprinkle with nuts. Freeze. (Wrap in aluminum foil.) May be frozen 1 week. THIS MAY RUN OVER IN FREEZER SO SET A PLATE UNDER IT.

*John and Pat Hanna: Edward '74*

# OSGOOD PIE

1/2 cup butter or oleo
2 cups sugar
4 eggs, separated
1 teaspoon cinnamon

1 teaspoon nutmeg
1 cup raisins
1 tablespoon vinegar
1 unbaked pie shell

Cream butter and sugar. Separate eggs and beat whites until stiff. Add yolks to creamed mixture and beat well. Blend in spices, raisins, and vinegar. Mix well. Fold in beaten egg whites. Pour into unbaked pie shell. Bake at 425 degrees for 10 minutes; reduce heat to 350 degrees and continue baking for about 45 minutes longer or until done.

*Mrs. Thelma Fennell: Sandra Davis '53*

# PEACH COBBLER

1 large can cling peaches
1 cup sugar

1/2 stick butter (or more)
1 teaspoon nutmeg

Mix the above ingredients in bowl. Make pie crust; roll out on well floured board until fairly thin. Pour cobbler mixture into baking dish and place crust on top of peach mixture. Bake at 425 degrees until brown and bubbly. Double recipe for larger pie. Crust can be cut into strips.

*John and Betty Shumaker: Katherine '82*

# CLARA JANE'S
# UNFORGETTABLE PEACH PIE

4 medium-sized, peeled and
  sliced, real ripe peaches or
  1 can, drained
1/2 teaspoon pure almond extract
1/2 teaspoon pure vanilla extract

1/2 teaspoon mace
1 cup brown sugar, packed
2 teaspoons cornstarch, dissolved
  in water
2 tablespoons water

Mix the peaches with everything else. Pour into best pie shell you can buy or make and bake at 350 degrees for 30 minutes. And pray to God it turns out like hers!

*Remember:* Clara Jane used Watkin's pure vanilla extract, Watkin's pure almond essence, and mace only. She combed her hair with a Watkin's comb and read her Bible 3 times a day. This may have been the secret to the pie. —copied

*R.G. and Lena Holcombe: Jimmy '57*

# SOUR CREAM PEACH PIE

4 cups peeled and sliced peaches
  (7 or 8)
1 cup sugar
5 tablespoons flour
1/8 teaspoon salt

1/2 cup sour cream
1/4 teaspoon cinnamon
1/4 teaspoon nutmeg
1 (9") double crust

Spread peaches in pastry-lined pie pan. Combine sugar (reserving 2 tablespoons), flour, salt, and sour cream. Spread over peaches. Adjust top crust and flute edges. Cut vents in top crust. Mix remaining 2 tablespoons sugar with cinnamon and nutmeg. Sprinkle over top. Bake at 400 degrees for 40 minutes or until peaches are tender and crust is browned.

*Note:* Summer's treat! Peaches and cream under spicy, sparkly, pastry cover.

*Ed and Dorothy Cook: Mike '68; Marcy '75*

# PECAN PIES
## (2 Pies)

1-1/2 cups sugar
1/4 cup flour
1/4 teaspoon salt
1 cup white Karo
1 cup coffee cream

1 teaspoon vanilla
2 eggs, beaten
2 tablespoons melted butter
1 cup coconut
1 cup chopped pecans

Mix dry ingredients; add Karo, cream, vanilla, eggs, and butter. Add coconut and pecans. Bake at 350 degrees for 50 to 60 minutes.

*Teacher's Pet: Pat Spencer*

# PECAN PIE

*(A not-too-sweet version of this "all-time" favorite)*

| | |
|---|---|
| 1 unbaked pie shell | 1 tablespoon flour |
| 3 eggs, beaten | 1 teaspoon vanilla |
| 1/2 cup sugar | 1/4 cup oleo |
| 1 cup white corn syrup | 1 cup broken pecans |
| 1/4 teaspoon salt | |

Beat eggs and sugar. Add other ingredients except pecans. Add pecans and pour into unbaked pie shell. Bake 50 to 60 minutes at 350 degrees.

*Variation:* Pour pecans in bottom of crust, then add filling.

*L.D. and Floy Robertson: Larry '56*
*Ted and Viola Page: Roger '58*
*Wayne Pollard '51*
*Billy and Sylvia Grimes: Rory '66*

# TEA TIME TASSIES

*(Mini Pecan Pies)*

| Crust: | Filling: |
|---|---|
| 1 (3-ounce) cream cheese | 3/4 cup brown sugar |
| 1 stick oleo | 1 tablespoon soft oleo |
| 1 cup flour | 1 egg |
| Pinch of salt | Dash of salt |
| 1/3 cup chopped pecans | 1 teaspoon vanilla |
| | 1/2 cup finely chopped pecans |

Blend together cream cheese and oleo (room temperature). Add remaining ingredients. Blend. Divide dough into 24 equal-sized balls. Chill dough. With fingers, shape each ball into a crust in mini-muffin tins. Mix filling ingredients and fill each crust 3/4 full. Bake at 350 degrees for 15 minutes then 10 minutes at 250 degrees.

*Johnny and Cricket Adams: Suzie '71*
*Kenneth and Nancy Helvey: Valerie '76*

Forgiveness is the ultimate revenge;
Indifference is the ultimate insult.

# SOUTHERN PECAN PIE

| | |
|---|---|
| 1 (9") unbaked pie shell | 1/2 tablespoon flour |
| 4 eggs | 1 teaspoon vanilla |
| 1 cup sugar | 1/4 cup melted butter |
| 1 cup light corn syrup | 2 cups pecan halves |
| 1/2 teaspoon salt | |

Beat eggs well. Add sugar, syrup, salt, flour, and vanilla. Add butter and mix. Beat well. Stir in pecan halves. Pour into unbaked pie shell. Bake for 60 minutes at 350 degrees or until the filling is set in the center. Cool pie completely on a wire rack. Serve.

*Note:* Prepare pie shell and refrigerate while preparing pie.

*Willie and Jean Brown: Jerald '77; Chevela '81*

# PINEAPPLE SOUR CREAM PIE

| | |
|---|---|
| 1 cup sugar | 1 cup sour cream |
| 1/4 cup flour | 1 tablespoon lemon juice |
| 1/2 teaspoon salt | 3 eggs, separated |
| 1 large can (1-pound 4-ounce) crushed pineapple | 2 tablespoons butter |

Combine sugar, flour, salt, and pineapple in saucepan. Add sour cream and lemon juice. Cook until thick. Add beaten egg yolks and butter. Cook until thick; cool. Pour into baked pie shell. Top with meringue made with egg whites.

| | |
|---|---|
| **Meringue:** | 1 teaspoon vanilla |
| 3 egg whites, beaten until frothy | 6 tablespoons sugar |
| 1/4 teaspoon cream of tartar | |

Beat egg whites; add remaining ingredients. Beat stiff. Spread on pie. Brown slightly in oven.

*Ross and Marie Crabtree: Larry '56; Donna '61*

# PUMPKIN PIE

| | |
|---|---|
| 2 eggs | 1/4 teaspoon ginger |
| 1-1/2 cups milk | 1/4 teaspoon cloves |
| 1/3 cup brown sugar | 1/2 teaspoon nutmeg |
| 1/3 cup honey | 1-3/4 cups pumpkins (1 can) |
| 1/2 teaspoon salt | 1 (9") unbaked pie shell |
| 1 teaspoon cinnamon | |

Beat eggs and milk; add sugar and honey. Add salt and spices; then add pumpkin. Blend. Pour into unbaked pie shell and bake at 400 degrees for 15 minutes. Turn oven to 350 degrees for 30 to 40 minutes. Check at 30 minutes.

*O.F. and Edith Hamilton: Linda '61 (submitted by Linda Hamilton Holder)*

## PUMPKIN CHIFFON PIE

1 cooked pie shell
1 cup cooked pumpkin
1/2 cup brown sugar
1/8 teaspoon salt

1-1/4 teaspoons pumpkin pie
    spice
2 cups Cool Whip

Combine all ingredients. Pour into cooled pie shell. Top with whipped cream or Cool Whip.

*Milton and Ann Brumley: Doug '73*

## RHUBARB PIE

Crust:
1 cup flour

1/2 cup sugar
1/2 cup butter

Blend together. Spread in pie pan and cook about 15 minutes at 375 degrees.

Rhubarb Pie Filling:
2-1/4 cups chopped rhubarb,
    cooked
1/2 cup sour cream

3 eggs
1-1/4 cups sugar
2 tablespoons flour

Mix all ingredients in double boiler and cook until thick. Pour into crust and chill. Yummy if you like tart desserts!!

*James and Joyce Guy: Scott '79*

## RITZ CRACKER PIE

20 Ritz crackers, crushed
3 egg whites
1 cup sugar
1 teaspoon baking powder
1 teaspoon vanilla
1 cup chopped nuts

Topping:
1 cup whipping cream
1/2 teaspoon vanilla
4 tablespoons powdered sugar
1/2 cup chopped nuts

Crush Ritz crackers. Beat egg whites until stiff; beat in sugar a little at a time. Add remaining ingredients. Pour into greased pie pan and bake 45 minutes at 325 degrees. Cool. (Best to set several hours.) For topping, whip cream; add other ingredients. Spread on cooled pie.

*Claude and Venice Danley: Chris '69*
*J.D. and Gertrude Lyons: Steven '67*

He that falls in love with himself
will have no rivals.
— Benjamin Franklin

## STRAWBERRY PIE

2 Graham Cracker Crusts
2 eggs, well beaten
1 cup sugar

Juice of 2 lemons
2 (10-ounce) cartons strawberries
2 cups whipping cream, whipped

Combine eggs, sugar, and lemon juice. Cook over medium heat until thickened. Cool. Fold in strawberries and whipped cream. Pile into pie shells. Freeze. Take out of freezer shortly before serving.

*Sam and Billie Hollis: Lynn '63*

## FRESH STRAWBERRY PIE

1 quart fresh sliced strawberries
1-1/3 cups sugar
1/2 cup water
1/4 cup cornstarch
3/4 cup cold water

1/8 teaspoon salt
1 teaspoon lemon juice
Red food coloring, optional
1 (9") baked pie shell

Clean and slice strawberries. Set aside. Bring sugar and 1/2 cup water to boiling point in saucepan over medium heat. Dissolve cornstarch in 3/4 cup cold water. Add cornstarch to syrup mixture. Cook 10 minutes over low heat until clear. Stir often. Blend in salt, lemon juice, and coloring to produce a bright color. Cool thoroughly. Pour glaze over strawberries and mix well. Pour into baked pie shell. Chill. Serve with sweetened whipped cream or Cool Whip.

*D.P. and Betty Thomas: Jerry '57; Betty '59*

## SWEET POTATO PIE
### *(Makes 2 pies)*

2 unbaked pie shells
3 eggs, beaten well
2 cups sugar
1/2 cup butter
1 cup canned milk

2 cups stewed sweet potatoes
1 teaspoon nutmeg (or desired
    amount)
Dash of salt

Beat eggs; add sugar, and butter; mix well. Add remaining ingredients and mix well. Pour into 2 unbaked pie crusts. Bake at 300 degrees for about 1 hour.

*Variation:* May add 1/2 teaspoon each of cinnamon, allspice, and nutmeg for the spices.

*A.L. and Lola Rhodes: Sue '49*

# SWEET POTATO CREAM PIE

1 baked pie shell
1/2 cup finely mashed sweet
   potatoes
1 cup sweet milk
1/2 cup sugar

3 egg yolks
(a little cornstarch, it too thin)
Nutmeg, to taste
A dash of vanilla

Cook and mash potatoes finely. Boil milk, sugar, and egg yolks until thickened somewhat. Mix in potatoes. Add the cornstarch, if needed. Add nutmeg and vanilla to taste. Pour into baked pie shell. Beat egg whites to make meringue. Spread. Brown in 350 degree oven.

*John and Nina Jones: Louise Jones Woolley; Huckaby High School '42*

# VINEGAR PIE

1-3/4 cups water
1/4 cup vinegar

1/2 cup sugar

Mix all together and stir until sugar is dissolved. Make regular pie crust, adding 1/2 teaspoon baking powder (crust should not have as much shortening as regular pie crust). Roll pie dough very thin in oblong shape. Take knife and cut in 3 strips. Dot freely with butter, sprinkle with 1/2 cup sugar and cinnamon and roll up. Press edges together and place in pan (casserole dish) where vinegar mixture is ready. Dot with butter and sprinkle with sugar. Bake until brown at 350 degrees.

*Milburn and Marie Nichols: Keith '65*

# NEVER FAIL PIE CRUST

3 cups flour
1 cup Crisco
2 teaspoons salt

7 tablespoons cold water
1 egg
1 tablespoon vinegar

Cut Crisco and salt into flour. Make a hole in center of dough. Add cold water, beaten egg, and vinegar. Handle as little as possible in working dough. Wrap in foil and store in refrigerator. Use as needed.

*Ross and Marie Crabtree: Larry '56, Donna '61*

Old men are always young enough to learn.

# FRIED PIE DOUGH

5 cups flour
1 cup shortening
1 tablespoon sugar
1-1/2 teaspoons salt

1 teaspoon baking powder
1 tall can milk
2 eggs

Mix together like regular pie crust. Divide into small balls, about the size of golf balls. Roll out very thin. Then place a saucer of desired size on dough. Cut around saucer. Place desired pie filling in middle; dampen edge on half of pie crust, then fold over and crimp along edge. Fry in deep shortening or oil at 375 degrees until brown. The pies are then drained and can be glazed with powdered sugar, water, and vanilla icing.

*Calvin and Zella Withers: Linda '55*

# BAKED FRIED PIE
# DOUGH AND PIES

1 (8-ounce) cream cheese
2 sticks butter

2 cups flour
Fruit fillings

Mix and chill overnight. Roll out dough to the size of a walnut. Cover with small amount of filling (apricot, apple, etc). Seal edges with fork and bake on cookie sheet until brown at 400 degrees.

*Weldon and Mary Ruth Ingram: La Vonne '51*

# PIE CRUST MIX

3 pounds shortening
5 pounds flour

1 quart water
1 teaspoon salt

Cut shortening with flour and salt; add water and knead just enough to make dough. Dough can be put in refrigerator and take off desired amount when you make a pie. (Cafe recipe.)

*Mrs. Rose Ancell-Smith Freddie (Red) '51; Jackie '56*

# PIE CRUST

3 cups flour
1 teaspoon salt
1 teaspoon powdered sugar

1-1/4 cups Crisco
1 egg and enough milk to make
1/2 cup

Mix dry ingredients; cut in half of shortening; blend well. Add remaining ingredients; blend. Beat egg and milk. Add to dry ingredients. Roll on floured board.

This makes an excellent cobbler dough, too. Keeps well in refrigerator 5 to 7 days. (This is my mother's recipe.)

*Fred and Jackie Hobbs: Darrell '66*

# APPLESAUCE-OATMEAL DROP COOKIES

| | |
|---|---|
| 1/2 cup shortening | 1 teaspoon cinnamon |
| 1 cup sugar | 1/2 teaspoon cloves |
| 1 egg | 1/2 teaspoon nutmeg |
| 1-3/4 cups flour | 1/2 cup seedless raisins |
| 1/2 teaspoon baking powder | 1 cup Quick Cooking oats |
| 1 teaspoon soda | 1 cup applesauce |
| 1/2 teaspoon salt | |

Cream shortening and sugar; add egg and mix well. Sift dry ingredients; mix in raisins and oats. Add to creamed mixture alternately with applesauce. Drop by teaspoon onto greased baking sheet. Bake at 375 degrees for 15 minutes. Do not overcook.

*Ted and Dorothy Hibbs: Carolyn '67*

# APRICOT CHEESE PASTRY

| | |
|---|---|
| 1 cup oleo | Apricot preserves |
| 1 (8-ounce) cream cheese, | 1 egg, beaten (yolk and white |
| softened | separated; white not beaten) |
| 1/4 teaspoon salt | Sugar |
| 2 cups flour | |

Cut oleo and cheese into flour and salt mixture until well blended. Lightly shape into one ball. Wrap in wax paper and chill. On floured surface roll dough to 1/8" thickness. Cut into small circles, using a tiny cutter.

Place 1/4 teaspoon apricot preserves in center of circle. Brush edges with slightly beaten egg. Top with another circle. Press edges together with a fork. Brush top with egg white and sprinkle with sugar or use decorator sugar in the colors.

Bake on greased cookie sheet 10 to 12 minutes at 400 degrees.

*Jack and Mary Nell Dodd: Jackie '70*

God made night,
But Man made darkness.
— Spike Milligan

# BROWNIES

| | |
|---|---|
| 2 sticks oleo | 1/4 cup Karo syrup |
| 1/2 cup cocoa | 1-1/2 cups flour |
| 4 eggs, well beaten | 1 teaspoon baking powder |
| 2 cups sugar | 1/2 teaspoon salt |
| 2 teaspoons vanilla | 1 cup chopped pecans |

Melt oleo and cocoa over low heat. Cool; add eggs. Gradually add sugar, vanilla, and syrup. Add mixed dry ingredients and nuts. Pour into greased 9x13" pan. Bake at 350 degrees for 45 minutes. (A good variation is to use 1/2 cup nuts and 1/2 cup coconut.)

| | |
|---|---|
| Brownie Icing: (good for above recipe or just leave plain) | 2 tablespoons cocoa |
| | 1/2 stick oleo |
| 1/2 box powdered sugar | 1/2 teaspoon vanilla |

Mix sugar and cocoa. Melt oleo. Mix all and add vanilla. Spread on brownies.

*Forrest and Vida Scott: Stanley '64; Larry '66; Carl '69*
*Johnny and Janie Swinney: Stephanie '77*

# MARSHMALLOW BROWNIES

| | |
|---|---|
| 2 cups sugar | 2 teaspoons vanilla |
| 1/3 cup cocoa | 1 cup chopped pecans |
| 2 sticks oleo | 1 small jar Marshmallow Creme |
| 4 eggs | or 4 cups miniature |
| 1-1/2 cups flour | marshmallows |

Cream sugar and cocoa with oleo. Add whole eggs, flour, vanilla, and pecans. Beat well. Pour into greased and floured 9x12x2" pan. Bake at 350 degrees for 30 minutes. While still hot in pan, cover with Marshmallow Creme. Let cool. Cover with Topping.

| | |
|---|---|
| Topping: | 1/2 stick oleo |
| 1 box powdered sugar | 1/3 cup Pet Milk |
| 1/3 cup cocoa | 1/2 teaspoon vanilla |

Mix well and spread on brownies.

*Joe and Faye Dutton: Diane '75*

## Hope is a waking dream.

# PERFECT BROWNIES

Measure into bowl as given, but do not mix until all ingredients are in:

| | |
|---|---|
| 1-1/2 cups flour | 1 cup oil |
| 2 cups sugar | 1/4 cup water |
| 1/2 cup cocoa | 2 teaspoons vanilla |
| 1/2 teaspoon salt | 1 cup chopped pecans |
| 4 eggs | |

Mix and bake in 9x13" loaf pan 30 minutes at 350 degrees.

*Debe Wells: Zac Miller '84; Morris Miller '86*

# BUTTERSCOTCH BARS

| | |
|---|---|
| 2/3 cup butter or margarine | 2-1/2 teaspoons baking powder |
| 1 (1-pound) box light brown sugar | 1 teaspoon salt |
| 3 eggs | 1 package butterscotch morsels |
| 2-2/3 cups flour | 1 cup chopped nuts |

Melt butter and mix in sugar. Cool 10 minutes (I don't cool). Add eggs and beat by hand with wooden spoon until smooth. Sift dry ingredients and stir into creamed mixture. Add butterscotch morsels and nuts. Mix well. Pour into 10x15" pan and bake at 350 degrees for 30 to 35 minutes.

*Robert and Janis Craig: Wendy '80*

# CARAMEL LAYER
# CHOCOLATE SQUARES

*(Caramel Fudge Bars)*

| | |
|---|---|
| 1 (14-ounce) package Caramels | 3/4 cup melted butter |
| 2/3 cup evaporated milk | 1 cup semi-sweet chocolate chips |
| 1 German Chocolate cake mix | 1 cup chopped nuts |

Melt caramels with 1/3 cup milk in double boiler. Stir frequently. Combine cake mix and remaining 1/3 cup milk. Blend and add butter. Spread half mixture into thin layer in greased 9x13" pan. It will be stiff so pat with hands. Reserve remaining dough for topping. Bake 6 to 8 minutes at 350 degrees. Remove from oven. Sprinkle chocolate chips and pecans over baked crust. Spread caramel mixture over chocolate pieces. Crumble reserved dough over caramel mixture. Return to oven and bake 15 to 18 minutes. Cool slightly and refrigerate 30 minutes to set caramel. Makes 30 bars.

*Gary and Sidney Gaston: Whitney '85*

# CARROT COOKIES

1 cup shortening
1 cup sugar
3 eggs
1 cup grated carrots
1 teaspoon lemon rind
1-1/2 tablespoons lemon juice

3 cups sifted flour
2 teaspoons baking powder
1/4 teaspoon salt
1 cup ground raisins
1 cup chopped nuts

Mix in order given, then drop from teaspoon on greased baking sheet. Bake at 375 degrees for 12 to 15 minutes. Makes 40 cookies.

*Elmer and Lee Ona Taylor: Danna '58; Lee Ann Haney '77*

# CHOCOLATE CHIP COOKIES

1 cup shortening
1/2 cup sugar
1 cup brown sugar
1 teaspoon vanilla
2 eggs
2 cups flour

1 teaspoon soda
1 teaspoon salt
1 cup chopped nuts
1 (12-ounce) package chocolate
  chips

Cream shortening, sugars, vanilla, and eggs until light and fluffy. (Don't underbeat.) Mix dry ingredients and stir into creamed mixture gradually. Blend well. Add nuts and chocolate chips. Drop by spoon onto cookie sheet and bake at 350 degrees about 10 minutes or until lightly browned.

*Note:* Use 1/2 cup dough and flatten to one-half inch for BIG ONES! (Patti uses 2-1/2 cups flour.)

*Dewain "Slugger" and Janice Matthews: Jason '85*
*David and Patti Redwine: Brent Henager '86*

# CHOCOLATE COOKIES
## *(Boiled)*

1 stick oleo
2 cups sugar
4 tablespoons cocoa
1/2 cup milk
2 teaspoons vanilla

3 cups (Quick) oats
1/2 cup peanut butter
1 cup coconut, optional
1 cup chopped nuts, optional

Combine first 4 ingredients in saucepan; bring to a full boil and boil 1 minute. Add remaining ingredients. Stir mixture and drop by spoon on wax paper. Allow to cool.

*Raymond and Joyce Tipton: Tracy '60*
*Bill and Marilyn Wheeler: Bryan '68*

# NO-BAKED CHOCOLATE COOKIES

1 stick oleo
2 cups sugar
1/2 cup milk
4 tablespoons cocoa

1/2 cup crunch peanut butter
3 cups oats
2 teaspoons vanilla

Mix oleo, sugar, milk, and cocoa; bring to a rolling boil and boil 1 minute. Remove from heat and immediately add peanut butter, oats, and vanilla. Stir mixture well; then drop by spoonful onto waxed paper. Cookies will harden. Makes 24 to 36.

*Curtis and Billie Arms: Bunny '67*

# CHOCOLATE SANDWICH GOBS

2 cups sugar
1 cup oleo, melted
2 eggs, beaten
4 cups flour
1/2 cup unsweetened cocoa
2 teaspoons salt

1 cup buttermilk
1 teaspoon soda
1 cup hot water
YOUR FAVORITE
 CHOCOLATE ICING

Combine sugar, oleo, and beaten eggs in large mixing bowl. Mix well. Sift together flour, cocoa, and salt; add dry ingredients to creamed mixture, alternating with buttermilk. Combine hot water and soda; add to dough, mixing until combined. Drop by spoonfuls on greased cookie sheet. Bake at 350 degrees for 10 minutes. Remove to cooling rack. Form sandwiches by placing icing between two cookies. Press together.

*W.R. and Doris Schooley: Coby '70*

# CINNAMON COFFEE BARS

1 cup shortening
1 cup brown sugar
1 egg
1/2 cup hot coffee
1-1/2 cups flour
1 teaspoon baking powder

1/4 teaspoon soda
1/4 teaspoon salt
1 teaspoon cinnamon
1/2 cup raisins
1/4 cup chopped nuts

Cream shortening, sugar, and egg. Stir in hot coffee. Sift dry ingredients and add to creamed mixture. Blend in raisins and nuts. Spread in greased and floured 9x13" pan. Bake in 350 degree oven for 25 to 30 minutes.

Icing:
1 cup powdered sugar

1/4 teaspoon vanilla
2 tablespoons butter

Cream together and spread over cooked bars.

*Jimmie and Virginia Hogg: Dickie '67*

# COCONUT MACAROONS
### *(Delicious)*

2 egg whites
1 cup sugar
1/2 teaspoon vanilla
1 cup coconut

2 cups cornflakes or other dry
    cereal
1/2 cup nuts, optional

Beat egg whites until stiff but not dry. Add sugar gradually. Add vanilla, coconut, cornflakes, and nuts. Mix well and drop by spoon onto a baking dish lined with foil (or teflon pan). Bake in 400 degree oven until macaroons are a delicious brown (about 15 minutes). Makes 3 dozen.

*Note:* Another version is to reduce sugar to 2/3 cup. Fold in 1 cup chopped pecans and 1 cup chocolate chips. Preheat oven to 350 degrees. Drop onto well-greased cookie sheet. Turn off oven; put cookies in and forget them. Remove from pan when cool.

*Bronce and Avalene Bristol: Boni '63*

# CONGO BARS

2 sticks oleo
2-1/4 cups brown sugar
3 eggs
2-2/3 cups flour
1-1/2 teaspoons baking powder

1/2 teaspoon salt
1 teaspoon vanilla
1 cup pecans, chopped
1 (12-ounce) package chocolate
    chips

Mix all ingredients well. Pour into greased baking dish. Bake at 350 degrees for 45 minutes to 1 hour.

*Charles and Kay Phares: Krista '77*

# COWBOY COOKIES

1 cup shortening
1 cup sugar
1 cup brown sugar
2 eggs
1 teaspoon vanilla
2 cups flour

1 teaspoon soda
1/2 teaspoon baking powder
1/2 teaspoon salt
2 cups rolled oats
1 (12-ounce) package chocolate
    chips, optional

Cream shortening, sugars, eggs, and vanilla. Beat until light and fluffy. Sift dry ingredients; add to creamed mixture and mix well. Add oats (and chocolate chips, if used). Roll into small balls. Bake at 350 degrees for 10 to 12 minutes.

*Variation:* 1 cup chopped nuts.

*Bob and Millie Speegle: David '65*

# DATE BALLS
# or SKILLET COOKIES

1 stick oleo
1 (8-ounce) package dates,
chopped
1 cup sugar
2 teaspoons canned milk
2 eggs, well beaten

1/4 teaspoon salt
1 teaspoon vanilla
2 cups Rice Krispies
1 cup chopped pecans
1 can (or more) coconut

Place oleo, dates, sugar, milk, eggs, and salt over slow heat and cook for 15 minutes. Remove and add vanilla, Rice Krispies, and nuts. While warm take out and mold into little balls. Roll in coconut.

*Kenneth and Cleo Cook: Carey '51*

# DATE PIN WHEELS

1 pound dates
1/2 cup sugar
1/2 cup water
1/2 cup brown sugar
1/2 cup white sugar
1/2 cup oleo

1 egg
1/2 teaspoon vanilla
2 cups flour
1/2 teaspoon salt
1/2 teaspoon soda
1 cup chopped nuts

In a saucepan, combine dates, sugar, and water. Cook over slow heat; stir constantly until thick (about 2 to 3 minutes). Cool. Cream brown and white sugar with oleo. Add egg and beat well. Add vanilla, then the flour, salt, soda, and nuts. Stir until smooth. Chill. Divide dough into two or three rolls. Roll out on board. Spread date mix on dough and roll up like a jelly roll. Place in freezer until frozen. To bake, slice about 1/4" thick and bake on greased baking sheet at 400 degrees for 8 to 10 minutes. Makes 8 to 10 dozen.

*John T. and Maxine Jones: Glenn '66*

# FUDGE COOKIES

2 tablespoons oleo
1 (12-ounce) package chocolate
chips
1 can Eagle Brand milk

1 teaspoon vanilla
1 cup flour
1 cup nuts (or cup coconut)

Melt oleo and chocolate chips over low heat (or hot water). Remove from heat and add remaining ingredients. Drop on greased cookie sheet and bake 12 minutes at 325 degrees. (Do not overbake.)

*James and Lois Russell: Billy '72*

# GOODIE, GOODIE
# OATMEAL COOKIES

1 cup shortening
3/4 cup sugar and 3/4 cup brown
   sugar
2 eggs
1 teaspoon vanilla
2 cups flour
1 teaspoon baking soda

1 teaspoon salt
2 cups oatmeal
1 (6-ounce) package chocolate
   chips
1 cup chopped pecans
3/4 cup raisins
Few drops of hot water

Cream shortening and sugars. Beat in eggs and vanilla. Mix together flour, soda, and salt; beat into shortening mixture. Add oatmeal; beat. Stir in chocolate chips, pecans, and raisins. Add a few drops of HOT water. Drop on greased cookie sheet. Bake at 350 degrees for 10 to 12 minutes.

*Len and Lynne Wilson: Mark '75; Kirk '78*

# GOODIES

1 cup sugar (1/2 white; 1/2 brown)
1 stick oleo
1 stick butter

1 cup pecans
1 teaspoon vanilla
Keeblers Graham crackers

Mix all except vanilla and crackers; cook 2 minutes. Break crackers and lay on jelly roll sheet. Add mixture and cook 10 minutes at 350 degrees.

*Kenneth and Helen Byrne: Susan '63*

# HAWAIIAN DROP COOKIES

2 cups flour
1 teaspoon baking powder
1/2 teaspoon salt
2/3 cup shortening
1-1/4 cups sugar
1 egg

1/2 teaspoon vanilla
1/2 teaspoon almond extract
1/4 cup crushed pineapple,
   drained
1/2 cup coconut

Sift dry ingredients; add creamed shortening, sugar, egg, and flavorings. Add pineapple and coconut last. Drop by spoonfuls on ungreased cookie sheet. Bake at 325 degrees for 20 minutes.

*Note:* Better if stored 24 hours. The coconut may be sprinkled on the cookies instead of added to the dough.

*Lyndon and Faye Martin: Tim '65*
*Edward and Roberta Martin: Bertie '54*

# LEMON BARS

First Layer:
2 cups sifted flour
1/2 cup powdered sugar

2 sticks oleo (or butter)
1/2 teaspoon salt

Mix and press into a 9x13" baking dish. Bake at 325 degrees for 20 minutes, or until lightly brown.

Second Layer:
4 eggs, beaten
2 cups sugar
6 tablespoons lemon juice

2 tablespoons flour
1/2 teaspoon salt
Powdered sugar

Beat eggs, sugar, and lemon juice. Sift flour and salt. Pour over baked crust NOT letting this mixture touch the sides of the pan. Cook for another 20 minutes at 325 degrees. When cool, sprinkle with powdered sugar.

*David and Patti Redwine: Brent Henager '86*
*R.J. and Bettie Sayers: Rollie '85*

# CRISP LEMON COOKIES

1 cup sugar
1/2 cup shortening
1 egg, unbeaten
1/2 teaspoon vanilla
2 teaspoons lemon extract

2 cups flour
1/4 teaspoon salt
1/2 teaspoon soda
2 tablespoons milk

Cream sugar and shortening; add egg and flavorings. Mix well. Sift dry ingredients and mix with creamed mixture. Stir in milk. Moisten hands with shortening and form into small balls and place on baking sheet about 2" apart. Flatten with a flat bottom glass dipped in sugar as each cookie is pressed. Bake 10 minutes at 400 degrees.

*Boyd and Delois North: Joy '62; Steve '65*

# MOLASSES COOKIES

1-1/4 cups flour
3/4 teaspoon soda
1/2 teaspoon baking powder
1/2 teaspoon salt
1 teaspoon cinnamon
1/2 teaspoon ginger
1/2 cup shortening

1/2 cup sugar
2 eggs
1/2 cup molasses or honey
1-1/2 cups oatmeal
1 cup raisins
1 cup chopped pecans

Sift dry ingredients and spices. Add creamed shortening, sugar, molasses. Add eggs and beat. Add raisins and chopped nuts. Drop by teaspoon onto cookie sheet. Bake at 350 degrees for 15 minutes for large cookies. Bake 12 minutes for small cookies.

*Russell and Faye Atchley: Russell '68; Carolyn '71*

# MOLASSES COOKIES
*(8 to 9 dozen)*

| | |
|---|---|
| 1 cup shortening (part butter) | 1-1/2 teaspoons ginger |
| 2 cups brown sugar | 1 teaspoon baking powder |
| 3 eggs | 6 cups flour |
| 1 cup dark molasses | 1 teaspoon soda |
| 1 teaspoon salt | 1-1/2 cups hot water |
| 1/2 teaspoon cinnamon | |

Cream shortening and sugar; add eggs and mix. Add and mix molasses, salt, cinnamon, ginger, baking powder, and flour. Mix soda and hot water and add. Mix. Drop by teaspoonfuls on lightly greased cookie sheet. Bake 8 to 10 minutes at 375 degrees.

| | |
|---|---|
| Glaze: | Dash of salt |
| 1 stick oleo | Powdered sugar, enough to make |
| 1/2 cup milk | consistency to spread |
| Vanilla | |

Melt butter with milk. Add other ingredients and keep warm while frosting cookies.

*Roy and Frances Buckner: Debbie '63; Spencer '65*

# NEIMAN-MARCUS SQUARES

| | |
|---|---|
| 1 box Yellow Cake mix | 1 (1-pound) box powdered sugar |
| 1/2 cup margarine, melted | 1/2 cup flaked coconut |
| 3 eggs | 1/2 cup chopped pecans, optional |
| 1 (8-ounce) package cream cheese, softened | |

Mix cake mix, margarine, and 1 egg. Press into 8x11" pan. Combine remaining ingredients. Spread over cake mixture. Bake at 375 degrees for 20 minutes.

*Joe and Pat Culp: (Hoermann) Tim Culp '70*

**Whatever you have,
you must either use or lose.**

# OATMEAL CHOCOLATE CHIP COOKIES

1 cup shortening
3/4 cup brown sugar
3/4 cup white sugar
2 eggs
1 teaspoon hot water
1-1/2 cups flour
1 teaspoon soda

1/2 teaspoon salt
2 cups oatmeal
1 cup chopped nuts
1 (6-ounce) package chocolate
chips (I use more)
1 teaspoon vanilla

Cream shortening and sugars; add eggs and hot water. Beat well. Add dry ingredients and mix. Add remaining ingredients and mix well. Bake at 375 degrees for 8 to 10 minutes. (I've used this recipe since 1942 when sugar was rationed and sweets a treat.)

*John and Ruth Tidwell: Sandee '53*

# OATMEAL CRISPIES

1 cup shortening
1 cup brown sugar, packed
1 cup granulated sugar
2 eggs, beaten
1 teaspoon vanilla
1-1/2 cups flour

1 teaspoon salt
1 teaspoon soda
3 cups oats
1 teaspoon cinnamon, optional
1/2 cup chopped nuts

Cream shortening and sugars. Add eggs and vanilla; beat well. Add dry ingredients and mix. Add remaining ingredients; beat well. Bake on ungreased cookie sheet at 350 degrees for 10 minutes. Makes 5 dozen.

*Variation:* Add 1 cup chocolate chips or 1/2 cup peanut butter along with the oats.

*Donald and Dee Cox: Cary '85*

# PEANUT BUTTER-CHOCOLATE CHIP-OATMEAL COOKIES

1 cup sugar
1/2 cup shortening
1/2 cup creamy peanut butter
2 eggs
1-1/2 cups flour
1/2 teaspoon baking soda
1 teaspoon salt

1/4 teaspoon nutmeg
1/2 teaspoon cinnamon
1/2 cup water
1 cup rolled oats
1 (12-ounce) package chocolate
chips

Cream sugar, shortening, peanut butter, and eggs. Blend dry ingredients and add alternately with water. Stir in oats and chocolate chips. Drop by teaspoons on greased cookie sheet. Bake 12 minutes at 350 degrees.

*Mrs. Tennison: Cindy '59*

# MY FAVORITE PEANUT BUTTER COOKIES

| | |
|---|---|
| 1/2 cup oleo | 1-1/4 cups flour |
| 1/2 cup peanut butter | 1/2 teaspoon baking powder |
| 1/2 cup granulated sugar | 3/4 teaspoon soda |
| 1/2 cup brown sugar | 1/4 teaspoon salt |
| 1 egg | |

Mix first 5 ingredients. Sift dry ingredients into creamed mixture and stir well. Chill dough. Spoon into little balls and place on greased cookie sheet. Press down with fork. Bake at 350 degrees for 12 to 15 minutes.

*O.F. and Edith Hamilton: Linda '61*

# PEANUT BUTTER FINGERS

| | |
|---|---|
| 1/2 cup butter | 1/4 teaspoon salt |
| 1/2 cup white sugar | 1/2 teaspoon vanilla |
| 1/2 cup brown sugar, packed | 1 cup flour |
| 1 egg, unbeaten | 1 cup oats |
| 1/3 cup peanut butter | 1 cup chocolate chips |
| 1/2 teaspoon soda | |

Cream butter and sugars. Blend in egg, peanut butter, soda, salt, and vanilla. Stir in flour and oats. Spread in greased 9x13" pan. Bake at 350 degrees for 20 to 25 minutes. Sprinkle with chocolate chips. Let stand 5 minutes. Spread chocolate evenly and drizzle with TOPPING.

| | |
|---|---|
| **Topping:** | 1/4 cup peanut butter |
| 1/2 cup powdered sugar | 2 to 4 tablespoons milk |

Mix and drizzle over chocolate chips. Cool; cut into bars.

*Mel and Shirley Funk: Todd '73*

# PECAN FINGER BARS

| | |
|---|---|
| **Crust:** | 3/4 cup powdered sugar |
| 3/4 cup butter | 1-1/2 cups flour |

Cream shortening and sugar. Blend in flour and mix until crumbly. Press into ungreased 9x13" pan and bake 12 to 15 minutes at 400 degrees.

| | |
|---|---|
| **Filling:** | 1/2 teaspoon baking powder |
| 2 eggs | 1/2 teaspoon salt |
| 1 cup brown sugar | 1/2 teaspoon vanilla |
| 2 tablespoons flour | 1 cup chopped pecans |

Mix filling ingredients and spread over hot baked layer. Bake 20 minutes at 350 degrees. Cool and cut into bars.

*Michael and Delores McDole: Paula '80*

# RANGER COOKIES

1 cup shortening
1 cup white sugar
1 cup brown sugar
2 eggs
1 teaspoon vanilla
2 cups flour
1 teaspoon baking powder
1 teaspoon soda

1/2 teaspoon salt
2 cups oats
2 cups Rice Krispies or 2 cups Corn Flakes
1 cup coconut
1 cup chopped nuts
1 cup raisins, optional

Cream shortening and sugar. Add eggs and vanilla. Mix and stir in dry ingredients with creamed mixture. Add oats, Rice Krispies, and coconut. Add nuts. Roll into small balls. Flatten out.

Place on greased cookie sheet and bake 10 to 12 minutes at 350 degrees.

*Elgene and Margie Mills: Jeanne '61*
*Clete and Margie Pope: Charles '51*
*Jerry and Barbara Detterick: Mike '73*
*Raymond and Robbie Casey: Darren '70*

# SAND TARTS

2 sticks oleo
2 cups sifted flour
1/4 cup powdered sugar

1 teaspoon baking powder
1 cup finely chopped nuts
3 teaspoons vanilla

Cream oleo. Sift dry ingredients and gradually add to creamed oleo. Mix well. Stir in nuts and vanilla. Form crescents with fingers and bake on ungreased cookie sheet at 350 degrees for 12 minutes. Roll in additional powdered sugar while still warm. Handle with care. Makes about 3 or 4 dozen.

*Fred and Ora Herrera: Freddie '78*

# SEVEN LAYER COOKIES

1/2 stick oleo
1 cup Graham Cracker crumbs
1 can coconut
1 (6-ounce) package chocolate chips

1 (6-ounce) package butterscotch chips
1 can sweetened condensed milk
1 cup chopped pecans

Melt oleo in 9x13" pan. Add ingredients by layers as listed. Bake at 350 degrees for approximately 30 minutes until ingredients are melted and lightly browned on top. Cool on rack for 15 to 20 minutes. Cut into 2" squares and cool completely.

*Pat and Jean Rushing: Rick '64; Mark '65*
*Clat and Noma Robertson: Grace '58*

# SNICKERDOODLES

1 cup soft shortening
1-1/2 cups sugar
2 eggs
2-3/4 cups sifted flour
2 teaspoons cream of tartar

1 teaspoon soda
1/2 teaspoon salt
2 tablespoons sugar
2 teaspoons cinnamon

Mix thoroughly the shortening, sugar, and eggs. Sift flour, cream of tartar, soda, and salt; add. Chill slightly. Roll into balls the size of small walnuts. Roll balls in mixture of sugar and cinnamon. Bake at 400 degrees for 8 to 10 minutes.

*Jim and Charlene Jackson: "Skeeter" '70*

# SUGAR COOKIES

1 stick oleo
1 cup sugar
1 egg
2 tablespoons milk

1/2 teaspoon vanilla
1-3/4 cups flour
1/4 teaspoon salt
2 teaspoons baking powder

Cream oleo and sugar. Beat in egg, milk, and vanilla. Mix dry ingredients and add to creamed mixture. Chill dough. Roll out dough 1/8" thick; cut with cookie cutter. Sprinkle with sugar and place on cookie sheet. Bake at 375 degrees for 10 minutes.

*Wallace and Marie Comeaux: Shirley Thatcher '67*

# SUGAR COOKIES

2-1/2 cups flour
1/2 teaspoon soda
3/4 teaspoon salt
1/2 cup shortening
1/2 cup oleo

1 cup sugar
1 teaspoon vanilla
2 eggs
2 tablespoons milk

Sift flour, soda, and salt. Cream shortening, oleo, and sugar. Add vanilla and eggs; add milk. Add dry ingredients. Drop by teaspoon on ungreased cookie sheet. Mash flat with bottom of glass dipped in sugar. Bake at 400 degrees for 10 minutes. GOOD!

*Brodie and LaRue Hutchinson: Brodie '62; Nedra '64*
*Bill and Betty Luck: Terri '63*

---

**It often shows a fine command of language
to say nothing.**

# SUGAR AND SPICE COOKIES

3/4 cup shortening
1 cup sugar
1/4 cup molasses
1 egg
2 cups flour

2 teaspoons soda
1 teaspoon cinnamon
1/2 teaspoon cloves
1/2 teaspoon salt

Cream first 4 ingredients. Sift dry ingredients and mix with creamed mixture. Chill for 2 hours. Form into balls; roll in sugar. Place on greased baking sheet and bake at 375 degrees for 8 to 10 minutes.

*Jerry and Billy Jones: Lance '79*

# OLD-FASHIONED TEA CAKES

3 eggs
3 cups sugar
1 cup Crisco
1 cup buttermilk

1 teaspoon soda
1 teaspoon vanilla
7 to 8 cups flour

Beat well, adding one ingredient at a time, in order given above. Leave as soft as you can to handle. Divide dough into 3 parts. Take one part at a time and work out on floured board. Roll out thin and cut into squares or round. Bake at 400 degrees for 7 to 8 minutes. (Do not get them brown!)

*O.W. and Ruby Hughes: Don '49*
*Jimmy Faye Todd (Sullivan) '49*

# THUMBPRINT COOKIES

1 cup shortening or oleo
1/2 cup brown sugar
1 egg yolk; whites
1 teaspoon vanilla
2 cups sifted flour

1/2 teaspoon salt
Chopped candied fruit, jelly, or
    icing
Chopped nuts

Mix oleo, brown sugar, egg yolk, and vanilla. Sift dry ingredients and stir into creamed mixture. Roll into 1" balls. Dip in slightly beaten egg whites and roll in finely chopped nuts. Place about 1" apart on ungreased cookie sheet. Bake 5 minutes at 375 degrees. Remove from oven and press thumb gently on top of each cookie. Return to oven and bake an additional 8 minutes. Cool. Place in thumbprints your choice of fillings (chopped candied fruit, jelly or icing).

*Icing:* Use 1/4 cup oleo, powdered sugar, and enough water to make the right consistency to spread.

*Jim and Doris Stone: Sarah '60*

# TING-A-LING DROPS

1 cup (6-ounce) chocolate chips     1/2 cup salted peanuts, chopped
1/2 cup coconut     1 cup Rice Krispies

Melt chocolate chips; remove from heat. Add remaining ingredients and stir until well coated with chocolate. Drop by teaspoonfuls onto waxed paper or greased baking sheet. Let cool to harden.

*Herman and Zina Patterson: Garland '55*

# APRICOT BALLS

1-1/2 cups ground dried apricots     (1 cup finely chopped nuts,
2 cups shredded coconut       optional)
2/3 cup Eagle Brand milk
    Powdered sugar

Put uncooked apricots through food chopper; combine with coconut. Add milk and mix well. Shape into small balls and roll in powdered sugar. Store in refrigerator overnight. Keeps well.

*Odis and Rose Schoolcraft: Linda '67*

# CHOCOLATE COVERED CHERRIES

1 stick melted oleo     1 small jar Maraschino cherries,
4 cups chopped pecans       chopped
1 to 2 cans coconut     1/4 pound paraffin
1 can Eagle Brand milk     1 pound semi-sweet chocolate
2 boxes powdered sugar, less 1 cup

Pour oleo over pecans. Stir and add coconut, Eagle Brand milk, and sifted powdered sugar. Add chopped cherries (add more cherries if desired). Mixture will be very stiff. Chill. Roll into small 1" balls and freeze or chill. Melt paraffin and chocolate. Dip balls into chocolate and place on foil. Chill.

*Note:* Cherries can be chopped in food chopper; use the amount desired.

*George and Evelyn Clements: Donna '62*

**When you show a little kindness
you show a lot about yourself.**

## COCONUT OATMEAL CANDY

2 cups sugar
1/2 stick oleo
1 teaspoon vanilla
1/2 cup canned milk

4 tablespoons cocoa
1/2 cup peanut butter
2 cups oats
1 can Angel Flake coconut

Mix sugar, oleo, vanilla, canned milk, and cocoa and bring to a boil. Boil about 2 minutes. Add peanut butter, oats, and coconut. Drop by spoon on cookie sheet.

*John T. and Maxine Jones: Glenn '66*

## DATE LOAF CANDY

1/2 stick oleo
2 cups sugar
1/2 cup Pet milk
1/4 cup Karo

1 (8-ounce) package dates,
   chopped
1 cup chopped pecans
1/2 teaspoon vanilla

Melt oleo in saucepan. Add sugar, milk, Karo, and dates. Bring to a boil and continue boiling until forms a very firm ball in cold water. Remove from heat. Add pecans and vanilla. Beat until it holds shape when dropped from spoon. (It becomes very stiff and hard to beat before it's ready.)

Pour onto wet cloth and form into roll. Wrap in wax paper or plastic when cool. Slice as you choose.

*James and Faye Bearden: Karen '66*

## DIVINITY

3 cups sugar
1 cup white Karo
1/2 cup cold water
Pinch of salt

2 egg whites, stiffly beaten
1 tablespoon vanilla
1 to 2 cups chopped pecans

Mix sugar, Karo, water, and salt. Cook until thread is formed when dropped from a fork, a long hair-like thread. Pour over beaten egg whites gradually. Add vanilla and beat until mixture becomes thick and begins to loose its gloss. Add pecans and drop on wax paper with a spoon.

*Sidney and Golda Ervin: Paul '52; Robert '54*

---

**If you dig a ditch to catch someone innocent,
You often fall into it yourself.**

# DIVINITY

2 cups sugar
1/2 cup light corn syrup
1/2 cup hot water
2 egg whites

1/4 teaspoon salt
1/4 teaspoon cream of tartar
1 teaspoon vanilla
1/2 to 1 cup chopped nuts

Combine first 3 ingredients; stir until sugar is dissolved. Cover and bring to a boil. Do not stir down crystals from the sides. Boil uncovered to firm ball stage (use candy thermometer). Slowly beat eggwhites until foamy; add salt and cream of tartar. Beat until they hold firm peaks. Slowly pour 1/3 of syrup over stiffly beaten egg whites. Cook remaining syrup to hard ball stage and add to egg whites slowly, beating at high speed until mixture begins to lose its gloss. Add vanilla and nuts. Quickly drop by teaspoons or tablespoons onto wax paper.

*Bill and Sue Craig: Susan '61*
*Raymond and Gladys Sharbutt: Ray '61*

# NO COOK DIVINITY

1 package Fluffy White Frosting
　Mix (dry)
1/2 cup light corn syrup
1 teaspoon vanilla

1/2 cup boiling water
1 (16-ounce) package powdered
　sugar
1-1/2 cups chopped pecans

In a small mixer bowl combine dry frosting mix, corn syrup, vanilla, and boiling water. Beat on highest speed until stiff peaks form. Transfer to large mixer bowl. On low speed, gradually blend in sugar. Stir in nuts. Drop by teaspoonfuls on waxed paper. When outside of candy feels firm, turn over, dry the other side.

*A.G. and Marzie McClure: Anita '56; Lane (grandson) '85*

# FUDGE CANDY

4-1/2 cups sugar
1 tall can Pet milk
1 stick oleo
1 jar Marshmallow cream

2 cups chopped pecans
3 (6-ounce) packages chocolate
　chips or 1 (12-ounce) package
1 teaspoon vanilla

Mix sugar, Pet milk, and oleo in saucepan; melt. Add marshmallow cream, pecans, chocolate chips, and vanilla. Bring to a boil and boil 7-1/2 minutes. Pour into buttered pan. Let stand in ice box 1-1/2 hours. Store in covered container.

*Melvin and Ruby Lipham: Marilyn '63; Ricky '64*

# PINEAPPLE FUDGE

2 cups sugar
Few grains of salt
1/2 cup or small can crushed
    pineapple, well drained

1/2 cup cream or evaporated milk
1 tablespoon butter
1 cup pecans

Cook to (very soft) ball stage; remove from fire. Add 1 tablespoon butter and allow to cool 5 minutes before stirring. Avoid scraping sides of pan as you stir. When mixture becomes almost cold and real thick, add pecans. Stir until ready to pour onto buttered dish or drop by teaspoon onto wax paper.

*Variation:* Add coconut to the above recipe or use coconut instead of the nuts.

*Note:* Use lots of pecans and big pieces or whole ones.

*A.A. and Millie Horn: Ronald '50; Gerald '54*

# QUICK FUDGE

1 can Eagle Brand Milk
1 (12-ounce) package chocolate
    chips

1 package miniature
    marshmallows
Roasted peanuts or chopped
    pecans

Mix Eagle Brand milk and chocolate chips; melt together and cool. Add miniature marshmallows. Fold in; some will melt. (You do not want all to melt.) Add roasted peanuts or pecans. (The roasted peanuts have a good flavor.) Drop on buttered cookie sheet.

*Gordon and Sharon O'Dell: Debbie '68; Kim '70*

# ROCKY ROAD FUDGE

1 small package chocolate chips
1 can Eagle Brand Milk
1 tablespoon butter

1 teaspoon vanilla
1 small package marshmallows
2 cups chopped pecans

Melt chocolate chips in milk. Add remaining ingredients. Mix. Drop on buttered cookie sheet or pour in 9x13" pan. Cool and cut. Makes a bunch. Good!

*Teacher's Pet: Earlene Fisher, Pam Fisher's mother-in-law*

He that speaks much is much mistaken.

# WHITE CHOCOLATE FUDGE

1-1/2 cups sugar
1/4 cup oleo
2/3 cup evaporated milk
1/2 pound white chocolate

2 cups miniature marshmallows
1-1/2 cups chopped pecans
1 teaspoon vanilla

Combine the first three ingredients in a saucepan and bring to a boil. Boil 3 minutes, stirring constantly. Remove from heat and stir in chocolate (cut into small pieces) and marshmallows. Stir until smooth. Stir in pecans and vanilla. Drop by teaspoonfuls onto waxed paper or pour into a buttered dish and cut into pieces. Makes 45 pieces.

*Novice and Ann Kniffen: Cristy '85*

# CHOCOLATE COVERED MARSHMALLOWS

2 (12-ounce) packages chocolate
   chips
1 can Eagle Brand milk
1 (7-ounce) jar marshmallow
   creme

1 cup chopped nuts
1 large bag marshmallows (large
   size) or more

Melt chocolate chips, milk, and marshmallow creme in double boiler. Add chopped nuts. With 2 forks, cover marshmallows with mixture. Place on waxed paper.

*Teacher's Pet: Lois Pack, sister*

# MARTHA WASHINGTON CANDY
## *(Chocolate)*

1 stick oleo, room temperature
   (melted)
2 boxes powdered sugar
1 can Eagle Brand Milk
2 teaspoons vanilla

1 can coconut
4 cups pecan
1 (12-ounce) package chocolate
   chips
1/2 block paraffin

Mix oleo, sugar, and milk. Add vanilla, coconut, and pecans. Stir well and roll into small balls. Chill 1 hour. Melt chocolate chips and paraffin in a double boiler. Using toothpicks, dip balls into chocolate. Place on waxed paper to harden.

*William M. and Georgia B. Peoples: Craig '67*

# MILLIONAIRES

1 (12-ounce) package caramel
   candy
2 tablespoons water
2 tablespoons butter

3 cups pecan halves
2 (9-ounce) Hershey bars
2 small Hershey bars
1/3 to 1/4 paraffin block

Melt caramel candy, water, and butter in double boiler. Mix in pecans. Drop on buttered wax paper; cool. Melt in double boiler the Hershey bars and paraffin. Mix until smooth. Dip caramels in this mixture. Drop on waxed paper.

*Charles and Billie Burkett: Buz '62*
*Charles and Ethel Pope: Sherri '82; Ginger '86*

# PATIENCE
## *(Very Good!)*

3 cups sugar
3/4 cup milk
1/2 cup Karo
1/2 cup sugar, browned

2 tablespoons butter
1 teaspoon vanilla
2 cups pecans

Combine sugar, milk, and Karo. Bring to boil. This must be boiling when browned sugar is added. Brown 1/2 cup sugar (good in iron skillet). Just shake pan while browning. Add slowly to first mixture, stirring. When soft ball is reached, add butter. Allow to sit 5 minutes. Add vanilla. Beat. Add pecans. Drop from teaspoon onto waxed paper.

*Note:* If too thick, just add a scant teaspoon water and start dropping again!

*A.A. and Millie Horn: Ronald '50; Gerald '54*

# PEANUT BRITTLE

1/2 cup water
2 cups sugar
1 cup white Karo
2 cups raw peanuts

1 teaspoon vanilla
1 tablespoon butter
2 teaspoons soda

In a deep pan (Pressure cooker is good to use), bring water to boil. Add sugar and Karo. Stir until dissolved. Bring to a boil and cook until it spins a 6" to 8" thread or 238 degrees. Add peanuts and butter and cook slowly until mixture turns a golden brown. Remove from heat; add vanilla and soda. Stir until soda is mixed; work quickly. (Candy is still foaming.) Pour on large buttered cookie sheet. Cool. Break into pieces.

*Alfred and Juanita Nieman: Ramona '70*

# MICROWAVE PEANUT BRITTLE

| | |
|---|---|
| 1 cup sugar | 1 teaspoon vanilla |
| 1/2 cup corn syrup | 1 tablespoon butter |
| 1 cup raw peanuts | 1 teaspoon soda |
| 1/4 teaspoon salt | |

Combine sugar and corn syrup; mix and microwave 5 minutes. Add raw peanuts and salt. Cook 3-1/2 minutes. Add vanilla and butter; cook 1-1/2 minutes. Remove from microwave and add soda. Stir until foamy. Pour out on greased platter. Cool. So good and easy; J.V. makes this often!

*J.V. and Alma Dill: Gaye '75*
*James and Wanda Mosley: Shirley '61; Jana '64*
*Ron and Sande Stover: Jason Neinast '84; Brad '85*

# PEANUT BUTTER BRITTLE

| | |
|---|---|
| 2 cups sugar | 1 pint peanut butter |
| 1 cup white Karo syrup | |

In saucepan, combine sugar and Karo and cook until golden. Remove from fire and mix in peanut butter thoroughly. Roll thin on buttered foil with buttered rolling pin. Cut into squares and loosen from foil quickly. This is my mother's original recipe.

*Mr. and Mrs. George Mossman: Julia '49; Georgia '51*

# PEANUT BUTTER-RICE KRISPIES CANDY

| | |
|---|---|
| 1 cup sugar | 6 cups Rice Krispies |
| 1 cup Karo | 1 package butterscotch bits or 1 |
| 1 cup peanut butter | package chocolate chips |

Mix sugar and white Karo; bring to a boil. Mix in peanut butter and Rice Krispies. Press into buttered pan. Top with melted butterscotch bits or melted chocolate chips. Spread on top of candy.

*Note:* Betty's variation uses 1-1/2 cups peanut butter and 3 cups corn flakes instead of the Rice Krispies. She omits the chocolate chips.

*Lyndon and Faye Martin: Tim '65*
*Magel and Betty Smith: Gary Phelps '71*

---

## Love all, trust a few, do wrong to no one.

# PEANUT CLUSTERS

4 tablespoons oleo
2 tablespoons white syrup
1/4 cup evaporated milk
2 tablespoons cocoa

1 cup sugar
1/2 teaspoon vanilla
1 cup shelled roasted peanuts

Melt oleo; add other ingredients and cook 3 minutes. Remove from fire; add vanilla and peanuts. Beat until thick and drop on waxed paper.

*Mr. Ross Baxter: Karen '80*

# PEANUT PATTIES

2-1/2 cups sugar
2/3 cup white Karo
1 cup canned milk
3 cups raw peanuts

1/2 stick oleo
1 tablespoon vanilla
Red food coloring, if desired

Mix sugar, Karo, milk, and peanuts. Bring to a boil. Turn heat to low and cook for 1 hour in iron skillet, stirring frequently. Remove from heat and add oleo and vanilla. Add red food coloring if desired. Beat until thick, and drop on wax paper or cookie sheet.

*Note:* Do the same for Pecan Pralines, except use pecans instead of peanuts (a few less) and do not add food coloring.

*Michael and Delores McDole: Paula '80*
*Alfred and Juanita Niemann: Ramona '70; Barbara ' 71*

# WESTERN PECAN CRUNCH

1-1/3 cups sugar
1 cup oleo
1/2 cup white corn syrup
1 teaspoon vanilla

2 quarts popped corn
1-1/2 cups pecans
1 cup almonds or pecans

Bring sugar, oleo, and syrup to a boil, stirring constantly. Boil over medium heat 10 to 15 minutes, or until it turns a light caramel color, stirring occasionally. Remove from heat. Add vanilla. Pour over popcorn and nuts, mixing to coat all grains. Spread on foil to dry. Keep in air tight container.

*Bill and Mickey Green: Cindy '67*

Those who can command themselves,
command others.

# MEXICAN PECAN CANDY

2 cups brown sugar
1/2 cup milk
1/4 teaspoon salt

1 tablespoon butter
1 teaspoon vanilla
2 cups pecans, chopped

Mix sugar, milk, and salt. Cook to soft ball stage tested in cold water. Add butter and vanilla and beat. Stir in pecans. Drop on wax paper.

*Mona Lea: Shyla '67*

# PECAN PATTIES

2-1/2 cups sugar
2/3 cup white Karo syrup
1 cup canned milk
2 cups chopped pecans

Few drops red food coloring
1 tablespoon vanilla
3 tablespoon butter
1/4 cup powdered sugar

Bring to boil and cook to firm ball stage sugar, syrup, milk, add pecans and coloring. Then add vanilla, butter, and powdered sugar. Spoon out on wax paper.

*Billy and Pat Morrison: Bill '77*

# PRALINES

2 cups sugar
1 cup buttermilk
1 teaspoon soda

Pinch of salt
2 tablespoons butter
2 to 2-1/2 cups pecans

Use a large pan (4 quart) to cook this in because it foams while cooking. Combine sugar, buttermilk, soda, and salt. Cook briskly, stirring frequently, scraping sides and bottom of pan for 5 minutes. Add butter and pecans. Stir continuously for 5 minutes or until very soft ball forms in cold water. Remove from heat. Cool slightly, then beat until candy thickens and is creamy. Drop by teaspoon onto wax paper. If they tend to thicken before you finish, add a few drops of water.

*Henry and Beth Mohr: Charles '75*

**We do not stop playing because we are old;
We grow old because we stop playing.**

# PRALINES
### *(Microwave)*

3/4 cup butter
2 cups sugar
1/4 teaspoon salt

2 cups chopped pecans
2 tablespoons butter
1 teaspoon soda

Stir all ingredients except soda in a 4-quart bowl. Cook on high for 12 minutes, stirring every 4 minutes with a wooden spoon. When ready, stir in soda and stir until foamy. Cook on high for 1 minute to give a caramel color. Beat (about 1 minute). Drop by teaspoon on buttered foil. Makes about 5 dozen.

*Jonnie and Linda Miller: Jana '84*

# CHEWY PECAN PRALINES

2 cups sugar
1-1/2 cups cream
1-3/4 cups Karo

1 cup butter
2 cups pecans
1 teaspoon vanilla

Combine sugar, cream, Karo, and butter. Cook until mixture reaches firm ball stage. Remove from heat. Add pecans and vanilla. Stir until thick; drop by spoonfuls on buttered platter. Cool. Wrap each praline separately in wax paper.

*S.P. and Bernice Echols: Delilah '51*

# STRAWBERRY CANDY

1 can Eagle Brand Milk
4 small boxes Strawberry Jello
(3-ounce)

2 cups coconut
1 cup chopped pecans

Mix all together; roll into little balls or shape like strawberries. Roll in granulated sugar.

*Jerry and Sue Fox: Sharry '80; Stacy '82*

"There is nothing so annoying as to have two people
Go right on talking when you're interrupting."
— Mark Twain

# "TURTLES"
### *So Good!*

1 (12-ounce) package chocolate chips
1 can Eagle Brand milk

1 large package miniature marshmallows
Pecans, to taste

Melt chocolate chips and milk over low heat. Let cool; add marshmallows and chopped pecans. Spoon out on wax paper. (The cooling is to keep marshmallows from melting.)

*Glen and Cleta Wieser: Karol '68; Kerri '74*

# HOT SPICY APPLE DUMPLINGS
### *(Furr's)*

Dough:
2 cups flour
2 teaspoons baking powder

1 teaspoon salt
2/3 cup shortening
1/2 cup milk

Mix dry ingredients; cut in shortening until mixture looks like coarse crumbs. Add milk. Roll out dough and cut into small squares. Then place a spoonful of the apple mixture in each square and pinch together. Place in a deep pan.

Apple Mixture:
1 can apples
3/4 cup sugar

1/2 teaspoon cinnamon
1/2 teaspoon allspice
1/2 teaspoon nutmeg

Mix all ingredients; place a spoonful of mixture in each square of dough.

Sauce:
1 quart water
1 cup sugar

1/4 teaspoon cinnamon
1/4 teaspoon nutmeg
1/4 teaspoon allspice

Mix together. Bring to a boil and when mixture begins to thicken slightly, remove from heat and pour over dumplings. Place in oven and bake until brown.

*Ken and Mary Sacke: Schaun '66; Corbi '70*

---

"A man can't be too careful
in the choice of his enemies."
— Oscar Wilde

# APPLE CRISP

4 cups cooking apples, peeled
and sliced or 1 can pie apples
1 teaspoon lemon juice
1 tablespoon flour
1/4 cup brown sugar
1/4 cup white sugar

1/3 cup flour
1 cup uncooked oats
1/3 cup brown sugar
1 teaspoon cinnamon
1/3 cup melted butter

Mix apples, lemon juice, flour, and sugar. Place in shallow mixing bowl. Top with the mixture of topping: flour, oats, sugar, cinnamon, and butter. Spread on top. Bake at 375 degrees for 30 minutes.

*Leland and Mona Hamilton: Angela '63; Julie '77*

# APPLE KUCHEN

1 stick melted oleo
1 box Yellow Cake Mix
1/2 cup coconut, optional
1 can drained pie apples

1 teaspoon cinnamon
1/2 cup sugar
1 egg
1 carton sour cream

Mix oleo, cake mix, and coconut. Put in oblong cake pan; slightly pat in bottom of pan. Bake at 350 degrees for 10 minutes. Pour drained pie apples on this hot crust. Mix cinnamon and sugar and sprinkle over apples. Mix egg and sour cream; drizzle over top. Bake 25 minutes at 350 degrees.

(This is Latisha's favorite!)

*Diana Henderson: Latisha Atwood '84*

# BLUEBERRY DELIGHT

Crust:
2 cups Graham cracker crumbs
1 stick oleo, slightly melted

1/2 cup powdered sugar
1/2 cup finely chopped nuts

Mix all together and press into 9x13" pan.

Blueberry Delight:
1 package (8-ounce) cream cheese
2 eggs
1 cup sugar

2 teaspoons lemon juice
1 can blueberry pie filling
(Comstock)
Dream Whip or Whipped cream

Mix cream cheese, eggs, sugar, and lemon juice. Spread this mixture over crust and bake at 350 degrees for 20 minutes. Cool and spread blueberry pie filling over cooked mixture. Cool. When ready to serve, spread Dream Whip or whipped cream on top.

*Johnny and Annette King: Danna '72*

# CREME CARAMEL

Creme:
4 eggs
4 rounded tablespoons sugar
1/2 teaspoon vanilla

3 cups milk
Caramel Coating:
4 rounded tablespoons sugar
1/2 cup water

Mix and beat eggs, sugar, and vanilla until fluffy. Warm the milk a little and add to egg mixture. Beat 1 minute. For the caramel coating, take the pan in which you wish to cook the Creme Caramel and mix the sugar and water in it. Cook over medium heat until it is brown. Tilt the pan so that coating covers sides. Add the creme mixture. Put pan in the oven in a pan of hot water and bake 1 hour at 300 degrees or until set.

*Leroy and Florence Burk: JuJu '85; Charmain Franklin '84*

# CHERRIES ON A CLOUD

1 stick oleo, melted
40 Saltine crackers, crushed
3 egg whites, beaten

1 cup sugar
1 Cherry Pie Filling
1 large carton Cool Whip

Melt oleo in 9x13" pan. Add crushed crackers (reserve 3 tablespoons of cracker mixture). Spread over bottom of pan. Beat egg whites. Slowly add sugar while beating until stiff. Spread on top of crumbs. Bake at 350 degrees for 15 to 20 minutes. Cool. Top with Cherry Pie Filling. Spread Cool Whip on top. Add reserved crumbs. Cover with Saran Wrap and freeze. Remove from freezer 30 minutes before serving. Slice into serving size pieces.

*James and Flo Whitcomb: Janet '53*

# CHERRY DELIGHT
## (Good)

20 Graham crackers, double size
1/2 cup melted butter
1 (8-ounce) package cream cheese
1 cup sugar

3 eggs
1 teaspoon vanilla
2 cans Cherry Pie Filling
2 packages Dream Whip

Mix Graham crackers and butter. Press and pan into large oblong pan. Mix cream cheese, sugar, eggs, and vanilla; beat thoroughly. Pour over crust. Bake 25 minutes at 350 degrees. Let cool and pour 2 cans of Cherry Pie Filling over this and refrigerate overnight. Whip Dream Whip and spread over all. Cut in squares.

*Ray and Doris Flowe: Rita '68*

# CHERRY TORTE

Crust:
1 stick butter, melted
2 cups Nabisco Sugar Honey
   Graham Crackers, crushed

1 cup chopped nuts
1/2 cup powdered sugar

Melt butter in 9x12" pan. Mix other ingredients and pat to form crust.

Cherry Torte:
1 (8-ounce) package cream
   cheese, softened
2 eggs, beaten
1 cup sugar

2 teaspoons lemon juice
1 can Cherry Pie Filling
Cool Whip
1/2 cup chopped nuts

Mix cream cheese, eggs, sugar, and lemon juice. Pour on top of crust. Bake 20 minutes at 350 degrees. Cool. Pour Cherry Pie Filling on top. Top with Cool Whip and chopped nuts.

*O.F. and Edith Hamilton: Linda '61*

# CHOCOLATE DELIGHT

1 cup flour
1/2 cup butter
1 cup chopped nuts
1 cup powdered sugar
1 (8-ounce) package cream cheese
1 cup Cool Whip

1 small package Instant chocolate
   pudding
1 small package Instant Vanilla
   pudding
2 cups milk
1 teaspoon vanilla

Combine flour, butter, and chopped nuts and mix to cornmeal consistency. Press in 9x12" pan. Bake 20 minutes at 350 degrees. Cool and spread with mixture of powdered sugar, cream cheese and 1 cup Cool Whip. Mix pudding mixes and milk. Add vanilla. On top of second layer, top with pudding mixes. Top with remaining Cool Whip.

*Sherman and Alice Boley: Barry '74*

Always forgive your enemies —
Nothing annoys them so much.

# CHOCOLATE DESSERT
## *(Mississippi Mud)*

| | |
|---|---|
| 2 sticks oleo | 4 eggs |
| 4 tablespoons cocoa | 1 cup chopped nuts |
| 2 cups sugar | Pinch of salt |
| 1-1/2 cups flour | Miniature marshmallows |

Mix all ingredients except marshmallows. Mix well. Pour into greased and floured 9x13" pan. Bake at 350 degrees for 20 to 25 minutes. Cover with marshmallows. Let melt.

| | |
|---|---|
| Icing: | 1 box powdered sugar |
| 4 tablespoons cocoa | 4 to 5 tablespoons condensed |
| 1 stick oleo | milk |

Mix cocoa and oleo. Mix in powdered sugar and milk. Mix until creamy. Spread on cake.

*Fred and Joyce Weir: Charlotte '68*

# CHOCOLATE DESSERT SQUARES
## *(Weight Watchers)*

Line an 8x8" dish with 9 Graham Crackers (or cover). Set aside.

| | |
|---|---|
| 1 cup Ricotta cheese | 1 large package Nutrasweet |
| 10 packages Equal sweetener | Chocolate Jello Pudding |
| 1/2 teaspoon vanilla | 1 cup Cool Whip |

Mix cheese, Equal, and vanilla. Layer over crackers. Mix Chocolate Jello Pudding according to direction. Spread over cheese mixture. Ice with Cool Whip. Refrigerate several hours. 6 servings.

1 fat; 1 protein; 33 calories.

*Dayton and Maezelle Wester: Gayle '58*

# CHOCOLATE DREAM DESSERT

| | |
|---|---|
| Step 1: | 1 stick oleo |
| 1 cup flour | 1 cup pecans, chopped |

Mix and spread in 9x13" pan. Bake 20 minutes at 350 degrees.

| | |
|---|---|
| Step 2: | 1 (3-ounce) package cream cheese |
| 1 cup powdered sugar | 1 cup Cool Whip |

Mix and spread on cool pastry.

| | |
|---|---|
| Step 3: | 1 package Instant Chocolate |
| 1 package Instant Vanilla | Pudding |
| Pudding | 2 cups milk |

Mix and spread over layer number 2. Spread 1 cup of Cool Whip over all pie. Grate Hershey bar over the top.

*Bob and Johnnie Shannon: Neva Jo Shannon (Bufkin) '51*

# CHOCOLATE LAYERED DESSERT

1 cup flour
1 stick oleo, softened
1/2 cup pecans
1 (8-ounce) package cream cheese
1 cup powdered sugar

1 large package chocolate Instant
   Pudding
2 cups milk
Cool Whip

Mix flour, oleo, and pecans and then spread batter into baking dish. Bake 15 minutes at 425 degrees. Mix softened cream with sugar and spread over batter. Prepare pudding with milk. Spread pudding over batter. Cover with Cool Whip and refrigerate.

*Mr. Ross Baxter (Karen '80)*

# CHOCOLATE YUMMY

Layer 1:
1 stick butter or oleo, melted

1 cup flour
1 cup chopped pecans

Mix together and use milk (if necessary, approximately 1/4 cup, if any). Press into bottom of 9x13" pan and cook at 350 degrees for 20 minutes. Cool.
Layer 2:
1 (8-ounce) package cream
   cheese, softened

1 cup sugar
1 cup Cool Whip

Mix together and spread on top of cooled Layer 1.
Layer 3:
1 large package Chocolate Instant
   Pudding

2 cups milk

Mix Pudding Mix and milk until creamy (1 to 2 minutes). Spread on Layer 2. Cover with layer of Cool Whip and chill.

*Wayne Turley '52: submitted by his wife, Anna*

# PINK CRANBERRY FREEZE

2 (3-ounce) packages cream
   cheese
2 tablespoons mayonnaise
2 tablespoons sugar
1 can whole cranberry sauce

1 can crushed pineapple
1/2 cup pecans
1 cup whipped cream
1/2 cup powdered sugar
Vanilla

Soften cheese. Blend in mayonnaise and sugar. Add fruits and nuts. Fold in whipped cream to which powdered sugar and vanilla have been added. Pour into loaf pan and freeze at least 6 hours.

*Henry and Beth Mohr: Charles '75*

# CREAM PUFFS

| | |
|---|---|
| 1 cup water | Cream for Puffs: |
| 1/2 cup butter | 2 cups milk |
| 1 cup flour | 1 cup sugar |
| 3 eggs | 2 eggs |
| | 2 tablespoons cornstarch |
| | 1 teaspoon vanilla |

Boil together the water and butter. While boiling, stir in flour. Take from stove and stir to a smooth paste. After this cools, stir in eggs and stir 5 minutes. Drop by tablespoonfuls on a buttered tin and bake at 400 degrees for 25 minutes. Do not let puffs touch each other on the pan.

Mix milk, sugar, eggs, and cornstarch. Cook to a creamy texture and add vanilla. Cool and fill cooked puffs.

*Bob and Joyce Luck: Cathy '68*

# FROSTY STRAWBERRY SQUARES

| | |
|---|---|
| Crust: | 1 cup chopped pecans |
| 1/2 cup brown sugar | 1 stick oleo |
| 1 cup flour | |

Mix all ingredients like a pie crust; spread in a 9x13" pan. Bake 20 to 30 minutes in 350 degree oven. Stir often with fork to crumble. Cool. (Reserve 1/4 cup for topping.) Spread the rest like a crust. Prepare filling.

| | |
|---|---|
| Filling: | 1 cup sugar |
| 1 (10-ounce) package frozen | 1 pint whipping cream or 1 pint |
| strawberries | Cool Whip |
| 2 unbeaten egg whites | 1/4 cup chopped pecans |
| 1 tablespoon lemon juice | |

Combine strawberries, egg whites, lemon juice and sugar in large bowl and beat at high speed for 15 minutes. Fold in whipped cream (or Cool Whip and pecans). Pour on top of crust. Top with remaining crumbs. Freeze. Serve with Cool Whip and fresh strawberries for garnish. (May beat egg whites first and then add other ingredients.)

*Harold and Norma Roberts: Morris '67*
*James and Lois Russell: Billy '72*

**If you get up early, work late,
And pay your taxes,
You will get ahead — if you strike oil!**

# FLAN

| | |
|---|---|
| 1 cup sugar | 3 eggs |
| 1 can Eagle Brand Milk | 1 teaspoon vanilla |
| 1 can sweet milk | |

Melt sugar and pour into a square pan (pyrex or Corning Ware). Cover bottom part of pan with melted sugar and set aside. Pour remaining ingredients into blender. Blend and pour mixture over melted sugar. Place pan in larger pan containing water and bake at 350 degrees until done. (It should be the consistency of custard.)

*Gerard and Lulabel VanDuist: Ryan '79*
*Jess and Halya Barrera: Martha '79*

# FROZEN SALAD DESSERT

| | |
|---|---|
| 1 (14-ounce) can Cherry Pie Filling | 1 can Eagle Brand Milk |
| 1 (12-ounce) can crushed pineapple, drained | 1 (10-ounce) carton Cool Whip |
| | 1 cup chopped nuts |

Combine pie filling and pineapple. Gently stir in milk. Fold in Cool Whip. Pat into a 9x13" pan and sprinkle with pecans. Cover with foil and freeze. Keeps forever in freezer! Also good with peaches or blueberry pie filling.

*Variation:* Some recipes also add 1 can mandarin oranges or 1 cup coconut and 1 cup marshmallows.

*William and Dorothy Ryan: Bobby '64*

# FRUIT PIZZA

| | |
|---|---|
| Drain separately overnight: | 1 (8-ounce) package cream cheese, softened |
| 1 large can chunk pineapple | 1 cup sugar |
| 1 medium can mandarin oranges | 2 bananas, sliced and dipped in lemon juice |
| 2 packages frozen strawberries | |
| 1 small jar cherries | 1 jar apricot preserves, heated (do not boil or simmer) |
| 1 roll sugar cookie dough, room temperature | 1/2 cup chopped pecans |

Preheat oven to 375 degrees. Trim a piece of foil to fit a large pizza pan. Butter the top of the foil and roll cookie dough on top of foil. Bake until golden brown (about 12 to 15 minutes). Cool completely. Mix cream cheese with sugar and spread onto cooled crust. Place drained fruit in layers on top of the creamed mixture. Place sliced bananas on layered fruit. Heat preserves just until they can be poured and pour 1/2 jar over pizza top. Sprinkle with pecans. Pour remaining apricot preserves over pecans. Chill for 2 hours.

*Milton and Mildred Oswalt: Johnny '52 (submitted by Johnny)*

# HEAVENLY HASH
### *"BEST"*

3 tablespoons sugar
2 tablespoons flour
2 well-beaten eggs
1 (No. 2-1/2) can crushed
pineapple, (drain and save
juice)

1 tablespoon butter
1 carton whipping cream,
whipped
1 cup chopped nuts
1/2 pound small marshmallows

Mix sugar and flour. Add eggs and pineapple juice. Cook in double boiler until thick. Add butter. Cool. Add whipped cream, nuts, and marshmallows. Chill.

*Olan and Iona Calvert: Bob '56*

# MARSHMALLOW DESSERT

Vanilla Wafers, enough to crush
and line large loaf cake pan
1 (No. 2) can pineapple chunks,
drained (save juice)
1 (10-ounce) package
marshmallows, diced into
small pieces

1 pint whipping cream
1 teaspoon vanilla
1/4 cup maraschino cherries
1/2 cup pecans, chopped
3 or 4 bananas, sliced

Line the bottom of the cake pan with crushed Vanilla Wafer crumbs. Melt marshmallows in pineapple juice. Cool. Whip cream with vanilla. Stir into marshmallow mixture. Add fruits and nuts, saving bananas until last. Pour fruit on top of crumbs. Spread top with bananas. Top with more vanilla wafer crumbs.

*Julian and Maxine Hart: Curtis '50*

# OREO DESSERT

46 Oreo cookies, crushed
1/2 cup butter, softened
1/2 gallon ice cream

1 (8-ounce) carton Cool Whip
1 small can chocolate syrup
1/2 cup chopped pecans

Combine cookies and butter in bowl and mix well. Press into 9x14" pan. Slice ice cream; press over cookie mixture. Spread with Cool Whip. Drizzle with chocolate syrup and top with pecans. Freeze until firm. DELICIOUS!

*Charles and Wanda Dye: William '80; Chad '83*

---

**We can't all be heroes because somebody
has to sit on the curb and clap as they go by!**

## PEANUT BUTTER CUPS

1 cup oleo
1 cup peanut butter

1 pound box powdered sugar
1 large Hershey bar

Melt oleo and peanut butter; add powdered sugar a little at a time, mixing well. Spread in buttered 9x13" pan or cupcake tins. Chill. Melt Hershey bar in microwave or in top of double boiler and spread over peanut butter mixture.

*Bob and Paula Hamilton: Scott '80; Jeff '81*

## PUMPKIN LOG

3 eggs
1 cup sugar
2/3 cup pumpkin
1 teaspoon lemon juice
3/4 cup flour
1 teaspoon baking powder

1/2 teaspoon salt
2 teaspoons cinnamon
1 teaspoon ginger
1/2 teaspoon nutmeg
1/2 cup chopped pecans

Beat eggs at high speed for 5 minutes. Gradually beat in sugar. Stir in pumpkin and lemon juice. Sift dry ingredients and add to pumpkin mixture. Spread evenly into greased and floured 15x10" jelly roll pan. Sprinkle pecans over batter. Bake at 375 degrees for 15 minutes. Turn out on towel sprinkled with powdered sugar. Roll cake. Cool. Combine all filling ingredients and beat until smooth. When cake has cooled, unroll and spread with filling; roll again. Slice to serve.

Filling:
1 cup powdered sugar
1 (8-ounce) package cream
   cheese, softened
2 to 4 tablespoons oleo

3/4 teaspoon vanilla
1 cup chopped nuts
Mix and spread on cake; roll
   again.

*Note:* Decorate with springs of holly and serve at Christmas.

*Juanita Hughen: Waymon '50; (submitted by Waymon and Ima Jean Hughen)*

When the well's dry,
We know the worth of water!

# RASPBERRY DESSERT

15 Graham crackers, firmly
    crushed
1/4 cup melted butter
1/2 pound marshmallows
1/2 cup milk

1 cup whipping cream
2 packages frozen raspberries
1 tablespoon lemon juice
1 tablespoon flour or cornstarch
    (more may be needed)

Mix cracker crumbs and melted butter. Put aside 1/4 cup of mixture. Press the remainder on the bottom of an 8x11" flat pan. Melt marshmallows in milk; cool. Whip cream and add to marshmallow mixture. Separate raspberries from juice. Add lemon juice to berries. Thicken raspberries juice with 1 tablespoon of flour or cornstarch. (Use enough flour to make the consistency of gravy.) Cool. Pour 1/2 of marshmallow mixture into pan. Add raspberries and juice. Mix together. Top with remainder of marshmallow mixture. Cover with the rest of the crumb mixture. Place in refrigerator 4 hours before serving.

*Clyde and Elah Broam: Ronnie '53*

# RASPBERRY DELIGHT

1 can Eagle Brand Milk
1/2 cup lemon juice
1/2 cup pecans, chopped
1/2 pint heavy cream, whipped

2 tablespoons seedless raspberry
    jam
1 box vanilla wafers, crumbled

Mix slowly milk, lemon juice, and pecans. Fold in whipped cream and jam. Make a layer of wafers in pan. Pour half of mixture over wafers; make another layer of crumbs. Cover with remaining half of mixture. Top with crumbs. Chill overnight.

*William and Grace Jordan: Sara '71*

He that scatters thorns, let him not go barefoot!

# HERSHEY'S VANILLA CHIP FRUIT TART

3/4 cup butter or oleo, softened
1/2 cup powdered sugar
1-1/2 cups flour

Vanilla Filling (recipe follows)
Fruit Topping (recipe follows)

Heat oven to 300 degrees. Beat butter and sugar until light and fluffy; blend in flour. Press mixture onto bottom and up sides of 12" pizza pan. Bake 20 to 25 minutes or until lightly browned; cool completely. Prepare Vanilla Filling; spread on cooled crust. Cover; chill. Prepare Fruit Topping. Cover; chill assembled tart. 10 to 12 servings.

Vanilla Filling:
1-2/3 (10-ounce) package
HERSHEY'S Vanilla Milk
Chips

1/4 cup whipping cream
1 (8-ounce) package cream
cheese, softened

In microwave bowl, microwave vanilla chips and whipping cream on high (100%) 1 to 1-1/2 minutes or until chips are melted and mixture is smooth when stirred. Beat in cream cheese.

Fruit Topping:
1/4 cup sugar
1 tablespoon cornstarch

1/2 cup pineapple juice
1/2 teaspoon lemon juice
Assorted fresh fruit

In small saucepan combine sugar and cornstarch; stir in juices. Cook over medium heat, stirring constantly, until thickened; cool. Meanwhile slice and arrange fruit on top of filling, pour juice mixture over fruit.

*Teacher's Pet: Donna Lambert, daughter*

# GOOD BANANA PUDDING

*(So good! Makes a lot, too.)*

2 large packages Instant Vanilla
Pudding
5 cups milk
1 cup sour cream

1 teaspoon vanilla
1 large carton Cool Whip
1 box Vanilla Wafers
3 to 4 large bananas, sliced

Make pudding with milk; fold in sour cream and vanilla. Then fold in 1/2 of large container of Cool Whip. Layer vanilla wafers in large bowl; cover with slices of bananas, then custard. Repeat and top with rest of Cool Whip and vanilla wafers.

*Note:* May be placed in two smaller bowls — share one with a friend. Serves large group (14 to 16).

*Teacher's Pet: Lana Albers, daughter*

# BREAD PUDDING

5 cups day-old bread, cut up
   (French bread is ideal)
1/2 cup raisins
1-1/2 cups sugar
1-1/2 teaspoons vanilla

1-1/2 teaspoons nutmeg
4 cups milk
6 eggs
1/4 cup butter

Mix bread, raisins, sugar, vanilla, and nutmeg. Mix milk, eggs, and butter; pour over first mixture and let stand 15 minutes. Mix well. Pour into buttered pan. Bake 45 minutes to 1 hour. (Bread Pudding will keep well overnight in refrigerator. The recipe is from the Water Works in Waco, Texas.

*John and Ruth Tidwell: Sandee '53*

# BREAD PUDDING

6 to 8 slices bread, crumbled
1 small can evaporated milk and
   enough milk to make 2 cups
3 eggs
2 cups sugar

2 teaspoons vanilla
1/2 stick oleo
Dash of salt
Coconut to taste, optional
Cinnamon

Mix all ingredients except cinnamon. Pour into 7x11" greased pan and sprinkle with cinnamon. Bake 25 to 30 minutes in 350 degree oven.

Bread Pudding Sauce:
2 tablespoons cornstarch
1/2 cup sugar
1 cup water

1/8 teaspoon salt
4 tablespoons lemon juice
2 tablespoons oleo

Mix cornstarch and sugar with 1/4 cup water. Add remaining water. Bring to a boil and remove from heat. Add remaining ingredients. Cool slightly. Serve over warm pudding.

*Harold and Cleta Garms: Staci '71*

# RICE PUDDING

3/4 cup rice
3/4 cup sugar
1 quart milk
1 can (14-ounce) evaporated milk

1 teaspoon vanilla
Raisins (optional)
3 tablespoons cornstarch
3 tablespoons water

In a large saucepan, cook rice according to package directions. Add remaining ingredients, except cornstarch and water; stir to mix, and let simmer for 20 minutes. Mix cornstarch with water; add to rice mixture and simmer for 20 minutes longer. Let cool before serving.

*Breland and Ann Bridges: Brenda '61*

# VINEGAR DUMPLINGS

Make pie crust dough and roll out thin. Sprinkle with sugar and cinnamon. Roll as a jelly roll and cut into thin slices; place in pan and cover with dumpling sauce.

**Sauce:**
3 tablespoons flour
1/2 pound brown sugar
1 quart water

1/2 teaspoon salt
1/2 stick oleo
2 tablespoons vinegar

Place flour and brown sugar in saucepan and mix well. Add 1 quart of water and salt. Cook slowly until thickened. Add oleo and vinegar. Pour over dumplings. Bake at 375 degrees about 30 minutes.

*William and Neva Lee: Sheila '69*

# BASIC ICE CREAM

1 can Eagle Brand milk
1 large can Carnation milk
5 eggs, well beaten
2-1/2 cups sugar

2 teaspoons vanilla or 1 package
   frozen strawberries, well
   crushed

Mix well. Finish filling can with milk and freeze.

*J.L. and Mary Varley: Susan '69*

# BUTTER-PECAN ICE CREAM

6 eggs
1-1/2 cups sugar
1-1/4 cups toasted chopped pecans
1 tablespoon butter
1 can Eagle Brand milk

1 pint whipping cream
1 tablespoon vanilla
1 tablespoon butter extract
1 teaspoon maple flavoring

Beat eggs and sugar. Toast pecans in butter in 400 degree oven. (Stir 1 or 2 times while toasting.) Add remaining ingredients to above mixture. Mix well and pour into ice cream freezer. Add enough milk to fill freezer. 1 gallon.

*Alvie and Doris McWilliams: Marilyn '59*

---

**After all is said and done,
More is said than done.**

# BANANA HEATH ICE CREAM

6 beaten eggs
6 mashed bananas
1 can Eagle Brand milk
1 cup sugar

6 Heath toffee candy bars,
   broken up
2 teaspoons vanilla

Mix all ingredients; stir well. Put in freezer container. Add enough milk to fill to freezing line on freezer. Freeze as usual.

*Note:* If you will put Heath bars in the freezer for awhile, they are easier to break up.

*Jerry and Rosmary Wilkerson: Brent Garymartin '79*

# HEATH ICE CREAM

1 (8-ounce) package cream cheese
1 cup sugar
3 eggs
1 teaspoon vanilla

1 package French Instant Pudding
1 can Eagle Brand Milk
4 to 5 crushed up Heath bars
1/2 gallon milk

Combine cream cheese and sugar; beat tar out of it. Add vanilla, pudding mix, milk, and Heath bars. Mix well. Add milk and freeze.

*A.L. and Betty Vickers: Sharon '65*

# HOMEMADE ICE CREAM

4 eggs, beaten
2-1/4 cups sugar
2 tablespoons flour
1-1/2 teaspoons vanilla

1 can Eagle Brand milk
Favorite fruits, flavorings, candy,
   etc.

Mix beaten eggs, sugar, and flour and beat. Add vanilla and Eagle Brand milk. Add fruits, if used and fill with milk to freeze.

(Mike's family recipe — from his grandmother: good with vanilla with toppings of all kinds.

*Mike and Lavern Fetner: Gina '80*

---

**If you tell the truth,
you don't have to remember anything.**

# MILKY WAY ICE CREAM

6 Milky Way bars
1 can Eagle Brand Milk
5 eggs

2 to 2-1/2 cups sugar
1 small can Pet Milk (can use large can)

Melt Milky Way bars and Eagle Brand. Beat together eggs, sugar, and Pet milk. Mix all above together. Pour into ice cream freezer and fill with milk. Freeze.

*Terry and Lena Wilson: Clay '85*

# PEACH ICE CREAM
## *(1 gallon)*

5 eggs
2-1/2 cups sugar
1 can Eagle Brand Milk
1 can evaporated milk

1 tablespoon almond extract
2 cups mashed peaches
Half and Half milk
1/2 cup sugar

Beat eggs until frothy; add sugar and beat well. Add milk and extract. Continue beating until well blended. Pour into gallon freezer. Add Half and Half to fill freezer to 4" from top. Freeze 5 minutes or until thick. Add peaches to which 1/2 cup sugar has been added. Continue and freeze until firm. Let set 1 hour.

*Bill and Sue Craig: Susan '61*

# VANILLA ICE CREAM
## *(6 quarts)*

4-1/2 quarts milk
7 eggs, beaten
2 tablespoons flour

2-3/4 cups sugar
1 pint cream
3 teaspoons vanilla

Scald 1-1/2 quarts milk; beat eggs. Mix flour and sugar. Add to beaten eggs. Add 1 more quart of milk to eggs and blend into hot milk. Cook to custard consistency, stirring constantly over medium heat. (This takes awhile.) Cool. Pour into 6-quart ice cream freezer; add rest of whole milk, cream, and vanilla. Freeze.

*Billy and Jane Lucas: Ricky '82; Randa '84*

There is just one way to bring up a child in the way he should go, and that is to travel that way yourself.
— Abraham Lincoln

# VANILLA ICE CREAM

2 cups sugar
2 heaping tablespoons flour
1/2 teaspoon salt
1 quart milk

1 large can Carnation milk
6 eggs
1 tablespoon vanilla
Extra milk

Mix sugar, flour, and salt with milk and Carnation milk. Stir well. Cook to make a soft custard. Beat eggs for a long time. Add some hot custard to eggs; mix; then add eggs to custard in pan. Do not return to fire after adding eggs! Add vanilla and enough milk to fill a gallon freezer within 3" of the top. Cool before freezing.

*Moody and Georgean Conner: Mr. Conner, principal*

# SHERBET

6 orange soda pops
1 can crushed pineapple

1 can Eagle Brand Milk
Freeze in freezer.

*Variation:* Use 6 strawberry soda pops in place of orange.

*Bobby and Frances Longshore: Trina '70; Mark '77*

According to the laws of aerodynamics,
the bumble bee cannot fly.

# Miscellaneous

Applying for Teaching Job 1937

*Reflections...*

# My First School — 1937

The idea of becoming a teacher came when I was a fourth grader. The fulfillment was a long and arduous mission; the Depression of the '30s made everything so very difficult. College was in the future, but no money! I thought I would literally die if I could not go to college.

Luckily, our rural mail carrier-neighbor became my banker, and I was able to go to John Tarleton College, ten miles from home.

But, going to college did not guarantee a teaching job. Each small school (and there were many in the county) had seven trustees that must be visited personally. This was done for two reasons. First, the status and importance of being a trustee in the community, and secondly, a majority of the seven trustees must be convinced that you were the best qualified applicant.

The foot work was as important as the persuasion. I have often laughingly said that I bought an after-five outfit to apply for schools because I was out way after five still looking for a school. Many days, and all day long, I kept going from trustee to trustee. The most likely place to find the farmer-trustee in the spring was in his field. So with my after-five attire donned (finest dress, hat, and high heels) I made my way across his fresh plowed furrows to plead my case.

That was not the end of the ordeal. Election night came! All applicants assembled at the designated school, sat outside, or sat in cars, and waited and waited (often into the wee hours of the morning) for your turn to go in before all the seven trustees and AGAIN convince them of your credentials.

It paid off. My first teaching job was in 1937. Monthly salary: $83.67; yearly salary: $669.38!!!

# PEACH HONEY

1 cup peach pulp                     1-1/2 cup sugar

Peel peaches and remove seeds. Grind through food chopper. Mix. Heat to boiling point and let boil approximately 7 minutes. When it begins to boil, skim off top foam. Seal in hot, sterile jars.

*Note:* The amount given is the proportions of fruit and sugar to use. Can make larger amounts.

Old recipe — very good and easy!

*Tome and Jerry Rehders: De Aun '63; Denesa '70*

# CHOW CHOW

2 large heads of cabbage              6 cups sugar
1 peck green tomatoes (8-quarts)      1/2 cup salt
5 medium onions                       2 tablespoons allspice
5 green peppers                       2 tablespoons black pepper
5 sweet peppers                       6 cups vinegar

Grind cabbage, tomatoes, onions, peppers. Combine and mix remaining ingredients. Cook 1-1/2 hours. Place in hot, sterile jars and seal.

*T.C. and Helen Anderson: Tana '70*

# EDDIE'S PICKLES

## (Crisp)

2 cups pickling lime                  1 teaspoon celery seed
2 gallons water                       1 teaspoon whole cloves
7 pounds cucumbers, sliced            1 teaspoon pickling spice OR 1
2 quarts vinegar                         teaspoon powdered
8 cups sugar                             cinnamon
1 tablespoon salt                     1/2 teaspoon tumeric

In an enamel or crock, mix 2 cups lime with 2 gallons of water. Add 7 pounds of sliced cucumbers. (Medium sized and cut in average thin slices.) Let set 24 hours. Rinse thoroughly and let set 1 to 3 hours in cold water. (I add ice to water.) Make a mixture of vinegar, sugar, salt, celery seeds, cloves, pickling spice, and tumeric. Heat till well dissolved; pour over cucumbers. Let set over night. Boil 40 minutes and seal in clean sterile jars.

*Danny and Ima Gene Thomas: Tammy '74*

# ENGLISH PEAR RELISH

| | |
|---|---|
| 1 peck pears | 2 pounds sugar |
| 8 large onions | 2 teaspoons whole spice |
| 3 green bell peppers | 1 teaspoon salt |
| 4 red bell peppers | 5 cups vinegar |
| 3 hot peppers | |

Grind pears, onions, and peppers. Mix sugar, spices, and vinegar in large cooker; bring to a boil. Add pears, onions, and peppers and boil 1/2 hour. Seal as you would any relish.

*Glen and Connie Haggard: Jay '80*

# MEXICAN RELISH

| | |
|---|---|
| 8 cups tomatoes, green or ripe, chopped | 2 cups onions, chopped |
| | 2 cups sugar |
| 4 cups sweet red peppers, chopped | 1 tablespoon cinnamon |
| | 2 cups vinegar |
| 8 cups sweet green peppers, chopped | |

Mix all ingredients; bring to a boil and cook 40 minutes. Pour into hot sterile jars and seal.

*D.L. and Zelma Dorland: Linda '50*

# TABASCO PICKLES

These pickles are crisp, tangy and disappear quickly. Very easy to prepare.

| | |
|---|---|
| 1 gallon jar sour pickles | more hot flavor is wanted, |
| 1 regular size Tabasco Pepper | increase Tabasco carefully) |
| Sauce (2-ounce bottle) (If | 5 lb. bag sugar |

Drain pickles and cut into rounds approximately 1/4" to 1/3". (Save and use juice.) Discard stems. Place sugar and Tabasco in large container that will hold all the pickles. (I use a plastic wash basin.) Mix as best as possible. Add sliced pickles and stir to melt sugar. When all is melted, return to gallon jar and replace lid. Place in refrigerator and shake at least twice a day for 3 days. Ready to eat on the fourth day. Give as gifts by putting in small canning jars.

*L.Z. and Mabel Brown: Sherry '53 (given by Sherry Brown Landry)*

## BE CHEERFUL!
Of all the things you wear,
your expression is the most important.

# BARBECUE SAUCE

1 gallon catsup
4 ounces Worcestershire sauce
4 ounces Liquid Smoke
1 pound brown sugar

1-1/2 ounces COARSE black
  pepper
1 ounce garlic juice

Mix and store in refrigerator.

*Tom and Helen Helms: Daryl '62 (submitted by Daryl)*

# LARRY'S BAR-B-QUE SAUCE

1 (14-ounce) bottle catsup
1/4 cup beer
1/2 cup honey

1 tablespoon Worcestershire
  sauce
1 tablespoon butter (or more, if
  desired)

Mix all ingredients and cover meat. Continue to baste meat as it cooks. (Use as long as sauce last.)

*J.D. and Ethel Collinsworth: Sandra '50*

# FRESH CRANBERRY SAUCE

1 large package Strawberry jello
1 cup hot water
1 pound fresh cranberries,
  cleaned and ground

1 can crushed pineapple OR
  apple OR both (drain
  pineapple)
1 orange, chopped
1 cup pecans, chopped (or more)
1-1/2 cups sugar

Mix jello and hot water. Cool slightly. Add other ingredients to jello mixture. Refrigerate to set.

*Bill and Mary Moren: Bryce King '68; Leighton Moren '78*

# MARINATE FOR MEAT

1 cup sweetened pineapple juice
1 cup golden cooking sherry
1/4 cup soy sauce

1/2 teaspoon Accent
1/4 teaspoon garlic powder
2 tablespoons granulated sugar

Mix and pour over meat to marinate.

*Diana Henderson: Latisha Atwood '84*

---

**Genius is 3% inspiration and 97% perspiration.**

# LEMON SAUCE
### *(For Grilled Chicken)*

1/2 cup melted butter
2 tablespoons sugar
1 teaspoon Worcestershire sauce
1/2 teaspoon pepper

2 teaspoons salt
1/2 teaspoon paprika
Juice of 1/2 lemon

Stir all ingredients together over low heat until well blended. Brush on chicken to be grilled. (I often baste after it has been grilled on one side, then baste the other side.)

*Teacher's Pet*

# CHEESE SAUCE

1/4 cup butter or oleo
2 cups milk
1/4 cup flour

1 can green chopped chilies
1/4 pound cheese, grated

Melt butter; add milk, green chilies, and cheese. Cook until smooth. Use for green enchiladas.

*Frankie Garrett: De De '72*

# CHEESE SAUCE
# FOR BAKED POTATOES

4 tablespoons oleo, softened
4 ounces sharp American cheese
    (Kraft Old English)

1/2 cup sour cream
1 tablespoon finely chopped
    green onion (include top)

Have all ingredients at room temperature. Whip oleo and cheese with electric beater until light and fluffy. Stir in sour cream and onion. Top baked potatoes with cheese mix, and sprinkle with additional onion, if desired. Can be made ahead. Tops about 6 potatoes.

*Teacher's Pet*

# PICO de GALLO

2 bunches green onions, chopped
4 tomatoes, chopped
1 chopped bell pepper
3 to 4 jalapenos (or amount for
    your taste)

1 tablespoon, fresh Cilantro,
    optional
2 avocados (not too ripe)
1 tablespoon garlic salt
1 teaspoon salt

Clean and chop all vegetables very fine. Mix and enjoy as a dip, or on Tacos, or on fajitas, or as a snack. DELICIOUS!

*Cindy Arnold: Devonian Elementary Secretary*

# ANN'S SALSA

3 large onions, chopped
3 long green chili peppers,
   chopped
3 bell peppers, chopped
8 Jalapeno
3 cloves garlic

2 teaspoons Cilantro
1/4 cup oil
4 large tomatoes, chopped
1 teaspoon lemon or lime juice
Salt to taste

Chop above ingredients and saute in oil; remove from heat before bright green color disappears from peppers. Cool thoroughly. Add tomatoes, lemon juice, and salt. Refrigerate overnight before serving.

*Ernest and Ann Thornton: Lane '76*

# AJI SALSA

*(From a friend in Ecuador)*

2 hot peppers (red and green chili
   peppers)
Tomatoes, fresh and chopped
Salt to taste
1/2 teaspoon dried parsley

Dash lemon juice
Olive oil and vinegar to taste
1 small chopped onion
Water, barely enough to cover
   ingredients

Chop fine ingredients; mix. Serve over rice.

*Note:* You can vary amount of tomatoes and oil that you like.

*Jack and Oleta Greaves: Linda '61; Donna '63; Randy '66*

# DIET MAYONNAISE

4 eggs
1/2 teaspoon mustard
1/2 teaspoon white pepper
1/4 teaspoon paprika
Garlic salt to taste (less garlic
   than onion)
Onion salt to taste (more onion
   than garlic)

2 packages artificial sweetener
   (or 4 teaspoons sugar)
4 tablespoons apple cider vinegar
4 tablespoons fresh squeezed
   lemon juice
3 cups Kraft Popcorn flavored oil

Place eggs in food processor until fluffy. Add all other ingredients and process. (Add oil in a small stream.) Makes 1 quart. 1 tablespoon equals 2 teaspoons oil allowance.

*H.F. and Nellie James: Betty Marie James '49 (submitted by Betty)*

---

**God never closes one door
without opening another.**

# DEL RIO SEASONING SALT

1 (26-ounce) box Morton's salt
1 (1-1/2 ounce) box ground black
  pepper
1 ounce ground red pepper

1 ounce bottle pure garlic powder
1 ounce bottle chili powder
1 ounce carton Accent

Mix thoroughly.

*Bob and Millie Henderson: Scott Flanagan '78*

# FRIED PINEAPPLE

1 teaspoon sugar
4 tablespoons flour
1 egg, slightly beaten
1/4 teaspoon salt

2 tablespoons milk
6 slices pineapple, drained
1/2 cup bread crumbs

Combine sugar and flour. Combine egg, salt, and milk. Dip pineapple in flour mixture, then in egg mixture, and then in crumbs. Brown in small amount of hot oil. If desired, pineapple may be fried without dripping in mixture. Serve as accompaniment to roast or other meat.

*James E. and Dell Nelson: Ted '54*

# MACARONI AND CHEESE

3 pounds macaroni
6 cups milk
2 pounds Velveeta cheese

1 can Cream of Celery Soup,
  undiluted
1 stick oleo

Cook macaroni according to directions in a BIG canning pot with plenty of water. Drain and rinse with cold water; drain. Heat milk and add cheese. (Do not boil). Add soup. Mix well and add oleo. Cool. Seal in zip-lock bags and freeze.

*Note:* Makes a large amount to freeze.

*Teacher's Pet: Nela Allison, sister*

A man can fail many times,
But he isn't a failure
Until he begins to blame somebody else.

# INDEX

Cleone Colvin
1004 N.W. 8th Place
Andrews, Texas 79714

Please send ____ copy(ies)                    @ $12.95 each _____
    Postage and handling                   @ 2.50 each _____
    Texas residents add sales tax          @ .95 each _____

Name _____

Address _____

City _____ State _____ Zip _____

Make checks payable to *Cleone Colvin*.

- - - - - - - - - - - - - - - - - - - - - - - - - - - -

Cleone Colvin
1004 N.W. 8th Place
Andrews, Texas 79714

Please send ____ copy(ies)                    @ $12.95 each _____
    Postage and handling                   @ 2.50 each _____
    Texas residents add sales tax          @ .95 each _____

Name _____

Address _____

City _____ State _____ Zip _____

Make checks payable to *Cleone Colvin*.

- - - - - - - - - - - - - - - - - - - - - - - - - - - -

Cleone Colvin
1004 N.W. 8th Place
Andrews, Texas 79714

Please send ____ copy(ies)                    @ $12.95 each _____
    Postage and handling                   @ 2.50 each _____
    Texas residents add sales tax          @ .95 each _____

Name _____

Address _____

City _____ State _____ Zip _____

Make checks payable to *Cleone Colvin*.